Seachanges

Of sea and seafolk

By

David Jackson

MAPLE
PUBLISHERS

Seachanges – Of sea and seafolk

Author: David Jackson

Copyright © David Jackson (2021)

The right of David Jackson to be identified as author of this work has been asserted by the author in accordance with section 77 and 78 of the Copyright, Designs and Patents Act 1988.

First Published in 2021

ISBN 978-1-914366-34-5 (Paperback)
       978-1-914366-64-2 (Ebook)

Book cover design and Book layout by:

    White Magic Studios
    www.whitemagicstudios.co.uk

Published by:

    Maple Publishers
    1 Brunel Way,
    Slough,
    SL1 1FQ, UK
    www.maplepublishers.com

A CIP catalogue record for this title is available from the British Library.

CONTENTS

Acknowledgements and thanks

This book could not have been written without the help of my good friend Bernard Perry, who spent hours teaching me how to write acceptable English and then not complaining when I forgot. He worked so hard that I deliberately omitted all the embarrassing bits about him…

I also wish to thank all the people who unwittingly gave me things to write about during the last 60 years. I have not mentioned names of the 'bad guys' for obvious reasons (although most of them are dead). If I have mentioned your name then you are one of the good guys, which have been in the majority during my life at sea. If you haven't got a mention then it is because this book is about the sea and you didn't do anything crazy enough when I was around to notice. Drunken 'runs ashore' do not count. Sorry Bob Venables.

Lastly I wish to thank the guys at White Magic Studios for their advice, and forbearing with me when I kept on adding to the 'finished' manuscript.

━━◆◆❨▷◆━━

Forward 1955-57

I don't want this story (which is as true as I can remember) to be about me, but about the sea, what has happened above, on, and under it, throughout my life. I have never kept a diary, but I did have to keep a flying logbook throughout my aviation years. This may mean that I have made a few errors in dating some of the events, but the events are true. Things often seem to happen when I am around. Maybe I am 'incident prone'. I was initially thinking that my tale about the sea started when I joined the Royal Navy, but on reflection, my nautical life started in 1955.

My Grandmother, who raised me, worked on the Palace Pier, 30 feet above the sea, in Brighton, every summer season, so it was natural that I would hang around with her during the school holidays. I became well known to the pier crew and when it was realised that I had discovered the technique of how to win a bar of chocolate for one penny on the slot machine, I was in demand by the crew and had pennies pressed into my hand at snack time. I was allowed into all the attractions free and when I was 12 years old I was asked, by David and Katrina Southard, if I would help in odd jobs. David and Katrina were impresarios. They did a mind reading act and had another act of 'Blondini', Brighton's version of Houdini. His act included eating light bulbs, lying on nails and having concrete slabs smashed on his chest etc. Blondini was supposedly buried alive in a glass tank, and it was going to be in it for a month. During the day and evening people would pay sixpence (two and a half pence in today's currency) to view him entombed.. For two week, things went well but then he was found drunk in a bar in the early hours of one morning. To cover this, a girl was paid to smash the tank, saying 'I don't want him to die'!!

I learnt out how to eat glass and razor blades and how to avoid being strangled by 4 men with a rope. Not surprisingly, no one has ever asked me if I was qualified in these things.

The following year I helped them in a sort of peepshow and received half a crown a day; 13p in today's currency.

When I was 14 years old, they had a new attraction '*Nantina, the girl in the tomb*'. Having paid sixpence, you would go into a dark room and eventually found yourself looking through bars at a graveyard scene. The graves were glowing green,(the effect of invisible UV light on 'sunshine' paint') and above and beyond them were the outlines of a large coffin. When sufficient customers were present, the coffin lid slowly started to open, and then dropped closed with a crash. That was good for a few girly screams. Again, the lid creaked open, and this time remain so. After a long pause, from one end of the coffin, came an elongated, green skeleton hand, with red fingernails. From the far end then came the other hand. They stopped, seemingly hovering above the coffin, then, like a pianist's hands, they moved towards each other and away again, and once more stopped. The hand closest to the audience extended a long, bony finger and pointed at a girl, which got another scream when it slowly beckoned. As this was happened the girls at the front tried to squirm their way towards the back,. hiding behind their companion. Slowly, a hideous, green skeleton face, with flame red hair floated out of the coffin.

That was me, dressed in black and wearing a mask and specially made rubber gloves and I was paid £5 a week.

Near closing time, the more intoxicated punters would come in and some would spit at me, so I bought a water pistol and squirted them back. Occasionally I got carried away and if there was a girl with a low-cut dress she would also be my target. This always got a scream from her and a laugh from her boyfriend. During one performance, I was a bit too exuberant with the water pistol and an irate punter forced his way back to the cash desk, through the incoming crowd, and shouted, 'I want my money back, that Bloody Mare in there has just pissed all over me'!

David and Katrina liked my performance and tried to talk me out of my dream of joining the navy, and join a show they were arranging, touring South Africa, but they had no hope of doing so. My mind was made up. I was going to be a sailor but the love of theatricals never left me and helped me many times in my future life.

⸻

Chapter 1
HMS St. Vincent, HMS Vernon 2, Gosport. Boys time under training 1958-59

On April 6th, 1958 a short, skinny, 15 years and 3 month old youth got off the train from Brighton at Portsmouth Harbour station, clutching a cheap attaché case, and looked nervously around. Noticing a gaggle of similar aged boys, who were gathered around an Royal Navy Petty Officer, he approached them and when asked his name replied 'David Jackson' and this name was ticked off on the PO's clip board. The group, when complete, was herded across a floating pontoon in Portsmouth harbour and then onto a harbour launch, which soon cast off its ropes and headed across the harbour to Gosport.

This was my day; the day that I had been waiting and dreaming of for the last 6 years. I was going to become a sailor. The dozens of books that I had read about the sea and the Royal

Navy were just history, I was going to become the navy of the future, the person they would write about – or so I imagined.

The trip across the harbour was the first indication that maybe things were not going to be so straightforward as I anticipated; the fumes from the launch's diesel engine, the overpowering, eye watering, stench from dozens of warships burning FFO (furnace fuel oil) to power their boilers, the smell of tar, paint and a myriad of other substances such as rotting seaweed and sewage, worked with the slight swell produced by wind against current to send me very quickly vomiting over the guardrails. My half-digested Mars bar and egg sandwich which Gran had so carefully prepared, sank to the bottom of the harbour, amalgamating with the detritus of my historical heroes. I knew that Nelson used to be seasick every time he went to sea and crossing Portsmouth harbour was not exactly an ocean voyage, but I hoped that it would count as a point in my favour.

That day I joined HMS St Vincent, a Junior Seaman training establishment in Gosport, and my home for the next year. St Vincent was an impressive Victorian establishment. After entering under an imposing archway, eyes were immediately drawn to a large figurehead of Admiral Lord St Vincent, and then to a tall mast (reputed to be 125 feet) on the far side of a huge parade ground. Someone joked that we would have to climb to the top – except it was no joke. Soon after completing 6 weeks of 'Nozzer' (new recruit) segregation and training, where we learned how to wear, wash and repair our uniform and the basics of marching and naval discipline, we were rated as Junior Seaman Second-Class and made to climb the monster mast and ridiculed if we went through the 'Lubbers Hole' at the first platform, about 50ft up, instead of monkey climbing outwards at 45 degrees to gain access over the edge via the 'Devil's Elbow'.

After that first ascent I lost all fear of heights and often, in my 'blues' periods, would climb to the very top for solace and solitude and play my harmonica. There were no Health and Safety at Work rules in those days. The so-called safety net was tarred cordage hauled so tight it felt like wire and a fall would have meant certain death but as far as I know there had never been an accident. The sense of self-preservation was so strong that our grips were as tight as a padlock. My pay for the first six months was 50p (10 shillings as it was then), per week rising to 75p when I became a Junior Seaman First-Class.

Half of every weekday was spent in academic school classes and the other in learning nautical subjects. We were taught how to wear our uniform correctly (to put on the Burberry raincoat you have to cross your arms and slide them into the sleeves whilst facing the coat and lift it over your head, whilst uncrossing the arms; if you don't, the blue collar of your serge jumper gets screwed up.) We learnt to march forward, backward, and sideways, with and without a Lee Enfield 303 rifle, which seemed to gain weight by the minute (especially when you had to double march (run) around the parade ground with it held above your head – a standard punishment for any misdemeanour). We were taught how to strip and fire the weapon, play sport and tackle assault courses. In between times there were kit musters, where every item had to be washed, ironed to a predetermined size, laid out in a special order, and inspected. We were given short lengths of rope and were expected to produce complicated rope work by the end of term. In our spare time we embroidered our name in red silk on all our kit, including underpants, and do general and personal cleaning.

One thing we all hated was the weekly 'early morning dhobying' when we were up at 0530 and marched to the dhobi (laundry) house where there were dozens of large washbasins plus two large enamel baths filled with cold water. No washing machine in those days. We had to strip naked, wash all our clothes and bed sheets by hand, with hard 'Pussers' navy soap, and after they had been inspected by the duty Petty Officer (no 'skid marks' allowed on our underpants!), rinsed in the icy baths. In the winter it was a bitterly cold task. So that we looked like real sailors we all made a special effort to lighten the colour of our blue collars by hard scrubbing, so they had a faded sea-going look.

Whilst a Second-Class Boy, shore leave was either Wednesday or Saturday from 1700 to 1900, and Sunday from 1300 to 1900 every other week. When rated a 'First Class Boy' it expired at 2100.As we had very little money, we just walked around, trying to look like real sailors – and fooling nobody, with our pimply faces and squeaky boots.

Once a week we had a 3 mile march to Pridoux's (Priddies) hard, which was St Vincent's boat yard. There we learned how to pull (row) 27ft whalers and 32ft cutters, heavy traditional wooden boats. We also had to do Ceremonial Oar Drill which meant throwing the oar up into the air, catching it and then waving it around smartly in unison. Whilst the rest on the course managed to gain some resemblance of nautical smartness, the weight of the oar was too much for my skinny frame and after I had managed to drop the oar a few times and send a couple of my mates to sickbay with suspected concussion, Willy Hartnel, our CPO boats instructor, suggested that perhaps I would be better off learning to sail. What an intelligent CPO he was, for I found that I was in my element pulling a length of rope attached to a sail and pushing and pulling a piece of wood to steer. My mess mates also agreed that I was less of a menace in a sailing boat than a pulling one and sickbay visits dropped radically. This love of sailing has stayed with me all my life and whilst in the RN I spent much of my free time dinghy sailing. I have since owned and raced yachts and became the Chief Instructor of sailing schools in both Oman and Turkey.

We often spend years planning and plotting our future but sometimes, for what may seem to be the most trivial reasons, your life can change completely. After six months training, we had to choose our SQ (Specialist Qualifications). As a Junior Seaman I had the option to become G (Gunnery), RP (Radar Plotter) or TAS (Torpedo and Anti-Submarine). After watching lots of war films I knew exactly what I wanted to be – a Gunner, strapped in behind my multi-barrelled Oerlikon anti-aircraft gun, saving the ship by shooting down half a dozen aircraft every day. To help us choose we visited each of the specialist training establishments, which were all in the Portsmouth area.

The first visit was to HMS Excellent at Whale Island, the gunnery school. Until I went there, I did not realise that to be a gunner you were also to be an expert in parade ground drills, marching, rifle drill and other BS. This was not part of my 'being a hero plan', and to cap things off, the dinner served in the dining hall was disgusting, even by the low standard that St Vincent had set itself and constantly failed to reach. When I asked the trainee gunners if the meals were always that bad, I was told that 'today was a good day'! When I looked closely, I also had trouble making out the gunners badge design – was it crossed guns or crossed telescopes? It looked pretty naff to me.

That afternoon we had a visit to an anti-aircraft simulator, where films of aircraft were projected onto the doomed ceiling and, strapped into my AA gun-mount, I could shoot them down, which I did with gusto. The CGI (Chief Gunnery Instructor) praised me and told me that I had a natural flair. With 5 other trainees we had a second go – and then I realised that the last thing in the world that I wanted, was to go to HMS Excellent and be a gunner: the marching, the yucky food and crappy badge were not for me, so I made sure that the only thing I hit was the ships superstructure! The GGI shook his head and said something about beginners' luck and that we would not be seeing each other again. I tried to look suitable crestfallen and managed not to smile until we were in the back of the Bedford lorry and returning to St Vincent.

The following week we visited HMS Dryad, the radar establishment. First impressions were good. Only a small parade ground and nobody marching was definitely a positive point. The badge that I would wear on my arm was a bit confusing; was it a spider's web or what? The lectures on radar were interesting but then I found out that the main job of the RP was not to peer intently at a radar scope, looking out for the sneaky attacker coming to sink the ship, but to write on a large, illuminated, Perspex board, backwards so that officers on the other side could read it and keep up to date on the threats. I hated (and still do) writing forward, never mind backwards. The final nail in the coffin of my potential radar career was dinner. It was another chef's disaster special that even 15 year old boys with renowned appetites found inedible. Another Specialist Qualification that I did not intend going for. I was getting worried, what would I do if the TAS branch was also a no-no? St Vincent was not the happy place I thought it would be and I had another eleven and a half years left before I could leave the RN, unless I flunked everything and got SNLR (Services No Longer Required). In those days, a boy signed on for 3 years Boys Service, followed by 9 years Man's. To leave the navy required payment of a large sum of money, SNLR (troublemaker or incredibly stupid) or to stand as a Member of Parliament. The money was impossible, the SNLR a disgrace and the Raving Loony Party had yet to be invented and so becoming an MP was also ruled out.

The final establishment we visited was HMS Vernon, the TAS training establishment with its torpedo tubes protecting the entrance of Portsmouth harbour. No strutting around the parade ground, the best meal supplied by the Queen that I had eaten. The intricacies of mines, torpedoes, depth charges and other underwater weapons and such like were fascinating to me and I revelled in the thrill of detecting and destroying an unseen, underwater predator – and to cap it all the badge was the largest in the RN; Crossed torpedoes and a harpoon with coiled line. I could not wait to become a TASI (Torpedo and Anti-Submarine Instructor) for then the badge would be surmounted by a crown and 2 stars above. A badge to be admired, the biggest in the Navy. I was going to become a TASI! When I asked how I could become one I was told by 'Buck' Taylor, our PO TASI, that the Underwater Control (ASDIC as it was then and now called Sonar) side of the branch was the most difficult, so if I started as an 'underwater controller' and became a UC 1 all I had to do was the easier UW

1 (weapons) course and the badge was mine. So, my future was decided by a good meal and a badge – well, I was only 15 years old. My St Vincent training now included TAS and I took to it with enthusiasm. I started to learn about mines, depth charges, torpedoes and ASDIC.

ASDIC, the device used to detect submarines by transmitting a sound pulse, was so called as it was the result of work done by the Anti-Submarine Detection and Investigation Committee, formed after WW1. Its successor, sonar, was the acronym for SOund Navigation And Ranging, first used by the USN

That autumn, my entry group (number 13) was sent Sea Training on HMS Redpole for a week. Redpole was a wartime-built Bird class sloop, which meant that it was smaller than a frigate and rolled like a cow on wet grass. We boys were laughed at by the crew when we called everyone Sir, and given the dirtiest jobs on board. After spending 3 hours of the forenoon watch deep in the bowls of the vessel, untangling stinking wet cordage; I managed to eat all my dinner before vomiting it up in the mess deck. Then I knew why a mess deck is so called. I am pleased to say that that was the last time I ever completely succumbed to Mal de Mar. I have felt 'rough' on a destroyer in a typhoon and a couple of times on yachts but have never vomited again.

HMS Redpole, as most small ships did before the 1960s, had a system of victualling called Canteen Messing. Every mess was allocated so much money per person for food, and the leading hand of the mess planned and costed a menu for the month and purchased the food through the Victualling Office. All money left over at the end of the month from the victualling was passed to the mess. This money was usually used on a 'Run Ashore' to the nearest pub. This system was open to fraud and as only the cheapest meals were chosen (breakfast was traditionally a cup of tea and a Woodbine cigarette) and, being cooked by amateurs, the quality went down even more.

The ship only had 2 cooks, one for the half a dozen officers and the other for the rest of the crew (other ranks). Daily, the

Leading Hand of the mess chose 2 members to clean the mess and then to cook the meal under the supervision of the trained chef and then they would then bring it to the mess to be eaten. In bad weather it was not uncommon for the 'cooks of the mess' to spill half of the food whilst transporting it in the mess 'Fanny'. All metal food and beverage containers in the RN were called Fannies. This name came about as when tinned meat was first introduced in the navy a young girl by the name of Frances (Fanny) Adams was murdered in 1867 and her dismembered body, in tin trunks, was sent to railway stations around the UK.

Another memorable moment was when we had to 'coal ship' on HMS Barfoss. Barfoss, a Boom Defence Vessel, was the last coal burning ship in the RN and the coal had to be carried on-board by the sacksful, and who better to do it that then a gang of teenagers who needed toughening up. We had to carry the coal from the alongside lighter (barge), up a ladder, across the deck and then down into the Coal hold. It was not long before we all looked like candidates auditioning for the 'Black and White Minstrel' show. Being the runt of the class was useful, as after an hour a broom was thrust into my hand and I was told to keep the decks clean whilst my fellow students carried on carrying.

On completion of our St Vincent training, we had examinations and to make sure that we were not too cocky it was made impossible to achieve 100% as trick questions were added:
- What ship, because of its unusual shape, burns two sets of navigation lights at the same time;
- In harbour what do a yellow light and a shrill ringing of a bell signify? (Answers at the end of this chapter).

Finally, with great relief, at being set free from the discipline and BS of basic training, in the summer of '59 the TAS trainees were drafted to HMS Vernon and accommodated at HMS Vernon 2, a wartime-built camp on the shores of Stokes Bay. We lived in wooden huts and were daily 'Bedforded' by lorry to the jetty at Gosport and then embarked on an HLD (harbour launch) to and from HMS Vernon on the other side of the harbour.

That summer was the hottest and sunniest for years and Vernon 2 was like living in a holiday camp. What a change from St Vincent. No GIs and no parade training. As well as shore leave until 2100 for three out of four days, we were allowed to leave the camp and walk along the beach whenever we liked, as long as we were 'turned in' (in bed) by Pipe Down at 2230. We were also allowed to buy Pussers (Navy issue) 'Blue liner' cigarettes (reputed to be the floor sweepings of BAT!) but at 3 shillings (15 p) for 300 who cared! Vernon was the happiest part of my Boy's training. I enjoyed the UCs training and, being able to tell whether a note was higher pitched or lower, did well on the course. After qualifying I proudly sewed on my large TAS badge. Life was great for a 16 year old sailor. It was with some regret that after 2 weeks leave (during which I wore my newly badged uniform every day!) I was drafted to Portsmouth barracks, a huge gloomy Victorian establishment, to await my first draft to a real ship.

Answers to exam questions

Two sets of Nav. lights – An Airship
Yellow light and bell – Harbour master on his bicycle.

HMS St Vincent

Chapter 2
HMS Albion 1960/61

I n 1959 the RN still had a sizeable fleet, albeit consisting of some rather old ships. There was a battleship, HMS Vanguard, which was mothballed in Portsmouth and 7 aircraft carriers: Albion, Bulwark, Centaur, Hermes, Victorious, Eagle and Ark Royal. My 'draft chit' sent me to the carrier HMS Albion which was not to my liking as I would have preferred to go onto an anti-submarine frigate to practice my newly obtained skills but when I realised that it was a 10 month trip to the Far East including Korea and Japan I saw the advantages, and stopped whinging.

Albion's air wing consisted of 8 Sea Hawk and 12 Sea Venom fighter jets, 4 Douglas Sky Raiders AEW (Air Early Warning – they had a big radar in the nose), a CoD (Carrier of Despatches – our mail aircraft) which I think was also a Sky Raider, 8 Whirlwind Mk 7 ASW helicopters and a Dragonfly plane guard heli. I can't remember the Dragonfly so maybe it did not accompany us, and a Whirlwind used instead. The plane guard's duty was to rescue any aircrew that crashed, and it was the first aircraft launched and the last recovered. It was sorely needed on that deployment. Naval aviation will always be dangerous, and I have survived two 'ditchings' and a handful of emergency landings but that deployment of Albion was a bad one for the squadrons.

On 9 February, 1960, only a week or so after we left Portsmouth, a Sky Raider, attempting a landing, hit the starboard aft catwalk, and crashed into the sea and the same day a Whirlwind ditched close to Gibraltar. That crew was saved. The very next day a Sea Vixen had an engine fire and the pilot ejected. 20 February a Whirlwind ditched on take-off, crew rescued. A month later 2 Sea Venoms collided off Malta, all crew lost. On the 6 September a Sea Hawk had a fire after launching and the crew ejected safely and on the 14th a Sea Venom hit the deck on landing killing both crew. 2 November a Sea Hawk had engine failure in the Indian Ocean and the pilot ejected.

It is unfortunate that not many people reading this will have had the chance to watch air operations from a carrier. The ship steams fast into the wind to give airspeed to the aircraft, so there is always a gale blowing down the flight deck, whipping away the steam from the catapults which launch the planes into the air. Aircraft are towed by heavy yellow tractor tugs and ranged on deck, angled facing forward and inboard, and lashed down and chocked to stop them moving. Jet engines are started and the air is full of the whining of turbines and then, after loud bangs as the starter cartridges fire, snarling and crackling, piston engines too. Two aircraft at a time unfold their wings, which have been folded to reduce their size. The Fairey Gannet (which later replaced the Sky Raider) had Z folded wings and they looked like huge insects metamorphosing into flies, whilst the jets have a simpler V arrangement.

With wings extended, lashings and chocks removed, aircraft taxi to the port or starboard catapult and then stop. Aircraft Handlers run to them and disappear from sight, attaching a Hold Back Strop at the rear and a Towing Bridal at the front, which is attached to the catapult shuttle. The flight deck, just behind the aircraft, is a massive water-cooled Jet Blast Deflector and it hinges up, protecting the after end of the flight deck, on which are the remaining aircraft, deck equipment and men. The Flight Deck Officer in his yellow sur-coat, waits for confirmation signals that all is correct while the handlers, called Badgers because of their brown and white coats, scurry out of the way, jumping down into the safety of the catwalks.

When ready, the catapult operator signals that the correct pressure of steam is in the cylinder (it changes with the type of aircraft and take-off weight). The pilot confirms that he is also ready and then the shuttle of the cat is moved slowly forward, tensioning the Hold Back Strop, pulling the tail of the aircraft down and allowing the oleo strut at the front of the aircraft to extend and the nose to rise, so that it is angled in the correct flying angle. The FDO then spins his flag or wand in fast circles, the pilot selects his afterburners (on the later generation of aircraft) and the plane strains against the Hold Back with massive blue burning flames roaring out its exhaust, like a hundred thousand welding torches, making the JBD smoke and burn despite its water cooling.

The Hold Back then disconnects and the plane is hurled forward at over 150 knots (nautical mph173 land mph) and off the flight deck, sinking initially, boiling the sea underneath it with the heat and power of its after-burning engines. Slowly at first and then faster and faster, it climbs away from the danger of the sea and a charging ship, raising its undercarriage. The noise of the engines on take-off is indescribable, not only of the volume but also of the power, for it penetrates all your body; you can feel this sound throughout your being. It quivers muscles and flesh; intestines vibrate as do eyes and brain and a catapult launch is something, even when experienced hundreds of times, always produces awe.

At night this awe is increased even more. It becomes a violent ballet watched with stroboscopic vision. Every member of the flight deck must learn their moves to perfection in the darkness of the wind gale. The ranged (parked) planes have dim navigation lights until the engines are started and then they flash. Glowing wands, like Jedi swords, are lifted, waved, pointed and circled. Every member of the flight deck crew has to trust each other as mistakes cannot be seen and corrected and the pilot has to trust everyone, including the engineers, ships helmsman, captain and all of the thousands of people onboard. If the chef has not washed his hands before preparing food now is not a good time to find out. In the dark, the screaming, scorching flames of the after-burners are more intense, bits of burning deck paint fly from the JBD and the strobing flash of navigation lights make it completely surreal and, there is that punishing, body churning sound. It is a disco from hell, complete with strobing lights and I would not have missed it for anything.

Deck landings on a carrier induce a different feeling in the watcher. There is a more gradual build-up of tension. The returning aircraft can usually be seen over a mile away, circling 'Mother', waiting to be fed into the landing pattern. When the ship is steaming into wind and ready, one of the planes astern alters course and starts to close. Slowly at first it seems, but then faster and faster as it approaches the stern. As the ship pitches and rolls in the waves and swell the plane tries to correct its angle of descent and direction to keep on the glide path, its wings rocking sideways. The wheels and the arrester hook at the rear of the aircraft are lowered, indicated that they are locked 'Down' to the pilot by glowing green lights in his cockpit. Suddenly the plane hits the deck with a bang, tyres squealing and engine roaring. Stretched across the flight deck are 4 to 6 thick wires which have massive shock absorbers at each end. These arrester wires are raised about a foot off the deck. The pilot, getting visual clues from a mirror landing aid on the ship, must avoid flying into the stern of the pitching and veering ship but catch the first of the wires with his hook. If the pilot misses the first one there are a few more to stop him but if he is too low, he, crashes into the stern. Power is kept on the engines to control the sink rate until the hook engages and then cut rapidly, but if no wire is caught the throttles are jammed hard forward to the stops, to gain enough airspeed to fly off the deck and join the landing pattern again. At night the arrester wire showers sparks, like a Chinese fire-cracker as it is pulled at over 80 knots (92 mph) over the deck, adding more excitement to the 'Goofers' as spectators are called. Unfortunately, it does not always work like this, fatal accidents happen.

The UK's new carriers, the Queen Elizabeth class, will not have catapults as Very Short Take Off and Landing (VSTOL) aircraft are envisaged. This means that they could be limited in their operation as other types of aircraft cannot be carried. I do not know if there will be arrester wires. Maybe the steam catapult has had its day - the Americans are experimenting with an electromagnetic version and it might be able to be retro fitted if the need arises. British sailors will possibly never again have the chance of experiencing this mid blowing, body pulsing experience.

Albion was still in refit when I joined and I was quickly initiated into the chores of chipping paint, using hammer, de-scaler and pneumatic (windy) hammer as well as to the use of red and chocolate primer and Pussers (RN) grey top-coat paint. Still being on the small size I often was given the job of working in confined spaces and one of these was the Engine room ventilator intakes, which were filthy. It was whilst working inside one of these that I first came across the unfairness of the RN discipline system. I was called out of a ventilator to meet my Divisional Officer for the first time and was black with grime and covered in paint chippings. He looked at me and told me I was filthy and to report to his office and await him. Standing outside his door I was rather bemused as to what was happening and as he approached along the corridor, I stepped back to give him space and kicked over an unseen pot of paint which had been left on the deck. Next thing I knew I was charged with being dirty and wasting Admiralty property and had 2 days stoppage of leave!!!

The job I enjoyed most, was painting the ship's side. As I had no fear of heights, I was used to rig the nets that hung from the protruding sponsons and had to be secured to the ship's side at the bottom. This required climbing down the hanging net and, causing it to swing towards the ship, throwing a securing line when close enough. These nets were used to reach all along the side of the ship when painting. Tarzan, eat your heart out! This was done 30 feet above the floating pontoons (cats) that kept the ship off the jetty. Once again, no hard hats, safety harnesses or health and safety.

On completion of the refit, I was allocated a new 'Part of Ship' and mess (accommodation). I became a Side Boy. I assume that it was because I spoke reasonably clear English (I had to use the Tannoy, the ship's broadcast system) and had qualified for a silver Bosun's Call and Chain as a 'Call Boy' at St. Vincent, having proved that I knew all the 'calls' or 'pipes' that were required.

The gangway staff on a large ship consisted of the First Officer of the Day (OOD1), Second (OOD2), the duty Midshipman, the Quartermaster (a leading Hand), a Bosun's mate and finally, right at the bottom of the chain, a Side boy, who was a Gofer (go for this, go for that). I had to accompany the OOD on his daily and weekly rounds, run errands around the ship and do morning shakes etc. which meant that I had to learn and memorise how to reach every one of the thousand compartment onboard. At sea I kept my 'watch' on the bridge and used the ships Tannoy to run the ship's routine. It was an excellent introduction for a youngster, teaching me how the Captain, Commander (Air) (who was in charge of the flying), Navigator and OOW worked and made decisions. From my position on the port side of the 'Island' (command centre) I also was able to watch all the aircraft launches. I saw how rules of the road between ships (ColRegs) were applied in reality and learnt the Morse code. It proved invaluable training for when I became a yacht skipper later in my life. My proudest moment as Side Boy was in Mombasa, when I was left by myself for two and a half hours on the 'working' gangway as the OOD1 and 2, Midshipman, QM and Bosun's mate had to man the ceremonial gangway on the other side of the ship, to welcome VIPs. Not only did I run the ship's routine, making routine pipes (normally I had to wait to be told to make them) but also made decisions way above my pay grade, as to where store and fuel barges had to be secured, what stores parties had to be mustered, arrange special parties by telling CPO and POs to come to the gangway to see me so that I could tell them my decisions etc. I was frequently told that the OOD was the Captains representative and if that is so I must have been acting Captain of an Aircraft Carrier at 17 years old as I was doing the OOD's job!

Keeping watches on the bridge allowed me to read the signal log – I have always been nosey!

Our helicopters were Whirlwind MK 7 and when one was 'burning and turning' on deck one of the flight deck crew had to stand with a small red flag just outside of the spinning rotor disc, as a warning not to get closer. Commander (Air) sent a signal to FONAC (Flag Officer Naval Air Command) *'Like the motor car I believe that the Whirlwind Mk 7 has now become of age and I intend removing the man with the red flag'!* This was approved by FONAC and is no longer seen.

The day prior to leaving the UK we slipped from our dockyard berth and anchored off Spithead for the night and I had my final 'run ashore' in Pompy, as sailors call Portsmouth. Supposedly, being a Junior Seaman, my leave was only until 2100, but the weather blew up, and all liberty boats back to ship were cancelled. With my chums, I tried to get accommodation at Dame Agnes Weston's Royal Sailors Rest, a charity Naval hostel (is that still in existence?) but it was full, so for the first time in my life I stayed up all night, walking around Pompy, trying to keep warm in the January cold. Next morning when the boats finally started running again, we arrived back onboard and after changing and having breakfast started work. Thus Albion weighed her anchor and sailed for the Med and Far East.

We were joined onboard later by Rear Admiral Le Fanu, who was Flag Officer, Second in Command of the Far East Fleet. He was a real sailors' admiral, admired by all the ships company after he 'Cleared Lower Deck' and gave us an entertaining and informative talk about our role in keeping world peace. He endeared himself to the crew by frequently talking to the most junior of us. I was on the flight deck with my camera and a friend was taking my photo, when the Admiral came along and asked, 'Mind if I come in on this one'. Now I have a photo of the Admiral Le Fanu and me.

Although Admiral Le Fanu was trained, and fought, as a gunnery Officer, he was one of the enlightened leaders who realised that the navy had to modernise and change direction. No more was the big gun to be the main weapon. He realised the advantage of missiles and changed the direction of the navy towards being an efficient anti-submarine force to be reckoned with. His early death in 1970 was mourned by progressive thinkers. His orders to stop the daily tot of rum caused anguish at the time but it was the correct decision to make for a more advanced and complicated navy. Every day half-drunk sailors were operating more and more complicated equipment. Every year sailors died by drinking too much rum. He was also instrumental in improving the pay and living conditions of all the RN.

After Albion had anchored at Gibraltar for a couple of days, the less experienced crew members buying the obligatory castanets and lighters, we sailed for Malta (God, the Gut, properly named Strait Street, which was on a steep hill in Valletta, and packed with bars and obliging woman, opened my young eyes wide!) before reaching Messina, Sicily. There something happened which affects me still. I joined a group who went on a 'Grippo' (visit) to a power station, hoping that there would be some hospitality at the end of it and was not disappointed. There were countless bottles of vino and a large bowl of grapes. Being a greedy 16-year-old, I grabbed a handful of these and, cramming them into my mouth, bit hard. What a shock – they were olives, which I had never seen before, and the salty bitter juices squirted down my throat, gagging me. I looked around for somewhere to spit them out but there was nowhere, so I had to swallow them. Even now, over 50 years later I cannot eat olives, which is a pity as I live in Turkey and they form a part of most meals. We also visited Piraeus, the port of Athens, Greece; I enjoyed getting the train to and from Athens and learning the Greek alphabet by reading the adverts.

Albion, en-route to the Far East, transited the Suez Canal – and ran aground, twisting 17 feet of our keel. A couple of Sea Venom jets were securely lashed to the flight deck and were used at full power to extricate us and get back into the main channel. Britain had a jet-propelled aircraft carrier! As usual we were surrounded by Bum boats and entertained by a 'Gulie-Gulie' man (sleight of hand illusionist). We stopped at Aden and it was arranged that some of us Juniors would trek to the crater. It was hot and dusty, and the town was extremely poor, but sold unbelievably cheap duty-free Japanese electronics. I decided that I would never willingly go to that part of the world again but after leaving the RN I went to the Sultanate of Oman on a two-year contract and enjoyed it so much that I stayed for nine!

Do you know that you can smell Singapore a day before you arrive? Well, it is probably not just Singapore but Malaysia also. It is an earthy, sweet, spicy, jungle smell – a never forgotten smell. Albion went into King George the fifth (KG V) dry dock for about 3 weeks to get the keel repaired, and most of us moved to HMS Terror, the RN naval barracks. Each mess, which took up a complete floor, could hold a small-ship's company. The air squadrons also disembarked ashore but they went to airfields at Sembwang, Seleter and Changi so they could continue flying.

I really enjoyed our time there. I was against having a tattoo but agreed to accompany an oppo (friend) who wanted one. After he had finished, the tattooist looked at me and said 'You next. What you want? ' I started to explain that there was no way that I would have one, just as a crowd of lads from the ship came in. How could I refuse? They would think that I had chickened out, so I hurriedly looked at his catalogue and choose the smallest design that I could see – a small dragon with writing underneath it. I told him I would have that one, without the writing, on my upper arm. Thank goodness for that because it was the Welsh dragon and I have no connection with Wales at all. Fortunately I had the sense to have it where it was hidden under my White Front RN shirt.

When Albion arrived at Yokohama, in Japan, the Padre organised an expedition for us youngsters. We camped at Lake Yamanaka, climbed mount Fujiyama and swam in the ice-cold snow-melt lake.

Inchon, in S Korea, was a cold and muddy mess, memorable for the war-scarred buildings and vehicles with bullet holes as well as the sight of woman digging ditches with very long handled shovels; One woman holding the top end of the handle and another two with a ropes tied to the lower end, lifting it, full of earth, out of the ditch. Hong Kong was great, especially as I was now an OD (ordinary seaman) and had all night leave! Subic Bay, the American base in the Philippines, was also a good 'run ashore' and it was there that I first ate monkey meat. Returning via Mombasa I filled up my locker with wood carvings, using any space left alongside the other worthless trinkets that I had so far collected. It was then back through the Suez Canal and a dash westward through the Med, to arrive back home in Portsmouth dockyard before Christmas.

If anybody tells you that the Med never gets rough, do not believe them. The waves may not reach Atlantic height, but they are close together and, instead of climbing up the face of the wave and descending the other side, you crash through them. If you are doing 18 knots into a westerly gale it is a very violent crash. Frequently waves buried our bow and foamed along half the length of the flight deck, splashing against the Island and covering the triple lashed aircraft that were secured on deck in spray, and likewise the lookouts keeping watch on top of the Island. The forward catwalk on the starboard side of the flight deck was of solid construction and that was partially torn off and hung halfway down ships side, the waves continuing to battered it and drag it into the depths. The port catwalk was constructed of heavy, metal gratings and many of these sections had been washed away and the frames that they had sat in were concertinaed as if we had been in collision with a solid object.

Lower down, nearer the waterline, were the large 'shell ports' where the fo'c's'le (fore part of the ship, in the bows) seamen, (which was now my part of the ship) passed out the shorelines to secure the ship in harbour. For protection from the expected bad weather, we had fitted heavy, steel, perforated 'storm doors', held in position by 2 inch diameter steel pins, for the first time. These had to be removed before entry into Pompy by cutting them free with oxyacetylene torches as they had been bent by the force of the sea and were immovable by hand and hammers.

Although I was no longer seasick, I was feeling the effects of the violent motion and for some unknown reason I decided that I wanted to eat NAAFI (Navy, Army, Air Force Institution, a civilian organisation that runs canteens etc on military ships and establishments) ginger biscuits by the packet. This habit has stayed with me - rough weather equals ginger biscuits. It was many years later that I read that ginger really does help to fight sickness (it is often prescribed for expectant mums with morning sickness) and now I tell my crew to drink cold water with a teaspoonful of ginger powder in it and usually it works but tastes awful. Personally, I keep a hidden hoard of biscuits!

We arrived back on our ETA date, 11 months after departure, no bands or press for our routine trip. Most of the crew went on leave the next day but a group of us volunteered to stay onboard and de-store ship. This was expected to take 5 days and we were promised an extra week's leave. We did it in 3 and still had our extra week off. We were dead chuffed at 'seeing off' Pusser (the navy)!

It was on Albion that I realised that my academic qualifications were non-existent, so in my own time and with the ship's Education Officer tuition, I managed to pass three 'O' levels. One PO did mention to me that I would end up as an educated idiot! During the next few years I increased that to seven 'O' levels, eventually passing City and Guilds 720 which qualified me to teach in Further Education in UK colleges. An unexpected bonus was that because of my 'O' levels I sometimes got paid extra by teaching Junior Rates, to enable them to pass the education test for promotion to Petty Officer.

On Albion I learnt to play the most popular mess deck game in the Navy, Uckers. This is based on the children's game of Ludo but with added rules. The board is larger and home-made, and the pieces are circles cut from broom-handles and painted. It is played normally by four people in pairs but if only two people play, they take two opposite colours. You can form walls (Blobs) of the same colour, which require 6s to be thrown to remove. If the blob is of two (friendly) colours, (Mixi Blob) then the opponent can pass or remove them and send them back to their 'Home'. If a piece is on the final approach to the finish he can be 'Sucked Back' by an opponent, stopping at the bottom of the approach and by saying 'Suck Back' and saying the number of squares that he requires and throwing only one die. There have been many serious arguments playing this game, with the board often being thrown on the floor.

HMS Albion

With Admiral Lefanu

Chapter 3
HMS Verulam, Sonar trials ship
1961/62

After 'paying off' Albion I spent a short time in Royal Naval Barracks Portsmouth before being drafted to HMS Verulam, based at Portland. I had hoped to be sent to an ASW frigate, but the ways of the Navy have always been strange and shrouded in mystery.

Verulam was a relic of the Second World War and had helped to sink a Japanese Cruiser. She had been converted to an ASW frigate and then, stripped of all her weapons and warlike equipment, became a sonar trials ship. It was all very 'hush-hush' and was the main target of the 'Portland Spy Ring', in which an ex Master at Arms, (Ships police chief) was a leading figure. Verulam and HMS Brockelsby were the 2 ships used by the Admiralty Under Water Weapons Establishment (AUWE). Brockelsby was another second war relic; a Hunt class destroyer built in 1941 but, like Verulam, had been converted. She was called 'Black Brock', as she was the only RN ship to have the upper deck painted black. This was because her old oil burning boilers belched black smoke constantly, contaminating everything down wind. I don't think that I am breaking any official secrets act after all this time when I tell you that we were the experimental trials ships for the 2001 sonar of the UK's first nuclear submarine, HMS Dreadnought. We had security lectures, but it was rather a waste of time as only the scientists, AUWE (Admiralty Under-Water Establishment) boffins and submariners were allowed anywhere near the part of ship which housed the secret equipment. I used to go ashore hoping that some beautiful Russian spy would try to seduce me to tell her what secrets I knew (nothing!) but it never happened.

What I could have told her, was that we would wait in harbour until the weather became bad and then went to sea waiting until the storm had blown itself out and then, when the sea became isothermal (warm and cold layers mixed up which gave the best sonar conditions) would have to endure days of vibrating 'pings' reverberating our hull as the powerful sonar was tested and put through its trials. Once, for almost a month, we went to Loch Fyne for different trials and the little village of Tarbat became our run ashore. It had one pub and a village hall where there was Scottish country dancing to McClarty's 5 piece band every week. We all became experts at the Gay Gordon's and Strip the Willow. The Scottish licensing law required all pubs to close to the public at 2130, so every night at that time, we would move into the back room. Shortly after, Angus, the village policeman, would come in and ask if we were all private guests and when assured that we were he would have a 'wee dram' to see him on his way and then cycle to the next village. We really enjoyed our visit to Tarbat, and the locals were sorry to see us leave, especially the girls who at last found partners for dancing.

Prior to entering Loch Fyne, and our long stay in the area, it was decided to paint the ship's side as our long periods at sea had stripped the paint, and Verulam was looking very rusty. Unfortunately, the northern weather conspired against us and on the chosen day it poured with rain. At least it loosened the encrusted salt but, of course, it stopped the paint adhering. The only answer, as far as our First Lt. knew, was to have extra men involved who would be equipped with bundles of rags and dry the ships side (in the rain) as the paint was applied. Needless to say, as soon as we went back to the North Atlantic the paint came off in sheets! I thought this idea of painting in the rain was hilarious and next morning I was told to make a pipe (announcement) on the ships Tannoy that 'HMS Verulam will be entering harbour at 1300 and all scuttles (brass portholes to non-matalots) are to be bright and shiny'. In keeping with the hilarious mood I was in, I modified the pipe to 'HMS Vewulam will be entwing harbour at Thewteen hundred and all scuttles are to be bwight and shiny'. It got many laughs, but the last laugh was on me – it took weeks for me to stop saying W instead of R!

The victualling on Verulam was Broadside Messing system, food supplied by the navy and cooked by a qualified cook and brought to the mess in large fannies. Often, because of the bad weather, pot-mess stew was on the menu for days, unused food being returned to the galley for recycling. Once, the adjacent mess found a sock in in their food fanny. Plates and cups were always scarce as crockery lockers would break open in the gales and 'twos up' on plates was common. We even resorted to using jam tins as cups, as Navel Stores had run out because we had exceeded our allowance. Thanks to ginger biscuits I was never seasick.

Verulum was the only ship I served in where we all slept in hammocks. It is quite surreal to go into the mess deck at night and, in the glow of the red police lights, see the 'micks' swing side to side in unison. A pity they could not do the same fore-and-aft as the ship also pitches. There was always the sound of snoring as the only way to sleep in a 'mick' is on your back. There are a couple of essential rules for slinging (hanging) your 'mick'. It must be hauled as tight as possible, and at the head end a length of wood, called a stretcher (often half a broom handle) with notches in the end, inserted across its width to allow space for the shoulders. Even with these precautions it is not the most comfortable way to sleep and the unavoidable sag cause back pain. In the morning it really was 'Get up and stow' as we had to fold in the sides and tie tight marling hitches down the length of the 'mick', making a tight sausage of canvas, and place it in the stowage called 'hammock nettings' even though it was a cage with no roof. It was customary to sling liberty men's 'micks' for them. If you didn't then you would be awakened by a drunken oppo (friend) trying to do so in the middle of the night. You could tell how popular you were by how well it was slung. A slack 'mick' and no stretcher, meant no friends. The story was told how one winter night in harbour everyone was awakened by a scream. The AB by the scuttle (porthole) decided he could urinate out of it without getting out of his 'mick' but he had forgotten about the electric heater directly below it!

One of my jobs was Boson's Mate, keeping harbour watches guarding the gangway (no weapons of course in those days) on duty at the gangway, and one night we were alongside in Cherbourg harbour with a large USN supply ship towering ahead of us. Sometime after midnight the Captain and First Lt. arrived back on board, in a not quite sober state, and told me to get the keys of the paint shop and bring a pot of red paint and two 2 inch brushes, which they then disappeared ashore with. Half an hour later they returned, giggling like naughty schoolboys, and returned the paint pot and brushes. As all was quiet, I decided to investigate what they had been doing. When I got abeam the USN ship I found, underneath the tall accommodation ladder which was the gangway, large red letters saying, 'Yanks Go Home'! So even senior Officers can act the ass.

A night or so later a group of our seamen came back onboard carrying a café table, two chairs and an umbrella. The OOD (Officer of the Day), who was present at the gangway, asked where they had got them from and, on being told 'The café lady gave it to us', said 'OK, put them on the quarter deck' and there they stayed for the rest of the commission, used by all in good weather.

You have probably read something similar on the internet, but unlike that story, this is true. At sea Verulam was always 'conned' (controlled) from the open, upper bridge, except in the worst of weathers. We had no radar up there and the Operations Room with radar was two decks below. One evening, at dusk, I was lookout on the port side of the bridge and the signalman was on the starboard. The OOW was a very officious officer (nicknamed Peardrop by the captain because of his body shape) who loved to put us mortals in their places. He would disappear from the bridge and go below to the ops room, looking at the radar for any closing contacts. After one of these absences, he shouted at me and told me that I had missed seeing a light (which he had expected to see as he had looked at the radar) and warned me that, if it happened again, I would be on a charge. I peered even more intently and sometime later I thought I saw a light, but it disappeared. Then Peardrop screamed at me 'You have missed another one! It is a naval ship. Signalman, challenge it.' 'But sir...' said the signalman. 'Don't but me boy, challenge it now' Peardrop shouted. So dutifully AA AA AA, was flashed on the 21 inch Aldis signalling lamp, which is unknown ships call sign and got a flash back. 'Ask him who he is', bellowed Peardrop and the signalman started to flash the signal and then got another flash back – and then another one. It was a lighthouse! The signalman and I just collapsed in laughter, hanging on to each other for support. Peardrop was, for once, speechless and stood there in mute rage, waving his arms, and then stormed off the bridge. It was at least a quarter of an hour later before he returned. For the rest of the watch, he remained mute, even when I reported seeing a light and softly added 'house' afterwards.

Verulam had more than its normal share of strange people onboard. We had many more gays than normal, and one of the three Captains we had was surnamed Dick – honestly. A very well-built leading hand insisted that everybody call him

'Tweakers'. One of the officer's chefs was madly in love with Shirley Bassey and, when she married, became inconsolable. He joined a religious sect and every day in harbour, at tot time, half a dozen white robed friars would visit him. I believe that he later committed suicide and left a note saying that his way of life did not agree with his religion.

One of the electricians who was painting aerials whilst in harbour dropped some paint onto the roof of the First Lieutenant's car, which was parked by the ship, – so he painted it completely white. An Able Seaman who was told, as the ship approached the jetty, to throw a heaving line (a line to be tied onto a heavy mooring line) to the jetty did exactly that – without uncoiling it or holding the end. The Dockyard Matey who had it wrapped around his head was not amused and being a shop steward told the others to 'down tools' and not to tie the ship up. Verulam had a very strange mix of crew.

All ratings received a Kit Upkeep Allowance and could buy replacement kit from 'Pussers Slops' (naval stores) or civilian Naval Tailors. Most of us made an allotment of pay to a Naval Tailor and that allowed us to buy kit or civilian clothes when needed and the debt was paid off monthly. Naval tailors would visit the ship almost daily in harbour. When matelots gave directions ashore, we used Pubs and Naval Tailors as 'way points' – 'Pass the Rising Sun, turn right at Bernard's and then left at Flemings and it is between the Sussex and Gieves.'

Verulam had a long maintenance in Portland and the crew was moved ashore into HMS Osprey, a barracks on the top of Portland Bill. I was given a new job, messman in Ospreys CPO mess. This was a cushy job, keeping their mess clean, making tea and, when duty messman, preparing '9 o'clockers', a small supper snack that was served at that time. The usual menu included a bowl of hard-boiled eggs which were mashed up with salad cream and seasoning, to a gooey mass which was eaten as a sandwich filling. One night, when I was duty, a Chief Petty Officer berated me and accused me of using powdered eggs, informing me that he had enough powdered eggs in the war. He refused to believe me when I told him he was mistaken and next day he complained to the Mess Caterer, who sent for me. When I explained what had happened, he asked if I had left any eggshell in the egg mash. When I replied, 'No. I was careful,' he told me that in the future I should deliberately do so. It worked, never again did that Chief complain about powdered egg, only about the eggshell!

Chapter 4
HMS Sheffield / HMS Bellerophon
Reserve Fleet Portsmouth 1962

My draft to Verulam only lasted a year and then it was back to Portsmouth and to HMS Bellerophon, the name of the Reserve fleet. We lived on the 'Flag ship', HMS Sheffield, a wartime cruiser which was called the 'Shiny Shef' as the people of Sheffield had paid for many 'Tiddly' extras. It was what was called a 'cushy' draft.

I was the only UC (Underwater Controller, an ASDIC operator) on the TAS party and a CPO Artificer, a 'Lecky (electrician) and myself were tasked to go around the reserve ships in Portsmouth harbour and check that the ASDIC was working. The Chief Tiff and 'Lecky had never worked on ASDIC before, so my job was to switch everything on, lower the ASDIC dome and checked that it pinged correctly. If anything did not work, which was frequently, I would sit and read the Daily Mirror for hours until it was fixed. I got quite good at the crossword. We limited our inspection to just two ships a day and this meant learning the harbour ferry launch routine and going from dockyard cafe to dockyard cafe to fill in the time before returning for lunch or 'secure', (finish work time). I had never drunk so much coffee before in my life.

The TAS party also had an extra perk. Once a month, on the fourth Friday afternoon, HMS Sheffield had Divisions (a parade) and Captain's inspection. It just so happened that every fourth Friday, one of the fleet of reserve mine sweepers, which were based at Southampton, had to have its magnetic sweeping cable replaced, so the entire TAS party travelled there in the morning to do the job. We normally finished by midday so we had a long pub lunch and arrived back on the 'Shiny Shef' just as Divisions finished. In six months, not once did I go to Divisions.

That summer, a draft chit arrived for me - another Aircraft Carrier. This was a real shock as I really wanted to use my ASW training, and carriers do not offer that. In fact, on Albion, we only closed up (on watch) once in the ACR (ASDIC Control Room, later called Sonar Control Room), and that was as we approached the Formosa straits and Korea - and it was for real, not an exercise. There were two of us closed-up in the ACR (for those who are interested in historical ASDIC, it was a 149 set with manual training and no bearing recorder. This set was so old that it was never mentioned on my UC's course). I gained good contact on ASDIC with a moving object which I was sure was a submarine and, having eventually found where the microphone was, tried to inform the bridge and ops room of a possible hostile contact, but no one answered. We screamed and shouted but to no avail. We were the only two people of the fifteen hundred onboard that knew about this potential enemy that could attack us and we could not tell anyone. It was 10 decks up to the bridge and too far to run, especially with hatches and doors clipped tight in defence stations, and when I lost contact after about 10 minutes we decided not to bother because we were sure to get the blame and as we were still afloat it obviously had not fired a torpedo.

Anyway, back to my draft chit, I bleated at the Chief TASI (my boss, with the big badge that I coveted) about this and he agreed with me and a week later the draft chit was cancelled and a new one issued for HMS Caesar, a wartime-built CA class destroyer. A sister ship, Cavalier, is moored on the Thames in London. It was not an ASW Frigate, which I wanted, but did have Squid (anti-submarine Mortar Mk 4) and a more modern ASDIC. Caesar was 'Captain 'D' to the 8th Destroyer squadron based in Singapore and it was an 18 month foreign draft, which was the new length of a foreign draft, recently being reduced from 30 months.

Chapter 5
HMS Caesar, Far East 1962/64

In those days, ships commissioned and decommission en-bloc. No 'trickle' drafting. Caesar's entire ships company flew by Britannia Airways (in Britannia prop aircraft) to Singapore, refuelling in Athens, India and at an overnight stop in Gan, Maldives islands. It took two days and was the first time that I had ever flown – and I never wanted to fly again. It was a noisy, vibrating, uncomfortable journey of boredom. In-flight entertainment consisted of endless games of 'eye spy', made exceedingly difficult by only seeing sea, sky and clouds. In-flight catering was a brown bag of curling sandwiches. Not in my worst nightmare would I have believed that one day I would become an air crewman.

The commissioning ceremony took place on the parade ground of HMS Terror (the RN barracks in the dockyard) and we met our Skipper, Captain B.D.O. McIntyre, a veteran of the Second World War. He emphasised how important our job was and explained that USSR influenced Indonesia, had recently obtained 2 Sverdlov class cruisers which had very thick armour plating, 12×6 inch and 12×4 inch guns and lots of smaller ones plus 10 torpedo tubes. Our task was to counter that threat with an armament consisting of a thin hull, 2×4.5 inch guns, 4×Mk 9 torpedoes, (first in service in 1930!), Squid (ASW mortar Mk 4) and a couple of Oerlikon anti-aircraft guns. Oh yes, we could also do 36 knots. 'No problem' we thought, there are 4 of us in the 8th Destroyer squadron and we are British!

We were accommodated at HMS Terror, the RN barracks, until the refit was completed. The entire ship's company was on one floor of an accommodation block and having just arrived from the UK the heat and humidity were overpowering. No A/C in those days, just windows with no glass, fans and big balconies. Being on the equator, the climate is tropical rainforest and consists of two seasons; Wet and Very Wet. When it rains (usually late afternoon) the drops are so heavy, falling from clouds towering over 5 miles high, that they actually bounce almost three feet in the air, causing a low level, very wet, fog just above the ground. As soon as it stops (1 – 2 hours later) the water starts to evaporate, steam rises, and the humidity is 100%. Mould continually grows on shoes and clothes that are stowed in lockers. During the very wet season it also rains during the night. As the rain comes from high cumulonimbus clouds, it is very cold, sometimes mixed with hail. In harbour, sun awnings were rigged around the ship to keep the decks cooler and every day the duty watch had to 'slope awnings' so that the rain would run off and not tear them with the ferocity of the deluge. We quickly learnt that the best dress for sloping awnings was swimming costumes and afterwards we took the opportunity to have an extra cold shower.

Caesar had no air-conditioning, and the messes were very primitive by today's standards. After about nine months an air-conditioning unit was installed in the Forward, Seaman's' mess. Unfortunately, the installers for this monstrous chunk of machinery had no idea how to fit it. There was no exhaust to vent the hot air; it just blew out the back making the mess even hotter.

There was not enough space in the forward mess, under the fo'c's'le and the 4 inch gun, for the standard size Pussers (Naval) kit locker and as one of the junior ABs I had to use a half size one that was a third part of a narrow bunk. It was then that I realised why St Vincent had taught us to fold our kit so small. My career up to then had been in a big ships and one without a wartime crew, not a fully manned destroyers, so I had to re-learn that lesson. My bed was a metal framed camp bed and as there was no room for it in the mess I (and others) slept in the flat (passageway) that led to the mess. I soon discovered that, in harbour, if I placed my camp bed on deck, in an exact position under the quadruple torpedo tubes, it was a cooler place to sleep but if I were an inch out in positioning there would be a soaking from the night rain. This berth could not be used at sea as waves would often sweep along the 'iron deck' as it was called, for it was scarcely six feet above sea level. Every morning watch at sea the watch on deck would search the iron deck for flying fish and squid and have them cooked for breakfast. The messing arrangement was 'Broad side' messing. This meant the food was selected by the Catering office and cooked by Chinese, qualified cooks. At mealtime the food was collected from the galley and we ate it in our mess. Although we never lost any food during the delivery it was sometimes diluted with salt water. The 'duty cooks' had to do the washing up afterwards. Apart from the Chinese chefs, who were good and induced in me a love of Chinese food, we also had a Chinese cobbler (Shoe-Shoe), tailor (Sew-Sew, from whom we bought skimpy working shorts and shirts) and laundry (Dhobi-Dhobi). They combined to run a soft drink (goffer) empire. We would buy a book of tickets on payday (every two weeks) and use them to purchase 'softies', which were kept cooled in a large tub of iced water. Additional books could be purchased on credit if required.

On one occasion, during a self-maintenance period, I had collected some Teepol (brown liquid soap), in a Coke bottle and as I passed a boiler room access, a stoker (Mechanical Engineer) friend, who was cleaning the boilers and who was black with soot streaked with sweat, came out, saw my Coke bottle, snatched it out of my hand, said 'Thanks for the Goffer' and downed it! It happened so quickly I was taken aback and by time I had gathered my wits he had vomited and ended up in the sickbay undergoing a stomach pump. I was on Captain's defaulters because of this and was charged with 'administering poison to a junior rating' and warned that this was a criminal offence, and I could have a lawyer if required. When I explained what had happened, I was asked whether I had tried to stop him and, if so, when. I replied truthfully 'When the bubbles came out of his nose Sir'. Even the Cox'n, who was in charge of discipline, (police chief), sniggered at this. I was admonished and ME Firth had new nickname – Frothy. I believe that he never drank Coke again.

A huge learning curve was encountered when I was tasked as Cox'n (driver) of the ship's boats. One was a 25ft motorboat and the other the 3-in-1 27ft 'motor whaler'. Both of these craft required a 'stoker' to sit amidships, who operated the engine according to the Cox'n's command, which was sent by blowing on a whistle. I just could not get the hang of coming alongside the ship or jetty, and had many mishaps, causing damage to the boat. Sometimes I stopped the boat so far away that the liberty men almost had to swim to get ashore or I ended up crashing against (and once up) the accommodation ladder or jetty very hard and everyone was sent sprawling in the bilges. The more cautious I became the more accidents and incidents happened. I just could not understand what I was doing wrong until one day the Officer of the Watch, who, incidentally until then I had little respect for, explained that the problem was. A) I was too slow and B) that I should approach at 45 degrees, not at a shallow angle. Disbelieving him, the next time I approached the ladder, with the OOW glaring expectantly down at me and the passengers crossing themselves and rubbing their lucky charms, I decided to do exactly as he said to prove him wrong and came in at high speed and at 45 degrees and went hard astern to stop. It was perfect come-along-side. So, they do teach some sensible things at Dartmouth Officers College. I now teach this method to my sailing students and once berthed a 50ft yacht in a 56ft gap with 35 knots of offshore wind in Greece this way. I had the locals, convinced that we were going to park on the jetty, running for safety as I came in at 4 knots, but with the aid of my crew at the bow calling the distance I stopped exactly in the centre and barely depressed the fenders. Thank you Lt.Cdr Stratfield-James. Your words were true. So, all you budding cox'n's, why not try it yourself. I also teach my students never to 'cut the corner' on blind bends. Once, when passing close astern of Caesar, I met my Oppo (opposite number, friend) in the other boat doing the same thing coming the opposite way! Looking back, it was an exceptionally good experience for me, because if a boat was damaged the Cox'n had to help the shipwright repair it (and no shore leave until it was done), so I learnt a lot about boat repairs. I do feel sorry for the Chippies as I gave them a lot of extra work. When they found out that I was duty boats crew they were like rats deserting a sinking ship, fighting amongst themselves to get ashore!

Getting safely alongside was a big step in my boat handling competency but there were still gaps, or perhaps I should say chasms, in my ability. After a very drunken 'run ashore' in Mombasa I returned onboard one morning, just before shore leave expired, very much the worse for wear. My first trip was to take the Navigating officer ashore in the motorboat. He sat in the bow on a cushioned thwart (seat) facing forward, enjoying the cool morning air, little knowing what was going to happen to him. I approached the jetty faster than normal, over-confident with last night's Tusker beer still in my system (which meant fast!) and placed the signal whistle between my lips and blew the signal for 'neutral', which the stoker (Frothy Firth) did. I then tried to signal 'full astern' to slow the boat as I turned hard to parallel the jetty, but the whistle shot out my mouth. I tried unsuccessfully to catch it as it disappeared into the bilges, leaving the tiller unattended and so we did not turn. Ahead of the boat was a sloping 'Hard', stone blocks laid on the seashore to enable boats to be pulled ashore. They were not intended for beaching a boat travelling at 4 knots! As we raced towards the shore the bow reared up and we came to a sudden stop. The Navigator, who until then been quietly sitting and enjoying the trip was catapulted up and forward and screaming, managed to grab hold of the bow to stop himself going overboard. I was thrown forward onto the stoker and we both ended up hard against the engine bulkhead. In my not completely sober state, I thought it very funny and could not stop laughing. Surprisingly, there was no damage to the boat and the 'Nav' never referred to the matter afterwards. Never again did I drive a boat not sober!

I have always craved new skills and information, especially if it was to my advantage. I undertook a cinema operators' course, as I realised that if you showed the weekly films onboard ship, the welfare fund paid you. That became a good source of pocket money but (there is always a but) my cinematographic career did not start well. Two days after qualifying, I was asked to show a film in the Officers' club. The film was rather old and well worn, with torn sprocket holes, so I constantly had to stop and adjust the film loop and I could not understand why there was no sound until I remembered to switch on the amplifier. I saved my biggest cock-up until the last reel when I failed to fasten the upper film spool on properly and, just at the exciting part, the spool fell off the projector and rolled down towards the screen, unwinding the film as it went and with me chasing it and getting the film wrapped around my ankles, Needless to say, the film tore, and it took about five minutes before I had everything working again. Perhaps not surprisingly, I was never asked to show a film in the Officers' club again.

I also did a paint spraying course but never had that job whilst in the navy. However, the knowledge I gained has proved invaluable, spraying cars, boats and recently my garden chalet. Knowledge is very seldom wasted. If there is a chance of learning something new go for it.

Another course I completed in Singapore was the Shallow Water Divers' course (forerunner of the Ships Divers' course).

Every ship is expected, in wartime, to be able to clear itself of any attached limpet mines, so SWDs were carried. We were trained in the use of a pure oxygen diving set and limited to 33ft (10 metres). The set consisted of 2 × 0.6 litre pure O_2 bottles plus 1 reserve. These had to be hand pumped to 3,000 psi, from a 500 psi 150 cubic ft supply tank, which took two men about 10 minutes hard pumping for every bottle. Not an easy job in the tropical heat. The pure O_2 flowed into a counter-lung, which is a bag that goes around the neck and chest, and breathed from, through a protosorb, which absorbed CO_2, and then back into the lung. On the upper part of the counter- lung there was a pressure release vent. When wanting to attack unseen, the lung would be completely deflated ,well clear of observers ,and the pressure release valve screwed closed. Now no bubbles could come to the surface. The problem is that O_2 is constantly flowing into the counter-lung, so buoyancy increases with time, making it difficult to maintain depth. The endurance of the set was 90 minutes. Unlike today's scuba gear the mouthpiece was not separate; it formed part of the full facemask.

The first days of the 4 week course consisted of fitness training – long swims and runs, theory, learning how to put on the rubber 'dry suit', (which required a buddy) and that had to be done in less than 3 minutes whenever the word 'Awkward' was shouted, and chipping chain links open underwater. To do the latter, a heavy weight was lowered to the sea bed on the end of a rope (a Shot Rope) and we descended the rope, sat on the bottom with the shot weight on our thighs and, using the shot as a work-bench, hammered a chisel into the chain until it parted. Nobody managed on the first day and when, eventually, the chain link parted it was brought to the surface and we were told to go back down and do another one. Another task was to swim down to some workbenches, complete with vices, which were anchored to the seabed, and using a hacksaw, saw through the chain. Unless you wrap yourself around the bench like an anaconda all that happens, as you try to saw, is that your body moves backwards and forwards and the saw stays still!

I will never forget the first night dive. A triangular, rope, 'jackstay' was laid on the seabed around 20ft depth, making a course of about 300 yards, and the task was to swim around it for 90 minutes. The water in the tropics is full of bioluminescence – as you move your hand the water turns fiery white, – and is also full of sea snakes. Once the novelty of the bioluminescence had worn off, my thoughts turned to sea snakes. I had a small head torch but as my dive time extended, the silt stirred up from the bottom by swimming constantly around the same track made it useless. Visibility became zero and I lost contact with the rope of the jackstay. I tried dragging my hand over the bottom hoping to find the rope but all that happened was a denser silt cloud. It knew it could not be too far away and I ended up using both hands, almost crawling along the seabed. Still no jackstay so I tried a different direction - until I touched something long, slimy, thin, and, I thought, wriggly. With a shout into my facemask I lunged for the surface and found that the water was only three foot deep, I was standing on the bottom, a hundred yards from the jackstay. The diving instructor was not very impressed. An extra 'Awkward' was awarded to me for that performance, and the sea snake? A length of old rope!

At the end of the course a practical test was to find some dummy limpet mines that had been hidden on a WW2 Japanese destroyer that had been quietly rotting away for the last 18 years. The weed on the hull was over a metre long and home to its own eco system. Fish of all sizes and colours were hiding in the fronds. Very beautiful. As I left the surface the instructor's final command of 'Don't forget to search the inlets' stayed with me. I discovered the easy one, the mine placed on the 'A' bracket of the prop shaft. Then I searched for the others. I found a couple of small inlets, nothing there, and then the main engine room inlet, a much larger hole. I felt around the edges, all clear. I thrust my arm in as far as I could reach, and something grabbed hold of my wrist and hung on tightly. I probably gave a full-bodied scream as I shot to the surface, emulating a Polaris missile.

The assistant instructor told everyone that my fins were flapping full speed a foot above the water but that was an exaggeration – I think. The poor little octopus whose home I had violated flew off my franticly waving arm and quickly swam back to the depths. Ever after that experience, I have always shone a torch into any underwater hole before I insert my hand. Despite my moments of comedy drama, out of the initial twelve who commenced the course I was one of the four who passed and was allowed to wear the diving badge on my forearm and to receive 4 shillings (20 p) a day extra pay.

Caesar spent countless hours practising torpedo attacks, usually with the other three ships of our squadron, Cavalier, Cavendish, and Cassandra. My torpedo attack action station was on the open, upper bridge and I passed the settings to the torpedoes in the tubes, called F, I, R and E (I suppose, it makes a change from 1, 2, 3, 4). The torpedoes had semi burner diesel engines, which meant they also had a compressed air tank, and could speed along up to 40 knots with a max range of 15,000 yards. These were not simple point-and-shoot weapons; settings could be applied: Depth chosen (shallow, deep) for different size ships, a 'Fore run' chosen, which was how far the torpedo would run on a straight course before starting a zig-zag pattern attack course, if selected. To aim the torpedoes, which were launched on the beam, at 90 degrees to the ships head, the ship turned. They were always fired in sequence, as the ship turned, to fan out. It was an exhilarating sight to see an attack. All four ships would increase speed to 35 knots and then alter course violently, first one way then the other, heeling so that waves were breaking over the iron deck. Black smoke would be forced out of our funnels by the uptake fans (we burnt Furnace Fuel Oil, FFO to power our steam turbines) and the smoke lay thick, sandwiched between the blue of the sea and tropical sky. Everyone onboard had to cling on tight or wedge themselves securely during these turns and the timing was irregular, to confuse the target. On one of the turns, the torpedoes would be launched, aiming to intercept the target, which was over 2 miles away, but we would continue our zig-zag approach so as not to signify we had attacked and would then turn away and escape back through our own smoke screen.

Well, that was the plan but when now I realise the Svervlod's capability, with guns that could sink us at 10 miles and there would be two of them, against four of us, and of course radar, which nullified our escape tactic of using the smoke screen, perhaps all may not have gone to plan. We practised these coordinated attacks by day and night. These practice attacks were carried out throughout the 18 month commission but only once were we allowed to fire a live torpedo. There is a large rock, rising to about 50 meters above sea level off Borneo, that had been used for years as target practice by the RN and this was going to be our chance to prove the weapon. We zigzagged towards it and launched our weapon without pattern run, (straight course, without zig-zag) and then slowed down to confirm that all went well. Unfortunately, the torpedo missed the islet but luckily exploded on a reef a hundred yards away or it would be lying on the seabed, waiting for some fisherman to recover a live and primed torpedo!! The Captain was infuriated and threatened that when he found the culprit, he would be fired at the rock to make amends. The blame was laid on the torpedo tube crew who had failed to ensure that the tubes were locked on the beam, and as the torpedo launched, the tubes moved slightly. The tube crew blamed the weapon artificers that the lock did not engage properly. The TASO (Torpedo and Anti-Submarine Officer) sulked and locked himself in his cabin.

When it was not a torpedo attack my action station was in the Sonar Control Room (ASDIC had then became Sonar). Caesar had a type-164 sonar which fired our Squid anti-submarine mortar. The days of rolling depth charges over the stern or throwing them over the side had long passed. The problem with that system, was that the ship had to pass directly over top of the submarine and Sonar contact would have been lost a minute earlier as the sonar could not be tilted down, it only 'pinged' a narrow, horizontal beam (and often, because of the effect of water pressure and temperature gradients the beam would bend up towards the surface.) This silent, period, when it no longer heard the attacking ship's sonar 'ping', warned the submarine that it was about to be depth charged and enabled it to alter course, undetected, and avoid the depth charges. Towards the end of WW2 a new weapon emerged, called 'Hedge-hog', which fired 24 small bombs ahead of the ship and, if one hit the sub, they all exploded. This enabled the ship to keep tracking the submarine after firing, providing the ship altered course. Later Mortar Mk 4, Squid, was developed. This was a depth bomb that could be thrown 400 yards (before the dead space was reached) ahead of the ship and was stabilised to allow for pitch and roll. The latest sonar, 164, fired the Squid automatically, allowing for different relative closing speeds. It also had an extra sonar attachment called Q that allowed us to keep contact with a deep submarine closer. We thought that this was high-tech, but everything relied on a length of string that pulled the stylus that give an accurate range and fired the mortar. The person required to use this weapon system was the 'First Operator' who controlled the direction of the sonar transducer and gave his opinion as to what he could hear, although the Range Recorder and Bearing recorder operators would also give input. The SCR Controller would then make his judgement and tell the TASO in the Ops room his verdict. The TASO, who would be listening to many speakers, including the sonar, would then give the final decree and tell the Operations Officer who would inform the Captain who would then say if the contact was to be prosecuted (jargon for attacked).. Later in my life, one of the things which endeared me to helicopter ASW was that it only involved the observer and the crewman to decide to attack. I would say it was a submarine and he would arrange the attack.

Squid depth bombs are much cheaper than torpedoes, and occasionally, we fired one. This made us incredibly happy, as afterwards we would lower the sea boat and collect all the dead fish and dined well for a couple of days.

Caesar was the hardest ship I ever served on; exercise after exercise and the conditions we worked and lived in would probably be difficult to tolerate by many peacetime sailors. After one long exercise one of our evaporators broke down, which meant no water could be distilled for use by the crew, so a canvas pool was erected on the Iron Deck and half filled with water and that was the ships' company's bath until we arrived back in Singapore. For the officers, the 14ft RNSA dinghy was used. Half a cupful of fresh water was issued morning and night for teeth cleaning. This did not stop the torpedo attack practices, day and night, action stations and other war-like exercises and of course we were still in the tropics.

For over a month we anchored off Adu Atoll, in the Maldives Islands. The local Government was in dispute with the British Representative, Sir Humphrey Hartington Davies, so we anchored in the lagoon to protect him, keeping in Harbour Defence Stations. We were allowed leave and we climbed palm trees, swam and dived on the coral etc. The second day likewise and the third, fourth, fifth...After a week we were getting bored. After two weeks we were doubly bored, and after the third week, having seen all the films on board, read all the books and running short of beer extremely bored so when the RAF made a mail drop, missed the lagoon and the mail canister broke open, it was almost the last straw.

I had one unforgettable experience. I had taken the Captain, First Lieutenant and Navigating Officer ashore in the motorboat to a meeting with the Sir Humphrey and was waiting on the beach for them to finish when a Dhonie (local boat) arrived, with armed men aboard. They looked at the boat's engineer and me as they stepped ashore, and started talking amongst themselves, casting glances in our direction and looking very sinister. The stoker and I looked at each other, not knowing what to do. We had no weapons. I eventually decided that I had better find the Captain and tell him but that would mean leaving the stoker alone. We pushed the boat back a few yards until it was afloat, and I told 'Stokes' to make sure the engine was ready for starting and if he heard shooting to get out to sea and wait. I walked passed the men and up the beach, following the jungle track leading to H.E's residence. I heard the click of bolts and the 'snick' of rounds being loaded. I tried to be nonchalant, but my legs felt weak and hairs really do stand up on the back of the neck when scared. As soon as I rounded a corner and was out of sight of the beach I ran at full pelt to the residence and burst into the meeting, without knocking. I breathlessly blurted out what I had seen – and Sir Humphrey laughed and said, 'It's only the rat-catchers, they come this time every month'!

Caesar also carried out anti-piracy patrol around Borneo and the Malacca Straits For this we carried a couple of local policemen. The pirates use to operate at night, with no lights on, and one night there was a loud crash as we hit one trying to cross our bow. Our Skipper intend to stop and rescue any survivors but the police said not to bother – it saved on the paper work. We never caught any pirates, as to work up to our top speed took a long time (had to light all the boilers which took time) and the pirates had very fast boats, with high revving outboard engines. I think that it was HMS Cavalier that managed to stop one, and its crew jumped overboard. Cavalier lowered a sea-boat to rescue them and as they approached a survivor hanging on to the rudder post of the sinking boat, drew a revolver and shot the RN bowman dead. That particular pirate suffered a lot of unfortunate accidents onboard Cavalier, before being transferred ashore to face charges. He was obviously accident prone. A surprising fact is that the bowman, Able Seaman Sutherland, was buried in a Christian graveyard ashore and in the next grave was another AB Sutherland who was killed by pirates exactly 100 years earlier! Our only serious casualty on Caesar, for the whole time in commission, was when our search party were unloading weapons and there was an accidental discharges which ricochet off the deck and bulkhead before removing a large part of someone's leg. One of the most dangerous things is a sailor with a gun – to his mates.

When we went ashore every department stuck together. There were no TVs in the bars and very few jukeboxes. For entertainment we sang, as did every department and every ship. There were always singing wars early in the evening and then we usually united. We sang songs composed onboard and pop songs but mainly sailors and rugby players' songs. We were Caesar's warriors and nobody had better deny it. Before I left the Navy this form of entertainment had died out. From what I have seen lately entertainment consists of Facebook and SMSing on mobile phones. I suppose the good thing about that is that it takes up drinking time whist singing makes you thirsty. There was a tremendous camaraderie on Caesar. Our football team, which always had a 100% turnout of Caesar's supporters was only ever beaten once and that was by the ships' team from an aircraft carrier. The star player was AB Dadd who, years later in the Falkland's War, was one of the true heroes when he defused live bombs on HMS Coventry.

On one occasion, whilst we were undergoing Self Maintenance in Singapore, the dockyard went on strike, but the MoD decided that sailors would maintain the essential services. One of these services was Anti Malaria Party. This required going around not just the dockyard but all of Singapore Island, spraying the stagnant pools and ponds with a diesel-like oil, which was carried on our backs in large containers and pumped. This oil spread across the surface and killed the mosquito lava. I was pleased to be selected for this job as it meant seeing places on Singapore Island that I had never been to before, and meeting and interacting with locals in their kampongs (villages). The first week we had a guide and in the following weeks dropped off by Bedford lorry, one by one, making our own way back, after spraying all day, to the rendezvous for the evening return to HMS Terror. It was magical, by myself for once, exploring the island. Discovering a water-fall that appeared to gush out of solid rock (Moses, eat your heart out!), idyllic pools in jungle clearings and seeing groups of giggling girls beating their washing on stones as their forbears had been doing for centuries except that now there were packets of Omo, Tide and Persil lying around. There was one occasion when I had been too enthusiastic in spraying a pool, allowing oil to float down to a washing area, and the girls were rather irate, but I was forgiven – eventually, when they had run out of Malay and Chinese swear words.

I was issued daily with a 'bag lunch' but often invited to eat with the natives as it was unusual for them to be visited by a European and they were appreciative of our efforts to control malaria. During the last week of the strike (I think it lasted for a month) I stopped at a friendly Kampong (village) and was offered a monkey in exchange for my almost full container of oil. This seemed a good idea at the time as it meant that I lazed around the Kampong, in the shade, for the rest of the day, so late afternoon I boarded the Bedford lorry with a new pet. At Terror, Caesar's ships company were as usual billeted on one floor of a barrack block and George, my monkey named after the Cox'n, was very popular. I kept him tied up and everybody fed him fruit. I used to walk him like a dog in the evenings. This enjoyable state lasted for almost a week until I returned from the ship one day and found that George had chewed through his lead and disappeared. We looked for him, but he had gone, back to the jungle we presumed. As usual that afternoon I went ashore to Nee Soon village or somewhere, returning in the early hours. Next morning when we 'Fell In' for work I was told that I was on Captain's defaulters and when I asked why was told 'You're about to find out lad'. I was very soon in front of the Captain and the charge was read out 'Did keep a pet onboard HMS Terror without permission'.

Unfortunately, George had not escaped to the jungle but had climbed the parade ground mast. The RN has always taken its tradition of 'Sunset' very seriously, especially on shore establishments. Five minutes before the prescribed time the Evening Colour party march to the foot of the mast, from which the large White Ensign flies. At the correct time, the Second OOW calls 'Sunset Sir', the OOW says 'Make it so', the Quartermaster pipes the 'Still', everybody stands to attention, the Colours Party salutes and the Ensign is lowered slowly and reverently whilst the Royal Marine Bugler plays 'Sunset', with the Ensign in the hand of the signalman and the bugler finishing at the same time. Unfortunately it was not to be, that evening. As the signalman started to lower the Ensign, George, high up the mast, decided that he wanted it raised so he grabbed the flag and pulled upwards. The signalman, feeling a resistance, pulled harder but so did George and a tug of war commenced. Still trying to get the Ensign down before the bugler finished playing 'Sunset', the signalman jumped up and put his full weight on the flag halyard, which was too much for George, but instead of letting go of the Ensign he let go of the mast and the Ensign, with the signalman pulling and George's weight helping, came down in a rush, enveloping the Signalman. George, seeing the shape of a human under the ensign decided to bite and scratch. The Royal Marine, displaying the quick thinking and bravery for which the corps is renowned, finished the last few bars of 'Sunset' at record speed and subdued the monkey, getting bitten in the process. This part of the story is agreed by all but some say that George managed to escape again and disappeared into the jungle whilst others are adamant that next morning the gunners party took him to the rifle range and used him as target practice. I hope he lived a long life back in the wild. I ended up by losing 1 day's leave but I think that the Skipper saw the funny side of it as a week later I was promoted 'Acting Local Leading Seaman', my first step on the promotion ladder.

I was that exceedingly rare beast, a U/A Killick (Leading Hand, so called because of the small anchor badge, called a Killick). On the Ships books I had 'U/A' against my name, which meant that I was Under Age to draw my daily tot of rum and I would have to wait half a year until, reaching the age of 20 years. Then 'G' for grog would be inserted, and I could join my mess mates sitting around the rum fanny every lunch time.

After I was rated 'Acting Local' Leading Seaman and Caesar was in Singapore's floating dock undergoing a refit, the task of the duty Seaman Killick was to drive the Harbour Master's 20 metre HLD (Harbour Launch, Defence) around on 'Guard Duty' in the evening. Whilst the ships company lived ashore in Terror barracks, the duty watch slept onboard the ship in the floating dock. There was no beer issue in harbour those days, so it was the customary, but unofficial, task of the Guard Boat to collect the beer order from the duty watch and then go ashore to Terror canteen with the 'mess fanny' (a large container) and collect the required number of pints of draught beer. The Standing Order for the skipper of the HLD was to collect charts from the Queens Harbour Master every evening before sailing but normally we didn't bother. One evening, having spare time, I decided to obey the rules and asked the QHM for charts, only to be told that they had none for me. This seemed not to be a problem, so I carried on as usual. I patrolled along the limits of the harbour as far as the Causeway and then came alongside the floating dock and got the fanny and beer order for the duty watch. It was then out on another patrol after leaving the fanny and beer order in the canteen. Whilst patrolling, I sighted some suspicious object and investigated but it was only rubbish. This delayed me a bit and as the beer would be getting flat and warm, I decided to take a short cut to the canteen and had almost reached there when I saw a strange black object in the water. I altered course towards it - and hit the seabed very hard. The object was a buoy marking a rocky patch. It was embarrassing, having to call for help on the VHF and getting towed back. The lads were really Pd.Offed .about not getting their beer that night. At the subsequent inquiry I was charged with 'Incorrectly performing the duty' etc. as the HLD damage consisted of a hogged keel, jammed gear box, bent prop shaft and tipped screws. In my defence I called the QHM who agreed that he had not given me a chart of the area and the buoy should have been lit. I failed to mention anything about a beer run and had 'Case dismissed'. I now meticulously check charts in unknown waters!

I was a rather ineffectual leading hand as I looked even younger than my 19 years and it is always difficult to 'take charge' of your mates with whom you have been partying with for over a year. Luckily, we were a very efficient and friendly ships' company, and everyone knew what to do without having to be told. I suppose I must have been acceptable as my 'write up' report enabled me to become a proper Leading Seaman shortly after leaving the ship, after having reverted to an AB on leaving.

In late Spring of 1964, we all flew back to the UK, again by Britannia Airways, with bag meals and aft facing seats (which are of course much safer than facing forward – they give much greater protection in a crash). During six weeks' leave I joined the majority of the Brits who were in in the grip of something called Beatle mania, referring to a pop group that we had not heard about whilst away.

HMS Caesar

Chapter 6
Diving at HMS Vernon 1964

After leave, my draft chit sent me back to HMS Vernon, Portsmouth, for a conversion course from Shallow Water Diver to Ship's Diver. Vernon was not only the Torpedo and Anti-Submarine but also the Clearance Diving training establishment. My course meant learning about and using compressed air 'Swimmers Air Breathing Apparatus' (SABA). Pure O_2 sets had become a thing of the past for all but the diving specialists, the Clearance Divers.

All diving courses at Vernon were carried out at Horsea Island, which was further up the harbour, and once again the Bedford lorry was our main means of transport. It was there that I first encountered the infamous Horsea Island Mud Run. To ensure that we were fit, most days we had to don our rubber 'Dry' diving suit (with thick under-suits) and then run about a mile over (through!) soft sticky mud, being urged on by the assistance instructors. It was widely believed that none of them had married parents! It was only a two week course but for the first time I found out about 'Stops', to avoid the bends, as now I could descend to 120ft/35 metres and how to read and use de-compression tables. I also had my first 'descent' in a Re-Compression Chamber, a large cylinder that was pressurised by air to simulate the water pressure at varying depths, and found out that we spoke in a squeaky, Mickey Mouse, voice. None of these things had been covered in my SWD course as our maximum depth was only 33ft/10 metres.

The first 120ft dive of the course was in the sea, off Spithead. As I swam down the weighted shot rope, the increasing water pressure caused the creases in the 'dry' rubber suit to pinch me, so I compensated by partially inflating it by opening a small, compensating, 'guffing up,' compressed air bottle. As often happens, a leak in the suit allowed very cold deep water to squirt in from around my buttocks and soon my under-suits were sodden and the water ran down to the lowest part of my body, which were my arms and torso, as the suit started to fill as I swam down to the bottom of the Solent.

I finally reached the seabed, and it was pitch black. I inverted myself so that I was head up, which meant that the cold water in the suit drained from my upper torso down to the dry area around my legs, now making me thoroughly wet and cold. Shivering, I waited for the signal tugs on my life-line, telling me to start returning to the surface, and after 10 minutes I commenced a slow ascent. The air, in the upper part of my suit, started to expand as the pressure decreased, which I should have vented by allowing it to escape by pulling on my wrist-seals but I was slow in doing so and I realised that I was at the first 'stop' point, where I had to wait, to avoid the bends.

I held tightly to the shot-rope but my inflated body continued rising and I became inverted, legs pointing towards the surface. This allowed all the icy sea water that had been around my legs, to again pour down over my upper body. I was now utterly wet, top and bottom, all the air in my suit was trapped in the legs, and there was no way to vent it. Now I began to feel extremely cold and it seemed hours until I got the next tugs on my lifeline, telling me to ascend to the next stop. To do this upside down I had to slowly allow myself to float upwards, keeping a firm grip on the shot rope. As I ascended, closer to the surface, the air in my suit expanded even more and I became more inflated and buoyant. My legs were like huge, black, cylindrical buoys, lifting me to the surface. It was with very great difficulty that I hung on to the shot-rope at that 'stop.' My cold hands became completely numb and cramped and when eventually, the signal to surface came, I just let go of the shot rope and shot to the surface inverted, with my legs in the air – an inflatable V sign.

With great difficulty I managed to right myself and vent the air from my suit via the wrist-cuffs and, of course all the water that had been around my upper torso cascaded back down to my legs. The instructor and the rest of the course thought this was very funny. I had such a weight of water in my suit (my suit legs were now full of water) that I needed help in climbing the ladder onto the diving boat and it was with a huge sigh of relief that I took off my SABA set and, bending forward and down, started to drain the water from my suit via wrist and neck seals, my body violently shivering.

The Clearance Diving Instructor managed to stop laughing and asked if I was OK. When I nodded 'Yes', he said 'Good, get your set back on, you are going down again.' I looked at him in amazement. I knew that I could refuse and take myself off the course - but could I do another dive?

With tears in my eyes and a sob, I belted myself back into the SABA with difficulty, hands numb, and with shivering, uncoordinated legs walked to the back of the boat to jump in. I gave a shaky thumbs-up to show I was ready and was just going to step into the water when I was told 'OK get your gear off and have a cup of hot soup.' Diving students were never failed; they took themselves 'off course'. RN diving is not for sissies.

After the Ships' Divers course, I was sent to work in the Shipwrights shop, which again improved my boat repairing skills. I had a Lambretta motor scooter in those days (the days of Mods with scooters and Rockers with motorbikes having the occasional pitched battle) and wanted a secure waterproof stowage box on it. I toured the bike shops but nothing was available, the usual reason being that 'Nobody wants them an' there ain't any'. Well, I wanted one and working in the 'Chippies shop' gave me the idea of making one out of wood. It was a success and popular and I soon started a production line until the Chief Chippy pointed out that the Queen would rather I used her wood to the benefit of the Navy and not me. It was well over a year later that I first saw a factory-made bike box.

At Vernon I also took the next step in my ASW career – and got a star under the TAS badge. I became an Under Water Controller Second class after a 3 month course and also my 'B13' promotion form arrived and I became a 'proper' Leading Seaman and took command of working parties. One duty weekend a group of CCF cadets were visiting Vernon and a young lad by the name of *Charles*, (who for some reason had a minder and who lived in big houses in London, Windsor and Scotland) joined my road sweeping working party. Years later, his younger brother *Andrew* was a student on my helicopter squadron, but that is another story.

During another weekend duty one Friday at 2200 I was summoned by the Duty Officer, given a pair of handcuffs, railway warrants to Glasgow and return, a ten pound note from the welfare fund for expenses, and told to bring a deserter back to HMS Vernon. This entailed an overnight train trip from Portsmouth, via London, to Scotland and I ended up in a Glasgow police station the next afternoon. A couple of British Rail snacks had used up £5 and I was rather hungry. I walked back to the railway station, with my prisoner, and, to spare embarrassment, draped my Burberry raincoat over the handcuffs connecting us. Two girls tried to walk between us and then, thinking we were holding hands called us 'Sassenach Poofs'. For the train journey back south, I managed to connect the handcuffs to the seat so that we did not attract any more attention, arriving back in Vernon Sunday evening after missing two nights' sleep and feeling ravenous. I had to pay back the 10 pounds to the welfare fund as I had no receipts and ended up paying for all of our food.

It was at Vernon, on my 20th birthday, that I started drawing my tot of rum. From the age of 20, we were issued a gill - ⅛ of a pint, of neat rum a day. Ratings had it diluted with 2 parts of water, making it grog (so called after Admiral Vernon enforced it on the RN. He wore a cloak of a material called Grogram and had the nickname of 'Old Grog'). Senior Ratings were expected to add the water themselves! This daily issue was finally stopped on 31st of July, 1970.

The tot was a currency on the lower deck. Debts were repaid and favours asked with it. It was a ceremony that stretched back hundreds of years and the unwritten traditions were passed down through the centuries. It started every forenoon when the pipe 'Up Spirits' came on the Tannoy at 1145. On board ship the 'Rum Bosun' of each mess would collect the rum fanny, which was dark brown and pitted inside, never washed out, and proceed to the spirit store where the Duty Officer, Duty Supply Officer (Victualling) and the Master at Arms or Cox'n supervised the Issue. The quantity of grog for each mess was mixed and measured by pouring rum from one measure to another. To make sure the measure was not short, extra grog was allowed to overflow into the mess rum fanny. The Rum Bosun (the senior alcoholic!) took the grog to the mess and sat at the head of the mess-table. On his left was the 'Ticker-Off', the next senior alky. He was armed with a Perspex peg board with the 'G' ratings names on one side and adjacent each name were 2 holes, one for tot 'Not Drawn' and one for tot 'Drawn'. In the 'Not Drawn' hole was a coloured peg. When the tot was drawn the appropriate peg would be moved to the 'Drawn' hole. This method ensured that everyone entitled had their rum. Only a limited number of glasses were used, no washing between uses.

After drawing the tot, it was traditional to offer the Rum Bosun and the Ticker-Offer, a 'Wet'. A wet meant the lips were moistened. A 'Sip' was a bit more, the rum reached the mouth. 'Gulpers' was a swallow of the tot and 'Half-a-tot' self-explanatory. 'Sandy bottom' was to drink the complete tot. You gave your friends a wet. A small favour would earn 'sippers'. 'Gulpers 'was for a great favour or perhaps a good friend's birthday and 'half a tot' for a sub (changing duties with someone, to your advantage). If your life had been saved, then maybe it would be 'Sandy bottom'. After they had drawn their tot, the hardened drinkers would sit and wait. After a while the ticker-off would be asked if so-and-so had been drawn. It was like vultures waiting for a body to die. When all the 'G' members had their tot there would always be some rum left over, because of the deliberate spillage when first being issued. In a large mess this could be a lot of rum. Now who did this rum belong to? It was obviously the Queen and was thus called. The Rum Bosun would measure out a tot of 'Queens' and he and the ticker-off would have a wet and then pass it around the mess table anti-clockwise, every one saying, 'The Queen, God bless her' as they had a wet. It was imperative that the person who drained the glass was the Bosun after it had been passed around everybody. This would be repeated until the 'Queens' was finished. When it is realised that some messes had 40-50 members, the Senior members would have drunk a lot of grog. It was customary to offer a birthday person a sip at least. Every year there were deaths caused by drinking too much rum and as the RN became more technical many mistakes in the afternoon could be attributed to it, but the upside was that dinner tasted good when the rum had titivated the taste buds. It was strictly forbidden to 'bottle' the tot for later consumption.

When the rum issue ceased, ratings could buy 2 cans of beer at sea and 3 in harbour. Chief and Petty Officers came out of it even better, at sea they could purchase 3 shorts of any spirit and 2 pints of beer, increasing to 3 or 4 beers, in harbour, depending on the Captain. For the first time, Senior rates had a bar in their mess. Drunkenness decreased significantly.

I enjoyed being back at Vernon and on course again and for the second time received the 5 pound prize for top student. Now

I could join the hunt for the submarine enemies of the Queen. Sure enough I was sent to an ASW frigate, HMS Torquay The bad news for me was that she was the Dartmouth College training ship and in the 18 months I served on Torquay, we had only 2 anti-submarine exercises.

Chapter 7
HMS Torquay. Portland 1964/65

Torquay was a type 12 ASW frigate and the first of her class. She was revolutionary as she was the first to have a V shaped hull, which improved her speed into a sea. The sonar onboard was the very latest, Type 170, which had 4 sonar transducers in a diamond array, instead of just one. This gave a better sound beam, greater accuracy, and greater depth. It was the controlling sonar for the Anti-Submarine Mortar Mk 10, known as Limbo. This was the first ASW weapon to have a variable range (up to 1,000 yards). It could fire in any direction and was fully stabilised for pitch and roll. This meant that the target would not know when we had fired and the movement of the ship in the waves was removed. The bomb would explode at a pre-determined depth.

Torquay spent a lot of time in harbour (Devonport) and we were one of three ships making up the Dartmouth Training Squadron. Our main task was to take Officer Cadets to sea for training. Somehow, I ended up as their seamanship instructor. I think that the Chief who was supposed to do that was averse to teaching. It was useful to me as I was studying for my Petty Officers Board (examination) and they do say that you do not know a subject until you teach it. It certainly helped me to pass my POs board. We did a couple of short passages abroad, to Spain and Malta (we were there for Malta's Independence Day ceremony, when the UK handed back the island to the Maltese) and another, longer one to North America; New York, Halifax and then up the St Lawrence seaway to Rochester.

We used to tease the cadets by giving jokey instructions, such as asking them to get green oil for the starboard (green) lamp, to ask the shipwrights for a long weight (wait) when they were kept standing for an hour, and asking for volunteers to go on a Maltese Dog shoot (Maltese Dog was our name for upset tummy). Another ploy was to ask who wanted to be Cox'n of the splash target, a device which was towed behind the ship, which aircraft attacked with live bombs, rockets and cannon fire. There were always volunteers for this!

When we visited Grand Harbour, Malta, I got into the routine of being Cox'n of the Seaboat and taking a 'Banyan' group away. This is the naval term for allowing sailors, when in harbour, to go ashore swimming. Our idea of swimming was a little different. The first stop was at the nearest bar to buy bottles of Mazivin wine – disgusting but unbelievably cheap. I would then take the Seaboat out of the harbour to a nearby cove and the Mazivin drinking was interrupted by the occasional swim until it was time to return to the ship, have supper and then go ashore and visit the 'Gut' (officially named Strait Street), a narrow street that was on a hill and continuously lined with bars. The Gut had been the sailors preferred 'run ashore' for hundreds of years and stank of old wine and urine.

On one occasion I took the 'Banyan Party' for the usual session and on return, despite being 'in a confused state' hoisted the Seaboat, as Torquay was sailing the next morning. I made sure that the bung was out to allow any water to drain, carefully positioned and tensioned the thick, wide 'Gripes' (straps) that held the boat tightly in the davits and connected the boat rope that allowed the Seaboat to be towed alongside if it was used at sea. Next morning Torquay sailed and then I was summoned by the Chief Bosun's Mate, who was the senior CPO in charge of all seamanship evolutions and maintenance. He was a large, quietly spoken man and he beckoned me to follow him and he led me aft to the Seaboat and without a word, pointed. I had done a perfect job of securing the boat for sea – the only thing wrong was that I had hoisted it facing aft instead of forward! As a boat intended for emergency use it was useless. On our return to Malta that afternoon I sneaked aft and lowered and re-hoisted the boat correctly. Amazingly, there was no consequence of my misdemeanour.

Whilst in Malta I managed to get all the diving qualifying time that I needed, which was 120 minutes every four months. Without this time I would lose my diving pay, 4 shillings (20p) a day. Most of that time we dived in Grand Harbour. Once to recover a pair of spectacles that had been dropped over the side and which, against all odds I found within minutes. Having a lively imagination, diving in Grand Harbour was always stressful for me. I kept on thinking of all the tens of thousands of bombs that the Italians and Germans had dropped on Malta during the second world war and realised that there must have been many unexploded ones that were still lying buried in the mud, waiting for an idiot like me to disturb them. I made sure that I kept well clear of any strange lumps and humps!

When Torquay visited N. America, we had a padre onboard and we were also accompanied by the two other ships of the squadron. Normally I am very anti-religion but I have a great respect and liking for that padre; Noel Jones I believe was his name. His sermons were very entertaining. I was Quartermaster, controlling the gangway during the middle watch (midnight to 0400) whilst in New York and the padre and other officers arrived back onboard in a 'Happy State', all with Bunny Club stickers. The padre also had a large teddy bear, which he said that he had won. I asked him if he had a name for it and he instantly replied 'Joyously'. I must have given him a quizzical look as he then quoted a paragraph in the Bible 'Joyously my cross I (eyed) bare (bear)'.

When we went to Halifax, Nova Scotia, I 'fell on bad times'. I had to get 120 minutes diving qualifying time and so I, with ships divers from the other ships of the squadron, went to the diving section of HMCS Granbury, the Canadian shore base. The first day, we dived in the St. Lawrence – it was numbingly cold and had only been re-opened for a week after the winter freeze. The almost freezing water produced a band of cold which seem to be crushing my head. Next day we were offered the option of a recompression chamber (RCC or 'pot') descent instead. Although not a real dive 50% of the time would count towards our quarterly minutes and we accepted with alacrity. We 'descended' to a depth of 250ft, which was twice as deep as we were qualified to, and then slowly 'ascended', with stops for decompression. When we went into Granbury's dining hall for dinner, we were welcomed by all and a tot put into our hands, followed by countless 'wets'. We all ended up very much under the weather and decided, still dressed in our 'number 8' blue working rig, to go down Bar Street, where all the clubs and dancers were. I really can't remember very much after the third or fourth bar except trying to climb up a pole with a dancer and almost tripping over as I tried to cross the gangway onto Torquay. When I awoke, next morning, I discovered that I was in my bunk under 'open arrest', which meant that a mess mate had to stand watch on me all night. Needless to say, I felt as in the final stages of sea sickness, when you worry that you will not die!

At 1000 I was on Captain's Defaulters, charged with 'Retuning from duty ashore drunk'. It appeared that the OOW had seen me and decided that he would rather not witness my return but the Royal Marine Young Officer felt it his duty to remain on the gangway, and after crawling over the gangway I had pulled myself up his leg and, saluting, said 'good morning' and fell down again. When this story had been recited to the captain he asked for my account. I realised that nothing I could say would stop me being demoted. I was doomed to becoming an Able Seaman again – that was until I said that I had undertaken a 'pot' dip to 250 feet and my defending officer (who was also the diving officer) said that I was only qualified to go to 120 feet. The captain looked at me and asked if I had any ill effects and then I saw a glimmer of light in darkness of my gloom. 'Yes Sir, I did not feel well at all.' 'Hmm', said the Skipper, 'I think that we had better get the Medical Officer here. Stand over until 1100.' As soon as I could I rushed down to the diving store, found the diving manual and started reading furiously.

At 1100 Defaulters convened again with the MO in attendance. 'OK Jackson, tell the MO what symptoms you had after your RCC descent.' I told him about pain in my joints, dizziness. sickness, tingling feeling, rushing noise in my ears, poor vision, shortness of breath, euphoria, and everything else I had read in the 'Poisoning' section of the diving manual. The MO was busy scribbling all of this down and referring to his books, I had described the symptoms of O_2 and CO_2 poisoning, shallow water blackout, nitrogen narcosis, bends and some ailments not yet discovered. After a while, the Captain asked the MO if this was possible and the answer came back that 'It might be.' Without further ado the captain pronounced 'Case Dismissed. Be more careful about how deep you dive next time.' So I was a free man - and still a leading seaman. I was astounded and could not believe how lucky I had been. I later found out from the captain's steward that the captain had been entertaining guests that morning from HMCS Granby and had told them about the case and they all had a good laugh, knowing exactly what really happened. I believe that the captain was Lt.Cdr. Martineau.

This episode and another, when I went ashore 3 times in New York intending to see the Broadway hit Funny Girl with Barbara Streisand and ended up in the bars instead (but I did see and hear the famous drummer Gene Krupper play – a disappointment as he was a gaunt shadow of his former talent), brought home to me the obvious fact that I was drinking too much and I decided that I would restrict my drinking. From that moment on I very seldom got drunk. I had grown up at last and I started to enjoy the countries I visited even more as I saw much more than just the bars.

My last months on Torquay were spent living in barracks at Devonport Dockyard, as Torquay was berthed in a dry dock there for a refit. As at all RN dockyard barracks those days, the accommodation was a huge room, stretching the complete length of a block and sub-divided by lockers and double bunks around cast iron stoves for heating. It could easily have held 500 men. My job at the time was Ships Postman, which entailed selling stamps for a short while every morning and afternoon, going to the Fleet Mail Office in the dockyard once a day to deliver and collect mail and to distribute the mail onboard Torquay. Not an onerous job – in fact, it was very boring. When I was not carrying out my postman duties I was supposed to be available to assist in the refit – which meant chipping paintwork! A friend of mine, Leading Seaman Jim Perry who was the 'killick' (Leading Seaman) in charge of ships boats, was also under employed, so we teamed up, acquired clipboards with paper and pencil so that we looked official and spent all our spare working hours wandering around Devonport dockyard and visiting the workers' canteens. I got bloated on coffee and Cornish pasties.

Devonport dockyard toilets were a monument to Victorian engineering. The cubicles stretched in a line, about 20, all sited above a long open drain but instead of individual flushing they were flushed all together every 10 minutes or so, a tidal wave of water starting at one end rushing along under the line of cubicles. A common event was for the occupant of the first cubicle to wait until just before the next flush, stuff toilet paper down the pan and into the drain and then lighting it so that as it went downstream on the flood the other occupants got a good singeing! Another, ploy was to call out 'fire below' making everyone jump up needlessly.

Chapter 8
HMS Royal Arthur. Corsham 1965

With the ship still in refit and having passed my Petty Officers board, at the end of my 18 months 'sea time' draft I was sent to undertake a 3 week Petty Officers Leadership course at HMS Royal Arthur, a small training establishment at Corsham, near Bath. I got off to a bad start. When the train stopped at Corsham I could not see the station name sign and asked another passenger if it was Corsham and was told 'No, next stop'. Unfortunately, the next stop was Chippenham and I had to retrace my route. This meant I arrived an hour later than planned. I was immediately placed on a charge of 'deviating from the route on my travel document' and had Captain's defaulters! Luckily for me the train detailed on my travel document for my journey from Plymouth to Bristol had the incorrect times written down so I had 'case dismissed', because if I had followed my proscribed time table I would not have arrived at all.

I enjoyed my course at Royal Arthur. Although only a Leading Seaman I was called Petty Officer (as were the other three leading hands on the course) whilst all the rest of the course were real Petty Officers. Also, for the first time in the Royal Navy I was given my own cabin! At Royal Arthur I found that I had an embryonic talent for teaching. My first lecture had to be on printing, a subject I knew extraordinarily little about – no Google in those days. To gain the interest of the rest of the course (my 'students') I commenced my lesson stating that many things were printed and held up a newspaper, a bank note and then a centre fold of Playboy magazine showing a buxom girl hiding truly little, a very raunchy picture for 1965. As I displayed the Bunny girl the door open and the Captain of Royal Arthur came in – stopped, stared at the picture, and then sat down. I felt the blood rush to my face, this was a disaster. First, I arrived late and now, I was showing a picture of a naked girl. I could see that for the rest of my life in the Royal Navy I would be chipping grey paint off rusty ships. Somehow, I managed to continue with my lesson and finished at the required time. The Captain stayed for about 20 minutes, not saying a word. After my lesson it was time for lunch and the course 'fell in' to a smart squad and we marched towards the dining hall. We were almost there, saluting the Captain as we passed, when he called out 'Petty Officer Jackson, fall out, come here'. My heart sank, I knew then that I was going to be 'returned to unit' in ignominy. I'd failed the course during the first week. 'Well done PO', the Captain said, 'That was a first class lecture. Keep it up.' I was speechless, bemused and euphoric.

Royal Arthur made major changes to my life for not only did I pass the course well, I also met there my future wife. On leaving Royal Arthur (and again being called 'Leading Seaman') I was drafted to HMS Vernon, not to be a student on a sonar or diving course, but to join the diving school. I was to be employed as an assistant instructor, helping the Clearance Diver Instructor in running Ships Divers and Search and Rescue Diver course. This time I made sure that I caught the correct trains!

Chapter 9
HMS Vernon, Portsmouth. Diving section 1965/66

M ost of the diving course was carried out at Horsea Island Lake, where I had done my conversion course from SWD to Ship's Diver. The lake was man-made and designed for testing torpedoes in 1889 and is 1,000 yards long. As the range of torpedoes increased it became obsolete before the First World War and eventually became the main diving training centre of the RN. The water (a mixture of sea and fresh) was dirty and visibility at the bottom very nearly zero. It also had a good quantity of urine from the thousands of divers who had used it over the years.

Being 'Second Dickey' on a diving course meant that I was expected to demonstrate procedures and drills. As part of the fitness programme for the students, a mile long run through the mud at low tide, was an almost daily event and the Second Dickey was expected to lead and encourage (shout at!) the students. As I was still a lightweight this was usually my job so I became very fit. My lack of fear for heights also singled me out for jumping into the water from high positions. Once, on a Search and Rescue (SAR) Divers course I jumped, in a suit and fins, from a 60ft crane. The diving set used by SAR divers, who were expected to jump into the water from a rescue helicopter if an aircraft ditched on taking off or landing from an aircraft carrier, was rather unusual. It was made by Normalair Garret. Instead of the usual mouthpiece compressed air was fed into the face mask. This was to allow the diver to speak to the aircrew and to pass them the mask so they could breathe underwater. It was disaster! The mask often got dislodged when jumping and if the seals were not perfect or the glass cracked the mask flooded and so the diver could not breathe.

On one of the SAR courses PO Tom Rush was the Clearance Diver Instructor (CDI) and when the course had graduated from jumping from cranes to jumping from an actual helicopter Tom confessed that he had never jumped from a heli and arranged with the pilot to do so. He was briefed that the heli would descend to 20ft and hover. When the pilot was ready for him to jump the crewman would tap Tom on the shoulder and he, dressed in a diving suit and wearing fins and a face mask, was to step out of the heli and enter the water. He would then be winched back up. Unfortunately the weather had freshened and the sea became choppy and out of limits for winching so the pilot, after hovering, instructed the crewman to tell Tom that the jump was cancelled and then increased speed and height to 20 knots and 60ft. Tom was rather nervous, this being his first time in a heli, and as soon as he was touched by the crewman to inform him that the jump was cancelled, stepped out of the helicopter and, caught by the slipstream, lost his balance and with arms waving madly, plummeted like a falling angel and hit the sea moving forward at great rate. His mask was dislodged and lost, one fin (which was just held in place by a heel strap) was driven up to his thigh and the other joined the mask on the seabed. Luckily the only injures were bruising and a bloody nose. Despite being out of limits Tom was winched up safely. He never volunteered for another jump!

SAR divers, like all helicopter crew, had to go into the Helicopter Dunker at Vernon. This was a large cylindrical tank, about 20ft diameter and around 30ft deep, standing on end, which had a heli cabin mock-up suspended by a crane above it. When the aircrew were strapped into this mock-up it was dropped into the tank, rolled over and filled with water. When the water stopped coming in, and was stable, the crew released themselves from their harnesses and escaped through one of two exits (the door or window), holding their breath, and waiting, until the person in front of them had escaped. As Second Dickey I was the safety diver in with them, ready to assist if required. As I was not strapped in, the first couple of times I was dislodged by the water rushing in and the rotation and became very disorientated. Luckily, my assistance was not need until the last practice, by which time I had become used to the turbulence and movement.

Another course I assisted on was a Ship's Divers course for Iranian Naval Officers. Again, Tom Rush was the CDI. The first day of the course, Monday, found the instructors at Horsea Island but no Iranians. Tuesday was the same. Wednesday, six Officers turned up and when asked where they had been replied 'Shopping in London'. It appeared that they did not want to do a diving course but when asked by the Shah 'Does anyone like swimming?' they had foolishly said 'Yes'! All six Iranians were small men and keenly felt the unfamiliar cold (it was during the winter and some morning ice had to be cleared from the diving board and floating pontoon.) They were only once made to do a 'skin swim' with no suits and their brown skins turned an unhealthy dusky blue in a short time.

Because of their small size and lungs, when they did their endurance swim they managed almost 90 minutes instead of the normal hour and were very close to hypothermia, so that exercise was not repeated. The SABA set that was used had a mouth-piece which was moulded into the face mask, allowing breathing even if water entered the mask. To clear the mask of water, the top of the mask was held tight against the forehead, and the bottom lightly pulled away from the chin, whilst air was blown out from the nose or lips. This air rose to the top of the mask forcing the water out the bottom. All the students except one managed this after a few attempts. That officer just could not manage it. It was the same mantra every morning and afternoon. 'In the water Sir. Let water into your mask. Now go underwater and clear it Sir'. He would disappear under the murky water and there would be a gush of bubbles of air coming to the surface and eventually he would surface and the mask was still full of water. On the final day of course, Tom explained to the student that unless he could clear his mask he would not qualify, which would displease the Shah, and disappoint him. Also. Once again it was 'In the water Sir, let water into the mask. Down you go and clear the water'. He submerged under the dirty, stagnant water and the usual maelstrom of bubbles rose to the surface and then the student followed them – with a clear face mask. 'Well done Sir. Very well done. Now do it again please.' said Tom. The student threw off his face mask and said, 'No Sir, I can't drink any more of that bloody stuff!!!' We rolled our eyes, clutching our throats and grimacing – we knew what had gone into that lake! He was not made to do it again and Tom said that any man who drank that much of Horsea Lake and not need a stomach pump deserved to pass the course.

Once again, I decided to volunteer to become a sonar aircrewman and this time would not be fobbed off with excuses. I saw the Captain of Vernon and he recommended me for training and told me that it would only be for two years, or three if I was subsequently chosen as an instructor. That was fine by me as I only needed two more sonar courses before I gained the large Torpedo and Anti-Submarine Instructor (TASI) badge that I had craved for as a spotty faced teenager. I was interviewed by the Aircrew Selection Board and was selected. After running through all the courses I had done, it was suggested that I may have a 'butterfly mind'. They were probably right as I still continued to enlarge my knowledge whenever possible.

My aircrew course would start at the end of the year and all I needed was to pass the medical examination. No problem – or so I thought. Firstly, I was reminded that I suffered frequently from sore throats and it was decided that my tonsils required removing. I explained that I had them removed as a child but was told that they can grow again. That was news to me! They were removed at the Royal Navy Hospital at Haslar, Gosport and my confinement there encouraged me to stop smoking. Not so difficult when the nurses have noses that can smell a cigarette half a ward away. I had been thinking of stopping smoking, so it was extremely useful. A side effect of non-smoking was that I started to hate the smell of stale tobacco and had to inform my fiancée that I could not kiss her unless she stopped too. My kissing must have been good because she did. The other health problem that was detected when I was in the hospital was small growths on both my eyes. The Ophthalmic surgeon advised me to have them removed (in one day and out the next) as they would grow and would be difficult to remove when larger. Thinking of the sick leave that I would get afterwards I agreed and, a few weeks, was re-admitted to Royal Navy Hospital Haslar. I should have known better! I spent over a week in hospital, blinded in both eyes for 3 days and 2 more in the other one, had a week's sick leave and then had another 3 days in-patient treatment.

I expected to have general anaesthetic but that was not so. After numbing drops in my eyes, they were held in a clamp and a large needle was used to inject anaesthetic. Imagine sticking a needle into a pickled onion. To make matters worse the doctor who operated was being advised what to do by the Senior Surgeon. I particularly objected to the advice of 'Be careful now or he will be blinded'!!! When surgery was finished on one eye I was asked if I wished them to continue and do the other eye or return on another day. I knew that there was no way I would return so I agreed that the other should be done right away. Ever since then I have always questioned medical advice.

An event whilst at the diving centre accelerated my move to HMS Osprey, the shore base that administered Royal Navy

Air Station Portland, where helicopter aircrew were trained. Every weekend, two of the duty watch of divers had to spend both Saturday and Sunday at Horsea Lake as guards, taking with them food to cook. They often complained that they did not receive their daily issue of rum (tot) to which they were entitled. One weekend I was one of the two duty men and sure enough no tot was delivered. On return to the diving centre, I went to the Regulating Office to officially 'State a Complaint' and was informed that it would be investigated. 'Stating a Complaint' meant going before the Captain of Vernon, which I expected to do within a few days, but nothing happened. A week later I again went to the Diving Regulating Office and was told that it was 'still being looked into'. This did not satisfy me so I decided that I would personally check with the Victualling Office why the tot was not issued to the duty divers and was told that it was and that the Duty Chief Diver and Duty Diving Officer collected it every Saturday and Sunday to take to the Horsea Lake guards. I was incensed to find that this rum was being stolen from us and again went to the Diving Regulating Office and complained. I was shouted at and told that it was a trivial complaint, I was a troublemaker and that it was always delivered. Next morning, I was summoned to the Regulating Office, told to pack my kit and the day after I was on my way to Portland, four months early, to do my Air Crewman course. It seems that the Duty Diving Chief and Diving Officer the weekend I was on duty at the lake were the Regulating Chief and my Divisional Officer!!!

Chapter 10
HMS Osprey, Portland 1966/67

Having arrived 4 months before my course started, the Air Station (RNAS Portland) had no use for me, so I was sent to HMS Osprey, the RN base at the top of Portland Bill. Osprey did not really have any employment (and probably Vernon had informed them that I was a troublemaker!) so a job was invented for me. I became the skipper of an HLD (a fishing boat size launch) in Portland harbour. This HLD had no regular employment, except every few months to go on a weekend trip to Guernsey as an 'expedition' vessel. The other crew member was Sid, a civilian engineer.

I was not given any instruction about my job and what was expected of me. The daily 'clean ship' took less than an hour and I soon became bored with drinking Nescafe and listening to old Sid droning on hour after hour. I often fell asleep and when I awoke Sid was still talking. To fill the time, I decided to do 'Chart Corrections' which were issued regularly with the official 'Notice to Mariners'. The boat had charts of all the seas around UK, Europe and the Baltic and corrections had never been done since the issue of the charts – years earlier. Chart corrections were new to me as on ships this was the Navigator Yeoman's job, so it was a struggle at times plotting lots of latitudes and longitudes without making a mistake. This plotting stood me in good stead when I eventually started Air Crew course. Because of the age of the charts, I often had to plot and notify an area and then in a later amendment had to delete or modify it.

One day I noticed that the buoyant smoke flare attached to the life buoy was cracked and in a poor condition, so I ordered a new one from stores to replace it. When it arrived I was in a quandary as to what to do with the old one. I could not throw it away as it could ignite and cause damage. I also couldn't use it in harbour as orange smoke billowing around would cause a lot of questions, so I hit on the idea of tying a heavy weight on it and just throwing it over the side, safety pin in to stop it igniting, eventually to be covered in mud and lost for ever. About an hour later I noticed a commotion on a ship berthed a hundred yards away, the other side of the harbour. People were looking over the side and pointing, the crowd getting bigger by the minute. I got the binoculars from the wheelhouse to see what they were looking at and then wished I hadn't. Bubbles of gas were coming to the surface of the harbour and then bursting into orange smoke. These bubbles were slowly moving along the length of the ship, aft to forward, as though a fire breathing dragon was swimming underwater, trying to escape from the harbour. The weight on the damaged smoke float had not been heavy enough to keep it on the seabed and the flood tide, after taking it into harbour had changed and was now ebbing, carrying the smoke float with it. Although the safety pin had been inserted water must have seeped through the cracks and ignited the smoke flare. The smoke was only supposed to work for 6 minutes but it took a lot longer and it was with a massive sigh of relief when I saw it had finally burnt itself out. Only I knew what had caused the phenomena and I certainly was not going to tell!

As winter approached it was decided that the HLD would no longer be required for expeditions to the Channel Islands and would be lifted out of the water onto the jetty for maintenance. I was out of a job so a new one was found for me as the assistant to Ospreys Accommodation Officer; another simple job that did not require any thinking. Apart from allocating accommodation to newly drafted sailors and grinding a new key for those that had lost their locker key, I only had to accompany the accommodation officer on his very occasional inspection of the messes for defects. Then suddenly things changed for me. We had a large influx of ratings and accommodation became short.

I was asked if I could find any sailor who would rather live in private accommodation instead of barracks. They would get lodging allowance, food allowance and travel allowance. Without any hesitation I and another Leading Seaman friend volunteered. We rented a caravan on Portland that was two minutes from a pub and moved in. We learnt where to buy cheap, out of date, food. Scrag ends of bacon and cheeses saved us enough money to allow us to have a few beers and a pie every night. As winter progressed the caravan became very cold and we had to light the coal burning stove to keep warm. This started to eat into our beer money so then I had the idea of taking my small RN attaché case every lunch time to where my friend worked in the dockyard. He had a coal burning stove to keep his workshop warm. I would fill the case up with coal and put it into my car. Sandwiches came in and coal went out. We never went short of coal again.

I stayed in the caravan until it was time to go on my annual two weeks Christmas leave. I was never to return as in the New Year I again had to return to Navy accommodation; This time I was going to the Air Crewman's mess, for I was starting Flying Training.

Chapter 11
RNAS Portland. Flying training 1967

I became a RAUT – Rating Aircrew under Training, at the mini airfield by the causeway that joins Portland Bill to the mainland. Although officially under the control of HMS Osprey we were completely self-contained except for main meals. We even had a different uniform. Serge navy blue battle dress blouse and trousers with vertical creases instead of 5 horizontal, blue shirt with tie, extra warm underwear (no heating in helicopters) and flying boots that could be cut back into normal-looking shoes if we crashed in enemy territory. Instead of a white cap we had berets. Personal flying clothing was issued: fabric flying suits for the summer, thick waterproof woven 'goon' suits for the winter. These immersion suits were in two parts. The trousers had built in boots and a rubber seal around the waist and held up with braces. The top was the same material with a long rubber seal at the bottom and pulled over the head, with rubber seals stopping water entering from the neck and wrist. When top and trousers were donned the top seal on the trouser and bottom seal of the top were rolled together and tucked under a flap to make everything watertight. We had our own Life Saving Waistcoats (LSW) which were called Mae Wests, one-man life-rafts, (which were worn as a backpack), inner helmets with earphones, throat microphones and a hard flying helmet to go over the top. We were also issued with aircrew watches and navigating instruments. Apart from our extra kit our living conditions also changed. Before night flying, we got an extra meal and if landing late at night, another one, whilst tea and coffee were always available.

On every ship and establishment in the RN, I had been issued with a 'Station Card' which had to be handed in when going on shore leave and collected on return. Leave times had to be strictly adhered to. One minute too early and you were not allowed ashore; one minute late back then you were on a 'charge'. In the Fleet Air Arm (FAA), to which I was now attached, these cards had been abolished for years. If you were not required for work you could do what you liked – go ashore, go to bed, whatever. Providing you turned up for your work, the time was yours. Unbelievable to us who had come from General Service (the ship navy) but as RAUTS, and later aircrew, very sensible, as flying, briefing and debriefing takes place any time of day and night.

There were about a dozen of us on number 17 RAUTS course, two petty officers and the rest of us leading hands and able seamen. Some were hoping to become SAR divers, others crewmen in commando-carrying helis and two sonar operators in ASW helis – AB Brian Harbisher and I.

The Whirlwind Mk 7 was the Basic Flying Training (BFT) aircraft, an old piston engine helicopter, using volatile petrol and which required a cartridge to be fired (with a bang) to start it – sometimes two. Unlike later helicopters, the pilot was separated from the crew, which could make things interesting at times. A common problem was failure of a micro-switch in the intercom system, which stopped the pilot and crew talking to each other. The intercom unit was situated between the pilot and crew and if there was a communication problem the first remedy was for the crewman to lean out of the door, in flight, and bang hard on the aircraft's side, adjacent to the unit, hoping to jar the micro switch to the operate position. If that failed the crewman had to climb out of the cabin and give hand signals. We slid open the cabin door, climbed up the steps outside the cockpit and tap the pilot on his right shoulder. In flight, often the first indication to the pilot that there was a problem was a tap on the shoulder and a grimacing wind deformed face at his window, sometimes at a height of thousands of feet.

We were taught how to navigate, allowing for wind, how to interpret ground and air maps and charts and how to calculate the wind vector at various heights. Meteorology was a big part of the course as well as rescue techniques. We had in-depth lectures on avionics, electrics, aerodynamics, engineering, fuel systems and about the publications and books concerning aircraft maintenance. We also had to go to HMS Vernon and go through the helicopter dunker. We got to know the Dorset area very well from 1,000 feet on our navigation exercises (NavEx). We also learnt about the uncertainty and caprices of the weather, sometimes waiting days for a suitable weather window to fly. We were taken out to the harbour in a boat and thrown over the side, to be 'rescued' from our life raft by heli, as well as winched from land. We practised 'Wet' and 'Dry' winching as crew, telling the pilot to go backwards/forwards/left/right up and down to get the rescue strop (sling) to the 'survivor', because when the heli was above, the 'survivor', the pilot could not see him.

We practised, as winch operators, single lifts (just the rescue strop was lowered) and double lifts (another crewman was lowered to assist the survivor, and both were winched up together). For the double lift the lowered crewman, the winchman, had to protect the survivor from being injured from hitting the underneath of the heli as they swung, so as they ascended, the face of the survivor (who hung lower than the crewman) was pulled into the crutch of the crewman until the crewman could hold the top of the heli crew door and, putting his feet on the bottom step, gave a thrust with his pelvis to push them into the cabin. We also practised picking up heavy loads from a hook slung underneath, using strops up to 80ft (25 meters) long. After 6 weeks on course and with 22 hours of flying, (23 sorties) most of us passed and then it was onto the 127 course Operational Flying Training (OFT).

The 'Pingers' (sonar operators) changed to the Wessex HAS (Helicopter Anti-Submarine) Mk 1, which was fitted with type 194 dipping sonar and had a small navigator's table for the Observer, a naval officer. The Wessex was a far superior aircraft. It had a more powerful jet turbine engine which was started with a very volatile fluid called AvPin. This sometimes resulted in an engine fire on start up. It had a flight control system and could also carry anti-submarine torpedoes and depth charges. Most of the OFT students were officers, pilots and observers. Brian Harbisher and I were the only two ratings.

Again, we had aircraft type pertinent lectures and at a greater depth of knowledge. We carried out all the previous flying exercise but this time to a higher standard. We had a thorough knowledge of our 194 sonar, that we lowered on a special winch and with 90ft of cable allowed us to ping below a shallow temperature layer where a submarine may be lurking, and we were given a lot of 'Secret' information, on tactics and manoeuvres, many which were developed during the Second World War, and which were kept in our personal safes. We were taught ASW tactics and code words that applied to ships, aircraft, and convoys. The observers and sonar operators spent hours in the Anti-Submarine Attack Training Unit simulator, where we changed jobs so that we could understand the problems as submarines 'attacked' ships and convoys. I loved being 'Captain' and 'Scene of Action Commander' of a ship and developed a flair for 'destroying' submarines. Unlike surface ships, which have 5 man team to detect, classify and ultimately to destroy the submarine, in a heli the sonar operating air crewman does it all. Detecting submarines was by listening for the returning echo as the sonar, which was lowered on a long wire whilst in the hover, emitted a pulse or 'ping' of sound. He told the observer what the contact was, where it was and its course and speed. The observer then told the pilots where to go or he 'vectored' another heli to drop a weapon on it (usually an electric homing torpedo as the traditional depth charge was being phased out). One of the weak links in the system was directing the weapon dropping helicopter onto the target (Vectored Attack or 'Vectac'). The attacking heli would over-fly the in-contact heli on a heading calculated by the observer, allowing for wind, the submarine's position and course and speed, and drop the torpedo at a certain distance on its port bow. The torpedo would then sink to the required depth, engine running, and commence an anti-clockwise search, pinging on its built-in sonar. When it detected the submarine, it would aim for it and then explode on contact. Depth charges were dropped just ahead of the submarine and sinking time calculated with submarine's speed so that the charge exploded in the correct position. The problem was that the submarine would try to escape by releasing decoys, turning and changing depth. This required new calculations by the heli observer and often the attack had to start again by overflying the controlling heli which could take many minutes. Another problem was that when the submarine came out of range of our sonar, the controlling heli had to re-position itself by raising the sonar, flying forwards into the wind to gain airspeed, and climb to 150ft before turning onto a course calculated by the observer, allowing for wind, and the submarine's last known course and speed. It then turned back into wind before decelerating into the hover, lowering the sonar to the correct depth and pinging again. This was termed 'Jumping' and could easily take 5–20 minutes which allowed the submarine, undetected, to alter course, speed and depth and being nowhere near where it was expected. If possible, at least two helicopters were needed, one 'jumping' and the other(s) 'in the Dip', to maintain contact. We had to wait for a more advanced ASW system, which included airborne radar to come into service before the dropping accuracy problem was solved whilst with active sonar (one that pinged) the maintaining contact problem always required more aircraft. More advanced sonar, producing more power, helped a bit but the problem with the sonar sound beam reflecting off the surface and refracting in different temperature layers is the main range limiting factor. Getting below a deep thermocline (temperature changed layer of water) was eventually helped by having a longer sonar cable. We also learnt about the 'Special Weapon' a nuclear depth bomb which would destroy anything within a couple of miles of its drop point. It was not our preferred weapon as the contamination it produced could also threaten 'friendly forces'.

The Wessex Mk 1 could fly and carry out all tasks at night and in poor visibility, so these were practised in the dark. Apart from no daylight, most of the 'back seat' work was the same as daytime. Instruments were well illuminated, and we had torches, but for the pilots it was very difficult. At least two pilots were failed because of a lack of night flying ability. What did prove more difficult for the crewman and observer was 'wet winching' – rescuing survivors from the sea. At night it is extremely difficult to judge distances from a small survival light, especially as it will be bobbing up and down on waves. The pilot, who cannot see directly below the heli, has to be 'conned' directly over the top and at the correct height. He gets all his information from his altimeter, air speed indicator, compass and attitude indicator. If told to go back and left 2 yards and up 5 feet he must follow the commands, interpreting the crewman's measurements, as everybody has a different guess as to the length of a yard (30 cms), and converting it into minute adjustments in height, airspeed, left and right movement. Apart from 'conning' the heli, the crewman is operating the rescue hoist and giving a running commentary to the pilot. When night wet winching, the stress level is always high as the sea is never flat calm and the height of the waves varies constantly, as does the wind.

For the first time in my naval career, I felt mentally stretched and enjoyed every moment of it. I realised that I was not only joining a small, select group, but I was a vital part of it. If I could not detect a submarine and correctly calculate its course and speed and estimate its depth, then using helicopters for ASW (Anti-Submarine Warfare) would be a failure, a complete waste of money and manpower. On the 14th of April 1967, after three months training, 79 sorties and 91 hours flying I was extremely proud to be awarded my aircrewman 'Wings' which were sown on my sleeve for the remainder of my time in the RN, for, despite the then current ruling that I was only 'on loan' to the Fleet Air Arm (FAA) for 2 years, it was eventually realised that our job was so valuable and training so deep and ongoing that it was not possible to have temporary aircrewmen. I never served as a seaman again. So began my happiest and most fulfilling time in the navy, which lasted another 16 years and which changed my life.

Chapter 12
First Front Line squadron. 820 NAS HMS Eagle 1967/68

After qualifying as an aircrewman (sonar), I was drafted to 820 NAS (Naval Air Squadron) which was the heli squadron of the aircraft carrier HMS Eagle, which was disembarked at HMS Seahawk, at RNAS Culdrose, near Helston in Cornwall, as the ship was being refitted. Shortly after joining the squadron I was promoted to Petty Officer, which had nothing to do with qualifying as an aircrewman. I still belonged to General Service, the ship navy and was only on loan to the Fleet Air Arm (FAA) for 2-3 years.

Eagle was one of the two largest aircraft carriers that the UK had ever built: the Audacious class. The other was the sister ship, Ark Royal, and building started in 1942 but, on the ending of the Second World War, completion was delayed, and she was first commissioned in 1951. After two major refits where the weight (tonnage) increased from 36,800 tons to 54,100 tons, an armoured, angled, flight deck, new catapults and arrester gear, new island and a greatly updated radar was fitted, she became the ship I joined as the most junior member of 824 Naval Air Squadron. Eagle's fixed wing squadrons, (helicopters are rotary wing) were Sea Vixens, Buccaneers and Fairy Gannets.

The de Havilland Sea Vixen was a twin boom (tail) fighter jet aircraft and the first in the RN not to have any guns. Its max speed in level flight was just below the sound barrier. The prototype crashed at the Farnborough air show in 1951, killing 29 spectators and after modifications became the RN fighter aircraft and remained in service from 1959 to 1972. Out of 145 built, 55 crashed and over 42 crew were killed.

The Blackburn Buccaneer was a very specialised aircraft. The design brief was for an aircraft that could counter the large cruisers, such as the Sverdlovsk, that the USSR was building. The same threat that, 5 years earlier when I served on HMS Caesar, we were training to counter with torpedoes. It was designed to fly fast, 500 knots and low, 100ft above the surface, to keep under the radar beam and then climb steeply and release its bomb in a long 'lob'. It was ideally suited to its job but difficult to fly in air to air combat. It served from 1958 to 1994.

The Fairey Gannet, a Turboprop aircraft, was an Air Early Warning aircraft and had exceptionally large and powerful radar. They were not fast but could stay airborne for up to 6 hours, relaying radar information directly into Eagles operation system. The Gannet was the electronic eyes and ears of the RN from 1960 until 1978 and the lack of the Gannet in the Falklands War is considered the main reason why RN ships suffered so much damage from the Argentinian air force.

The Commanding Officer (CO) of 824 Sqd. was Lt.Cdr. Tony Casdagli and the Senior Pilot Ben Bathurst. Both made Flag Officer later in life, as did Lt. Peter West, the Squadron QHI (Qualified Helicopter instructor.) We had 6 Wessex Mk 1 helicopters, fitted with 194 type sonar. The Wessex Mk 1 could carry depth charges, torpedoes or the 'Special Weapon'. They also had rescue winches and could carry under-slung loads up to about 2,000 lbs, providing not too much fuel was carried. Most times the speed was around 90 Kts (knots) but it could fly at 120 Kts. Whilst flying on ASW work our standard transit height was 120ft and max altitude was 12,000ft, although we never went higher than 10,000ft as we did not carry oxygen. The longest sortie (flight), without refuelling, that I have in my logbook is 2 hours 20 minutes. That would have been about the limit of endurance. Longer flights were carried out, with landing and refuelling, of up to 3hrs 50 minutes but were very tiring because of the weight of the flying clothing, and the one-man life raft, which was continuously carried on our backs.

Also attached to the squadron were 2 Wessex without any sonar. These were used as SAR (Search and Rescue) and Plane-guard aircraft and carried an SAR diver (I had been an assistant instructor on one of these courses at the diving centre, HMS Vernon, a year earlier). The concept of an SAR diver was formed after a tragic accident in 1958, which the UK press observed. They had been invited to see the embarkation (arrival) on the aircraft carrier HMS Victorious, of the air squadrons. The CO of 803, Scimitar squadron, caught an arrester wire on landing but the wire failed, and he was unable to gain enough flying speed to take off again and retry. He crashed into the sea and within a very short time the Plane-guard Whirlwind heli, which had been airborne and positioned ready for this sort of emergency, hovered above the still floating aircraft ready to rescue the pilot as soon as he had opened his Perspex canopy. Unfortunately, the canopy had jammed, and the Scimitar slowly sank, with Lt.Cdr. Norman, the pilot, still struggling to get out. The heli winchman, who was hanging from the rescue winch wire, was unable to help once the plane sank. This tragic event was filmed by a Pathe News cameraman, who was in the plane-guard heli, and made world-wide viewing. After this accident it was decided that a diver, with light-weight diving equipment, should jump from a heli and be trained how to jettison canopies and hatches. If the aircraft sank, he could offer the pilot oxygen when underwater. These divers saved dozens of lives, aircrew and civilians, until the specialisation was stopped in 2006. Probably, because with no aircraft carriers, it was thought that there was no need for such specialist. Maybe it will be re-introduced before the new carrier, HMS Queen Elizabeth, embarks its air groups. Although I was never officially an SAR diver, my training experience required me to be used as one whenever there was a need for someone to jump into the water, on all my squadrons, during the rest of my time in the RN.

If I thought that I had learnt everything an aircrewman needed to know I was very quickly disabused of this during the three weeks at Culdrose, prior to embarking on Eagle. After an area familiarisation flight, I was tasked as the observer (the navigator) to go on a pilot continuation training flight called a JumpEx. I had never used the radio before, and never had to calculate the courses required to enter the hover, to simulate prosecuting a submarine. I had to ask one of the other crewmen how the tables and graphs worked and fumbled my way through the flight. It was a good job that the weather was clear, and I avoided flying into the cliffs around Falmouth Bay. The radar controller at Falmouth Radar did have to warn me a few times that I was close to the boundary of the exercise area. A day or so later I was again the observer and I was a little more confident, knowing that Falmouth Radar would be keeping an eye on me. The first 30 minutes went well and then Falmouth Radar stopped working, so I was on my own, with no one to help with the navigation. We continued with the JumpEx until the first pilot said that it had started to get foggy and we had better return to Culdrose and asked for a course to steer to take us to the south bank of the Helford River, which was the route to return to Culdrose. After countless letter S jumps (going to and coming from the hover required flying into wind) and with no radar assisting me for half an hour, I was completely unsure of my position. The fog was getting worse and at 150 feet height even seeing the sea was becoming difficult. I made a guess and gave a course and time to fly. It was a really wild guess and I felt sick in my stomach. After some time, I was asked again how far to go. I thought we should have been there by then, so I made another guess and said, 'two minutes sir'. Two minutes went by and again the pilot asked how long when abruptly he said

'I have the Helford Buoy, passing overtop now. Turning left and climbing, following the south bank.' I started breathing again. After landing, at the crew de-brief, I was told 'Well done, spot on navigation Leading Hand'. If only they knew how lucky we were!

Another new skill was learnt when we had to move troops and Wombat guns for the army, on Exmoor. This had to be done with minimum fuel because of the weight. I had lifted loads on my course but not guns. I had also not learnt the routine for carrying troops.

Eagle had finished her refit and we embarked, at sea, and disembarked whenever she returned to her base port of Devonport Dockyard. The flying tasking was mixed. We did combined anti-submarine exercise (Casex) with Eagle and her consorts, ferry trips from ship to shore and back, wind turbulence trials to assess the turbulence in the wind wake that 54,000 tons of steel moving at 30 knots makes, night flights to assess the flight-deck landing lights and moving stores, food and ammunition from the supply ship to Eagle, as well as squadron specific flying such as continuation training for all crew, day and night SAR from land and sea, check-test flights after maintenance, navigational exercises over land and sea, and constant practice of JumpEx.

One operational task was to recover a Sioux helicopter which had ditched off Scotland. This meant using a long strop and lifting it to Royal Navy Air Station Lossiemouth, where it would be repaired. The pilot was the squadron CO, and with me in the back was PO Bob Venables, who would show me what to do, this being my first aircraft lift. After putting the crashed heli on the ground we took off for our return to Eagle, who was somewhere at sea. A radio call was made to Lossiemouth, asking for an update about Eagle's position and the call was answered by a WRN (Women's Royal Navy Service) radio operator who was less than helpful. In frustration, on the heli's intercom, the CO said, 'Those WRNs are only good for one thing!', to which Bob Venables, in the cabin with me, said. 'My wife's a WRN sir.' The CO did not say a word for ages. The RN was not PC in those days.

Eagle was not planned to sail to the Far East until later in the year, so I arranged to be married the first week of August. In the last week of July, the signal came that the sailing date had been advanced, and it would now be 10 days after my wedding and return would not be for another 11 months. When we did, I was greeted by my wife and baby son. As we used to say, 'That's life in a blue suit'. The thing that did annoy me was that at Christmas, when Eagle was in Singapore, the ship had arranged for wives of newlyweds to be flown out but my DO (Divisional Officer) had not applied for it or told me.

Eagle visited Gibraltar, Cape Town, Singapore, Hong Kong, Perth – Australia, and Mombasa. We were involved in the British withdrawal from Aden. From there we lifted out dozens of refrigerators for use on the ship (the centre of the hanger had a long line of them), as they were not standard issue to messes or crew rooms. The air squadron's excuse for needing one was to keep a stock of film for their Hasselblad recognisance cameras. It was quite amazing how photographic film started looking like soft drink cans and chocolate! In Aden, one of our heli's was fired on and hit but no one knew until a hole was found in the underside. Luckily, the rubber fuel tank had not been pierced. It was off Aden that I had a search for a lost seaman, the first of many searches. We found no one.

Whilst in Singapore I learnt how to assist in a heli's compass swing (assessment and adjustment)

In a special magnetic free area, the heli would turn and land onto a chosen direction and I would set up a tripod, perfectly horizontal, by use of spirit levels, sight down the centreline of the heli and, with arm signals, pass the error to the crew. One degree of compass error equals one mile every sixty flown. This was a routine job for the crewman but not mentioned in training.

During our disembarked period at RNAS Simbang I was sent on a jungle survival course. This was my first experience of navigating through the jungle, hacking away at thick creepers with a machete to make a path, and being constantly wet; hot during the day but cold at night. Leeches found their way up our trouser legs and shirt sleeves requiring a burning cigarette to make them drop off. If pulled off, the head would stay attached, festering, and causing running sores. We we shown how to cut a vine for the potable water it contained and make 'Bashas', temporary shelters.

The flying was routine for a deployment away from the UK. We had many Casexs, lifted underslung loads between ships, transferred people from ship to ship (winching them on small ships) and spotting the accuracy for our Buccaneers 'long lobbing' the 'enemy' which was a target that was towed behind the ship and sent a plume of seawater into the air. It was amazing how accurate they were.

One of our pilots, Bill Hutchinson, got the nickname of 'Foot and Mouth' by the other officers, as when he opened his mouth he often 'Put his foot in it'. I had first-hand experience of this when we transferred the admiral and his senior staff officers to HMS Albion. Our communication in the heli was by using a throat-mic and by earphones built into a soft helmet, worn under our protective helmet. The admiral and staff officers only had the inner soft headset with earphones. After we had taken off from Eagle and gained radio contact with Albion, Bill gave the admiral a report and asked if he was enjoying the flight. As the admiral and staff had no throat-mic I said, 'The admiral can't speak to you sir', to which Bill replied, 'Thank God for that'. The admiral turned white and clinched his teeth and his staff officer turned red with apoplexy and his lips disappeared. I then informed Bill in a quiet voice, 'But he is listening to you sir'. The heli dropped about 50 feet and a strange moaning sound could be heard on the intercom. We landed on Albion, the admiral got out and was met by Albion's captain whilst the staff officer rushed up the pilot's steps and proceeded to severely assault Bill with his index finger, pinning him to the back of his seat. Bill ended up being Duty Officer very frequently during that month. I never saw Bill Hutchinson after I left Eagle and often wonder how he later got on.

Sailors, especially the younger ones, are always buying presents for their family and loved ones. These gifts seem to multiply very quickly (I ended up with two full Norataki China 6 piece dinner/tea/coffee sets). Because of their preponderance to multiply, these gifts are known as 'Rabbits' and at the latter end of a voyage, spare lockers and compartments are opened to stow them. These are called 'Rabbit Warrens'. I had also bought a carved teak and camphor wood chest as well as dozens of other knick-knacks. When Eagle arrived back at Devonport in June the squadrons flew ashore the day before but because of my heavy gifts I managed to stay on the ship until after it arrived in harbour. Bedford lorries were arranged to take all the squadron's tools and spare parts etc. to Culdrose and I loaded my 'Rabbits' with them and by gifting a box of 100 duty free cigarettes persuaded the driver to take a short detour and drop my belongings at my wife's home. After eight months away I now had three weeks' leave.

I re-joined the squadron, after leave, at RNAS Culdrose, not far from the house which I had rented with my young wife and child. Continuation training kept us busy with a few days of Casex off Portland and the usual check test flights. I had my first SAR rescue in the middle of August. A motorboat had ended up on the rocks at the cliff edge to the east of Falmouth and I was duty crew. This was the first time that I had to rescue anyone for real and it was not a simple rescue because of the closeness of the cliffs. The gusty SW wind which we had to head into placed our tail and tail rotor very close to danger. The pilot was Ben Bathurst, the senior pilot and he held the heli rock steady despite the gusts and turbulence. I winched up a man and woman and the man was upset that we hadn't lifted his boat, which was wedged up against the cliff, as well. We returned to Culdrose with them and afterwards found out that he was a wine merchant, so we had hopes of a liquid donation to the squadron, but it was not to be.

I left the squadron at the end of August and wondered what the flying navy next had in store for me. What was important was my next squadron. Should I volunteer or just wait until the aircrew drafter decided for me? Because the total number of sonar aircrewman was so small (about 40 maximum) the drafting was done on a personal nature by Lt.Cdr. Charlie Wines, at Lee on Solent and it was not unheard of for people to telephone him to discuss things. After talking to other crewmen, I concluded that the least wanted draft was to RNAS Culdrose in Cornwall, so if I volunteered for there, I would certainly get it. Another unpopular draft was Northern Ireland so that also I applied for. As my wife was Cornish, Culdrose would be good for us and a married accompanied draft to NI could be enjoyable, so I put these preferences to Charlie Wines, and I was promised I would get them. But the ship navy still had a say in my future. I was told that first I would be attending a UC1 sonar course at HMS Vernon. Another step closer to gaining the biggest badge in the RN –although now it did not seem so important.

The NI squadron had been equipped with a different version of the Wessex, the Mk 3 and it was decided that I had better do a course before I joined. I had a familiarisation flight at Culdrose, on 706 NAS, a training squadron, before I left Cornwall, and moved to Portsmouth in September to start the course at Vernon.

Wessex 1

HMS Eagle

Chapter 13
HMS Vernon, Portsmouth. September 1968/March 69

737 NAS Portland April 1969.

After almost 2 years in the Fleet Air Arm (FAA), it felt strange being back in the surface navy, with parades and regulated leave. This was the winter when Her Majesty's Government decided to keep 'summertime' throughout the winter, to reduce road deaths. It was very successful in this but bad publicity by the press stopped it happening in subsequent years. Every morning, before we went to instruction, we would have to parade on Vernon's unlit Parade Ground, and the Officer Of the Day came around with a torch to inspect us!

I commenced my UC1 course and had a refresher on things I had learnt earlier and a lot of new knowledge about the latest surface ship sonar, type 177. Modern sonar was no longer the simple, trainable, transducer that put out a pulse of sound like a searchlight. Now it was a massive array of transducers that were stationary and put out a rippling wall of sound. The movement of any contact no longer just gave a 'ping' which we heard and changed its pitch as it moved towards or away but bands of filters on a visual display showed the actual speed it was doing so. The visual display became the main way of detecting submarines, the audio less. Because of the many Casex's that I had been on over the last 2 years and the fact that in a heli I was doing a job that, on a ship, took a team of 4 people, I did very well on the course. Instead of just saying 'I have a contact bearing 123' I would say 'I have a confident 3 (submarine) contact bearing 123. Speed 4 knots, course 300'. I think all UC (sonar) aircrewmen would have done the same. Again, I managed to get the £5 prize for top student. One more course, the UW 1 (Under Water Weapons course) and I would become a TASI and get the big badge I had been working towards for the last ten years.

I have used a lot of abbreviations in this book and I sometimes have been caught out by them. As usual, part of the course was 'Sea Training' on a ship, instead of the simulators that were at Vernon. With my course, on board HMS Hardy, was also a course of trainee TAS Officers. I was in the Ops room, bent down and hidden, aligning equipment, when a group of officers came in. Their instructor pointed in my direction and said 'LOPO' (Local Operation Plot Officer), to show his work area. Thinking he was speaking to me I stood up and said, 'Hello Sir'! The Officers saw the funny side of this, and my red face.

One of my fellow students had a wife that was not the brightest lady in the world, and this was during the time of the famine in Biafra, and collections were being made to help these starving people. On Christmas Eve there was a knock on her door and when she opened it, there was a lady, shaking a collection box, who said, 'Buy a Biafrian baby for Christmas?' The wife replied, 'No thank you, we're having turkey', and closed the door!

Having finished the course, which I did not realise at the time would be the last sonar course I would ever do there, I was sent to 737 NAS at Portland, where I had completed my basic flying training. This time I was going to learn about the Wessex Mk3 on a two-week conversion course.

The new sonar in the Wessex Mk 3 was a Type 195 and completely different to the old 194. The body, which was lowered into the water, was much bigger, heavier and rectangular, unlike the ball of 194. It was multi frequency, more powerful, had a visual display like the Type 177 I had used on my sonar course, and had 250ft of cable, allowing it to go much deeper in the water and go below deeper thermoclines (temperature layers).

The Wessex 3 had also undergone a make-over. The engine had been up rated and had a 'Paloust' jet engine to start it, although it could be started by battery if required. It had a flight control system that would accelerate and climb it out of the hover, turn it onto a chosen course, and then automatically turn it into wind, decelerate, and descend into the hover. No more Jump Tables required by the observer. Once in the hover and the sonar lowered, the heli would keep over the vertical sonar cable. There was also, for the first time, radar, which could be used in a 'true-motion' mode as the heli had Doppler navigation. If an acetate chart was laid on the large radar display, the land stayed still as we flew over it.

Because the course only lasted two weeks it was very intense, and we only had enough time to learn our own job. There were only 13 sorties, of which seven were submarine hunting Casexs.

After this course I had two weeks leave which was long enough to see my second son born, and leave him a week later, with his brother and my wife, to join me in NI a month later.

—◦◦◄❖►◦◦—

Chapter 14
819 NAS. RAF Ballykelly. Northern Ireland 1969-70

8 19 Squadron was unusual. It was not attached to a ship, but to an RAF Airfield. RAF Ballykelly, near Londonderry. Instead of being above sea level, when we landed, our hardstanding (the area where we landed and where our headquarters and hangers were) was actually about 4ft below. Officially we were part of HMS Sealion, the RN Base at Londonderry but the only reason that I went there was to go diving, (to stay qualified as a Ship's Diver).

The squadron spent a lot of time away from base on various ships and sometimes operated ashore living in hotels. We used to do a lot of trials of new tactics and testing of equipment with NATO forces. We were also involved in Casexs, SAR and Casevac – Casualty Evacuation. I arrived before the last 'Troubles' erupted, and half the squadron were Irish, many from Bogside, 'Derry. The CO was Lt.Cdr. 'Bushy' Shrubb, the Senior Pilot (SP) Lt.Cdr. Dave Mallack and the Senior Observer (SObs) Lt.Cdr. 'Jock' English;

three very experienced whisky-loving, (Glenfiddich!) leaders. All with extremely high standards, which were very demanding at times.

We had 6 Wessex MK 3s, the same heli that I was converted to in Portland in March. The Wessex 3 was very distinctive because it had a prominent hump on the top, behind the engine and main rotor, housing the radar, and the last operational one, on HMS Endurance in 1982, was called Humphry for that reason.

Within one week of joining, we embarked on RFA Olmeda, an oil-tanker and supply ship specially designed for the RN. The Royal Fleet Auxiliary (RFA) is a civilian manned fleet of tankers, supply ships and landing-craft, which support the RN world-wide. It is a very highly trained fleet that not only has to follow the Merchant Navy rules and regulations but are also trained in NATO tactics, including operating helicopters. It is not unusual to see a supply ship steaming at 20 knots, with an aircraft carrier 100 feet on one side, connected by pipes pumping fuel or ropes transferring stores, whilst on the other side another ship is doing the same. They will then zig-zag, in perfect formation, to confuse enemy submarines.

I soon learnt how to get the best out of the new 195 sonar as we participated in many multi-national exercises. We landed on Dutch as well as RN ships to refuel. A new thing with the Wessex 3 was that it was possible to do in-flight refuelling. Not from another aircraft, but by hovering over a ship with no heli pad and winching up a refuelling hose, connecting it just forward of the cabin door. This required good station keeping by the pilot, assisted by the crewman, as ships veer from side to side and rise and fall on waves.

Although I had been told how to operate the radar in the Wessex 3, because it was the observer's job, I had never actually done it. The first time I undertook this task was departing from a ship and returning to Ballykelly. I had just about discovered how to switch it on and get it aligned as we landed. It was noted that I needed to do some continuation training in this skill. After an hour's training flight, I became as little more competent, and the next day another sortie was scheduled. This was to include a more advanced technique of a 'Self-controlled Radar Approach' to land at Ballykelly, to simulate landing in thick fog. On my first attempt I thought I was just about doing okay. I directed the heli downwind of the runway, told the pilot the course to steer, allowing for slight wind drift and told him to descend and at the final point told him to decrease speed and come to the hover. When we were in the hover the pilot told me to look out of the window, so I removed the blackout blind, which was needed to see the radar, and discovered that we were hovering over a train in Limavady station. Thank goodness it was good visibility and only a 'training fog' or we would have been on a train ride instead of a plane glide! After the next few practices, I improved and finally reached a good standard and was trusted. I also practised approaches to a moving ship, which was more complicated.

It is imperative that all pilots remain qualified in instrument flying. In poor visibility pilots fly the aircraft only by looking at their instruments, and this takes constant practice. The Wessex can be flown by one pilot but, during instrument flying training, two were always used. The pilot doing the instrument flying practice wore blue lensed goggles and had yellow Perspex on his windows, which allowed him to see his instruments, but not out of the cockpit. The other pilot, who could see out of the cockpit, was a safety pilot who would take control if the other pilot became disorientated. There was a period that the squadron had fewer pilots than required so the observers and aircrewmen were trained as safety pilots and were used in instrument flying training. I never reached a standard where I could land a heli on a ship but could manage to control the heli in flight and land on an airfield – somewhere!

One of the trials we carried out was a new tactic called a Didtac. The aim of a Didtac was to visually identify an unknown vessel at night so that it could be attacked if it was a hostile vessel. We tried various techniques. We dropped parachute flares that slowly descended; we fired small flares towards the target; we used our landing light and even our small hand-held signalling lamp. The problem was that we had to get extremely close to the ship to make a positive identification.

At the de-brief with the admiral's staff officers, after a week of trials, we were unanimous in our report that none of these methods were worthy and when asked 'Why' we stated that every method would result in us being shot down by the enemy. The staff officer replied, 'Well, that would be a successful outcome, we would then know it was hostile'!!! Thankfully that was the last we heard of the Didtac but the identification problem was never really solved. I came up with a suggestion that we could use our sonar in passive mode (listening only, not 'pinging') miles away from the contact, and with practice we would learn to identify the fast patrol boats that were the main concern, but this idea was not taken seriously.

We had a very enjoyable deployment to Denmark, living in a hotel. Getting the aircraft there was easy, we flew, but moving the engineers and crates of tools and equipment from NI created a problem, which was solved by Thomas Cooke. They arranged everything. My only complaint about our hotel was that directly below my window was a pornographic book vending machine, and the clink of Danish Kroner and the metallic clunk of the dispenser seem to go on all night.

The squadron operated from a Danish airfield at Jutland, called Fredriks Havn. We flew from Ballykelly to an RFA, which took us to the North Sea and we flew off from there. On approaching Fredriks Havn the lead aircraft called on the radio, in a typical English accent, 'Fredricks Haven, Fredricks Haven this is Royal Navy 123, over'. No Answer. 'Fredricks Haven, Fredricks Haven, this is Royal Navy 123, over'. Again, no answer. Again and again, rechecking radio frequencies, we tried to make contact until, when we were only a few miles from the airfield, a Danish voice said 'Flight 123, this is Freed Haawn, Are you calling me?' It had been overlooked that pronunciation was somewhat different in Danish.

The language problem also came up on a British ship, RFA Olna, from which we operated for a couple of weeks. The first night onboard I was talking to a ship's engineer, who was from Newcastle, and he asked, 'Wen gang yam?' Seeing I didn't understand, he repeated it. I looked in askance at another squadron member and he shrugged. Luckily, another of Olna's crew translated and said, 'He asked when you are going home'. I told this story years later to a Danish friend and she told me that she understood perfectly as it was Danish. It seems that the Norsemen left a lot of their language in the northern part of England.

Early one morning, as duty crew, I was called out on a Casevac. An American nuclear submarine had a casualty onboard that needed airlifting to Scotland. For secrecy, the submarine would surface a long way out to sea, and we would be required to contact it using secret codes and authentication (we did not have secure radio then). This position was near our maximum range and when we reached the R/V a periscope and radio aerial popped up and we exchanged code and passwords. When it came to the surface, the captain appeared on the tall fin and just looked at us. Normally, on a sub, a handling party would have been on the deck to help but it stayed deserted. My observer winched me down onto the heaving deck casing and I released myself from the winch hook and the heli moved away so that I could talk to the captain. He looked at me. I looked at him. Nothing was said. Eventually I broke the silence and, 'Good morning sir, I have come for your casualty'. After a pause he asked, 'You got any ID?' I was dressed in my waterproof flying suit, clearly marked 'PO Jackson RN'. I pointed to that and then at the heli, hovering 100 yards clear, marked with Royal Navy and the British roundel, and said, 'My helicopter'. Another long pause, then, from the captain, 'You want coffee fella?' I told him I did and would like it white with sugar. The captain then bellowed down into the sub, 'Two coffees Elmer, one black and bitter, one blonde and sweet.' Obviously, I was blonde and sweet. I finished the coffee and still did not know the nature of the casualty. Did I need a stretcher to lift him? After another five minutes, a man dressed in civilian clothes appeared, fully fit. 'OK' he said, I signalled for the heli to come overtop and lift us both up and we took him to Scotland. Not a Casevac at all but an urgent passenger ferry.

I did have a real Casevac, which meant flying to Eire and on to Belfast. This required getting diplomatic clearance to cross the border. We landed at Letterkenny Hospital and I was introduced to the patient, who had a broken back. He was in an inclined bed, with weights on a line which was attached to a frame around his head, to apply traction to his spine. The doc there thought we were a properly equipped air ambulance and was surprised when I told him that there was only just enough room for a lightweight stretcher, and it would not be possible to rig up any traction device. We consulted and agreed that we could apply traction manually throughout the flight. He was carefully lifted, in our stretcher, into the cabin of the heli and, with the doc pulling on the frame around the patient's head to keep the spine in traction, we lifted off and headed for Belfast in NI.

I had given the doc a headset and throat mic and he kept say 'Don't worry, you'll be in hospital soon', every time the patient spoke. We could not hear the patient, because of the engine and rotor noise. I relieved the doc and took over pulling on the patient's head frame, with the patient constantly talking and looking even more agitated, with the doc still saying, 'Don't worry, you'll be in hospital soon'. After about 5 minutes I wondered what the patient was saying so I removed my throat mic and placed it around his neck, only to hear him say 'I can't breathe, I can't breathe'. It seems that I was overdoing it with the traction! As soon as I eased pulling, his body relaxed, his chest rose and fell rapidly a few times and kept quiet for the rest of the trip. I hope that he did not suffer any lasting effects from my inexpert attempts at being a paramedic.

Every summer, it was traditional that 819 NAS would send a heli to participate in the annual festival in Londonderry. This was held in a large field on the outskirt of the city and took the form of a flying display. Normally there was a flypast of all the helis which were available, followed by a demonstration such as winching 'survivors' or lifting a stretcher. Part of the show was always a 'sweetie drop'. We bought a lot of wrapped sweets and spent days tying them onto paper-handkerchief parachutes. As we flew over the spectators, the sweets were thrown out to the crowd. It usually resulted in chaos with adults and kids fighting to gather as many sweets as possible.

The first year I participated coincided with an advertising campaign by the RN to recruit more pilots and the slogan 'Join the Navy and fly a Camel', showing a picture of the Wessex 3, with its distinctive radar hump, was well publicised. To reinforce the campaign, we had a heli, with its winch wire led around the wheels and forward, flying just above ground at a slow walking speed. I, dressed in Arab costume and holding the winch wire, appeared to be dragging the Camel heli across the field. This got a quite an applause, but the following year's performance was the one remembered by many.

The blockbuster film that everyone was talking about was Batman, so it was deemed that our display must have a Batman theme. Somehow it was decided that Batman, on a bicycle suspended from a heli, would fit the bill and I would be Batman. We hung a 'Pusser's Red Devil' bicycle (as Navy bikes were called), with me on it, from the rescue winch, to test how we would fly. The answer was, not very well, as I just spun in circles, so it was decided to add a length of wood with a stabilising tail plane, behind the bike. This worked well in the test flight and I faced the right direction. The day before the display we had a dress rehearsal and decided we wanted to make a bit more of a statement, so on the tail plane we attached two Day and Night distress flares. These were double-ended flares that gave out red smoke at one end, for day-time use, and a very intense orange/red flare at the other end for night. They were operated by a ring which was pulled, so string was tied to the rings and, when pulled, thick red smoke billowed out. The dress rehearsal was a success, so we looked forward to the cheering of the crowd on the following day.

Next day was bright and sunny and after the flypast, whilst the usual melee and ruck was taking place after the sweetie drop, my heli landed just out of sight of the crowd and we paid out the winch wire and attached it to the bike and me. I had my improvised Batman's clothes on – black trousers, black shirt, black mask, a black helmet and, of course, a long black cape. The winch operator was Mick Dollin, the senior aircrewman.

The time came; the heli lifted off and climbed and as the bike and I cleared the ground, continued to climb whilst Mick paid-out more winch wire to keep me about 50ft above the ground. As the heli moved forward and gained airspeed the tailplane started to work and, as I flew through the air, my cape blew behind me and I started to pedal the bike. Just before we reached the boundary of the display field, I pulled the strings to ignite the red smoke. As we approached the spectators, I could see that they were really enjoying the display. They were jumping and pointing so I waved back at them. I could almost hear the Oh's and Aha's. I then glanced up at Mick Dollin and he was also enjoying it – or was he? He was mouthing something and pointing down at me. I gave him the 'thumbs up' and a grin, but he shook his head rapidly and pointed down and behind me. I turned to see what the problem was and discovered that my long black cape and the wooden tail plane were on fire, and instead of red smoke, orange flames were shooting out. The Day/Night flares had been put on the wrong way. No wonder the crowd were so excited, they were watching Barbequed Batman being burnt on a bike!

I rapidly gave the signal to Mick to land and we just cleared the hedge to the next field. As I touched the ground, I peddled like mad to achieve a running landing and, as soon as the bike touched the ground at about 20 miles an hour, I released my Quick Release Box to detach the bike and me from the winch wire. The bike and I fell over onto the grassy ground, as the heli soared away, winching in 150 feet of trailing winch wire. I rolled in the grass to extinguish the flames from my cape. Unfortunately, the downdraft of the heli then caused the burning grass, set on fire by me and the still burning flares and tail plane, to spread downwind towards the display field. I could imagine the news headlines, 'Batman barbeques city Fete'. Luckily, with the flares dying away, I managed to extinguish the grass fires by beating them with the remains of my smouldering cape, and the heli returned to pick me up. Apart from a small bruise or two from the landing I suffered no injury. After any flying incident the Squadron is required to submit an incident form, but I can't remember seeing one; far too embarrassing. Even today, I am sure that there is nothing in HeliSops (Helicopter Standard Operating Procedures) that covers fires on Batman on a bicycle.

A very enjoyable deployment was Gibraltar. Two of our helis were at RAF North Front, the airfield that sticks out into the sea by the border with Spain. We were accommodated for a week in a 5-star hotel and had a whale of a time. We were there to provide helicopter opposition against a course of trainee submarine captains. After weeks of training in various waters was the final examination for these students. Commanding Officers Qualifying Exam – COQEX, is often held in the entrance to the Mediterranean. This is because it is a busy area for shipping and the currents and different layers of water make it difficult for the submarine to maintain the correct buoyancy, whilst the same layers can help the submarine to remain undetected.

The cool Atlantic sea comes into the Med. and circles it in an anti-clockwise direction, along the African coast. As this water continues east towards Egypt and Israel and returns on the north side, it starts to evaporate and becomes salty and heavy. By the time it gets back to Gibraltar, years later, it is warm but so dense with salt that it sinks below the cooler, fresher, water coming in from the Atlantic. This means that there is a surface layer of cool Atlantic water entering the Med. at the Straits of Gibraltar, moving east, and a warm, salty layer underneath it, moving west. Normally warm water is less dense than cold and lies above. The speed of the sonar sound beam becomes distorted, refracted, and reflected by these different layers and it can be exceedingly difficult to detect submarines as they change depths to hide. It is precisely because of this sort of problem why helis, with long sonar cables, are used for ASW. They can transmit sonar at different depths, in different layers. The heli will automatically hover directly over-top of the submerged sonar to stop it dragging and tilting, thereby ensuring that the cable is perfectly perpendicular. That will not work when the sonar transmitter is in a layer of water moving westwards, whilst the heli is hovering over a layer of surface water moving eastwards. To allow for this, the crewman adjusts the hover so that the heli moves the same as the lower layer of water. It was off putting to the pilots that when we were in the hover, 'Pinging', we were moving sideways and backwards at almost 4 knots over the surface. It took some explaining, in the bar the first evening, to the junior pilots.

I enjoyed that exercise. Because I had proved my submarine detection skills and understanding of how the propagation of sound is affected by temperature and salinity layers, I was allowed to choose my own sonar depth and estimated ranges. Traditionally, the observer told the sonar operator the settings to use. Despite the submarine constantly changing depth, course, and speed, as well as ejecting decoys, I managed to keep in-contact with it and carried out successful 'attacks'. I had eventually become a good aircrewman sonar operator, thanks to the intensive training I had received.

Many of the squadron personal, including me, lived in Married Quarters or private accommodation, but some single men lived in RAF accommodation. A few days before a deployment to a ship, I was given the job of accommodation Petty Officer. This meant I had to check that the 'Mess deck', as we insisted on calling it, was in good condition etc. I found out where it was and asked the 'Lads' if there were any problems and was told there weren't any. A day or so later we embarked on a ship and returned late one Friday afternoon a few weeks later.

When I arrived at the squadron on Monday morning I was told that there had been a minor fire in the mess. A bed had been placed too close to a 'black' electric heater and the blankets had smouldered and caused some smoke damage.

The next day I was told that the RAF would be holding an inquiry and I would have to be present. I attended the inquiry, which consisted of 3 RAF Officers and Lt. Mike Bumpfry, one of 819 squadron observers, and was greeted with the words 'It appears that you may be responsible for the fire, and you can have a lawyer to represent you'. To say that I was flabbergasted would be an understatement. I was asked if I had briefed the inhabitants of the mess about fire precautions. I told the inquiry that I hadn't, and when asked why I replied that all ratings in the Royal Navy were trained to fight fires and I could see no reason to do so. The Inquiry Board then said 'RAF Ballykelly's Standing Orders states that the Warrant Officer in charge of accommodation is to instruct the inhabitants about the dangers of electric heating'. I did not know that this book even existed, never mind the duties of the Accommodation Warrant Officer. This book was not held by 819 NAS. I then pointed out to the Inquiry Board that I was not the accommodation WO as in the RN there was no such rank as WO. I was a Petty Officer. This threw the Board into confusion and I was told to wait outside of the room. I could hear heated discussions and I was called back in. 'You are a Petty Officer, undertaking the duties of a Warrant Officer'. I said, 'No sir, if I was, I would be getting a lot more pay'. This seemed to upset most members of the Inquiry Board, and I was told to leave and remain at my squadron until the findings were published. I went back to the squadron feeling very nervous and sorry for myself, and, later in the afternoon, I was told to report to the CO's office.

When I entered, I was confronted by the CO, SP, SObs and Lt. Mike Bumpfry. The Boss (CO) had a sheet of paper and said,' I have read the result of the Board of Inquiry regarding the fire and have listened to Lt. Bumpfry. I have here the recommendations of the board'. There was a long pause. I held my breath. The Boss screwed up the sheet of paper and threw it in the waste bin. 'That's all PO. Carry on'. What a relief. I never heard anything more about the fire, but I did go the mess and remind everybody that they were not allowed to set fire to RAF establishments.

Every Friday 819 had a traditional task. A navigational exercise (Navex) was arranged, which always included landing at a small airfield at Macrahanish, Scotland. As soon as the heli had landed a van would drive up to it and boxes of fresh fish, lobsters and crabs would be loaded onboard, a brown envelope containing money passed to the driver and then the heli flew back to Ballykelly. This was our weekly fish supply.

One of the last flights I had on 819 was on 17 December '70. A fishing boat from Douglas, the Isle of Man, (FV Verbona) put out a distress call after being caught in a force 10 severe gale and sank. The Manx lifeboat and a Shackleton aircraft searched for them unsuccessfully all night. The duty crew, which included me, took off at first light and it was decided that a search height of 500 feet was suitable for a visual search for the life raft they said they were getting into. The pilots searched the ahead sector, the observer the port side and I the starboard and below. I caught a glimpse of something small and orange and thought it was a buoy, as we had almost flown over top of it but to be on the safe side, I told the Boss, who was the captain of the heli. He had not seen anything but decided to investigate and turned and descended. It was the life raft. We quickly winched up the crew of two fishermen, despite the 20ft waves, took them to RFA Sir Geraint and after being checked by the doctor, returned them to the Isle of Man. When we returned to Ballykelly I decided that I would familiarise myself better with the Search and Rescue Manual and I subsequently became respected for my knowledge. One thing I discovered was that the optimum height for searching at sea was 100 feet, not 500.

In December 819 NAS left it's Irish home (and re-formed the following year, with new aircrew, at Prestwick, in Scotland). Two weeks' beforehand, my wife had driven my two young sons, in a car loaded with our personal effects, via the overnight ferry to Liverpool, to Cornwall. A 36 hour journey. Days later I followed by train in much greater comfort.

Wessex 3 the Camel

Chapter 15
706 NAS, RNAS Culdrose, Cornwall.
Jan -August 1971

706 was an Advanced Flying Training Squadron for pilots. Most came directly from Basic Flying Training and had never been on a Front Line (operational) squadron. A few pilots were converting from other helis and were more experienced. We had a mix of aircraft. There were Wessex 3s, Wasps, and the new Sea King Mk1.

The Westland Wasp, a small, jet turbine powered heli, had been 'Marinized' for the Fleet Air Arm. It derived from the Westland Scout which was used by the British Army. As it was required to operate from small ships, such as the Type 12 Frigate, it had some unique features that the Scout lacked. The undercarriage was strengthening for use in rough seas and had swivelling wheels to allow it to be pushed sideways. The rotor blades could give negative pitch (negative lift) so that the Wasp would stay on the deck as the ship rose and fell with the waves. Small ships mean small decks and hangers, so the rotor blades and the tail boom could be folded. Normally it flew with one pilot and a navigator (observer or aircrewman) and its main purpose was to carry 2 homing torpedoes to drop on submarines. As it had no sonar it had to be vectored to the dropping point by an ASW heli or a ship.

The Wasp had no radar or sonar, but crewman flew in these helis as navigator or winchman. I was allowed to fly one, with an instructor, and managed a reasonable level flight, despite it having no flight stabilising system, but my hovering left a lot to be desired. I ended up doing figures of eight over the landing spot. The instructor took control and told me not to give up my day job!

The Westland Sea King was a great improvement on the Wessex 3. The radar and sonar were the same, but the aircraft was much bigger. It could fly for 5 hours and was faster than the Wessex. It had 2 Rolls Royce Gnome jet turbine engines, which did not require external power to start and the 5 bladed main rotor folded automatically. The heli could lift a small lorry, underslung. The main wheels retracted into buoyancy sponsons that gave the Sea King a water take-off and landing capability in an emergency. The rescue hoist had much more cable and was faster. At night, when in the hover rescuing people, adjustments to the position was made by the winch operator. The RN Sea King derived from the USN heli of the same name, and with upgraded engines, superior digital flight control systems and excellent radar and sonar became a reliable; a versatile workhorse, until well into the twenty-first century.

The aircrewmen on 706 were usually used as observers (navigator and radar operators) and were also required to lower the sonar into the sea to simulate ASW. By this stage I had reached a good level of competence using the radar and navigating and enjoyed the responsibility. If there was no officer available, we also acted as Duty Officer, responsible for keeping the planned flying programme operating as well as fielding numerous telephone inquiries.

The pilots under training had a rigorous syllabus to cover. There was intensive 'ground school', that covered the theory and gave intricate knowledge of the mechanics, hydraulics, electrics and avionics of the aircraft. The tightly structured flying course commenced with starting the engines, then taxiing, take-off, landing, flying with and without the flight control system, instrument flying, load lifting, winching, and 'dunking', (which was lowering the sonar to simulate detecting and prosecuting submarines). It was in the last sections, load lifting, winching, and dunking, where backseat crew were always required but, if the weather was bad, we often flew on other lessons to provide extra safety.

The difference in flying a fixed wing plane and a helicopter (rotary Wing) can be summed up in a short sentence. A FW plane wants to fly, a helicopter does not. The lift from a helis rotating blades is not uniform. When flying forward, the blade that moves forward, into the airflow, gives more lift than the retreating blade the other side, which moving out of the airflow gives less lift, so the heli wants to 'roll' one way. As the blades spin in one direction, the torque tries to turn the heli the opposite way, so a tail-rotor is fitted to counteract this. The tail-rotor also acts as a rudder to turn the heli (yaw). To make the heli go forward or backwards the main rotor (rotor disc) angles forward or backwards, making the heli 'pitch' in that direction. To climb, the rotor disc increases the angle of attack of each blade, to give more lift. The rotor disc turns at a constant speed. The biggest problem is that when one adjustment is made, the pilot needs to adjust everything to keep it in balance. If you are in the hover and want to move forward, the rotor disc angles forward. This means that the heli no longer has the correct amount of upward lift and will descend. To stop this, a greater angle-of attack is applied to the rotor disc. This means the torque increases, so the tail-rotor increases its angle of attack to stop the heli yawing. All this extra work requires more power, so the engine power is increased. It is because of all these complications that helis have a flight control system. Any one movement, whether it is in pitch, roll or yaw, requires adjustment in the other two and the engine power. A pilot is required to have the skill to fly when the automatic flight control system fails.

On most of my sorties on 706 I was acting as observer and I eventually was very comfortable doing this. There was one SAR, when Royal Naval College Dartmouth, the officer training college, had the yearly sailing race to Fowey in 40 open whalers (27ft boats). The weather became bad and boats capsized. I did more than 6 hours searching for people in the water but was unsuccessful in finding any. Unfortunately, two young sailors died after their boats capsized and nineteen were rescued. 4four boats were washed ashore. The other heli with us caused great consternation, by reporting of 'Bodies' visual in the water instead of 'Survivors'. The Captain who authorised the race was probably ready to grasp his ceremonial sward and commit Hari-Kari!

Another occasional task was to assist in trials of dropping torpedoes and these were often done by aircrewmen. The drop was filmed at high speed and analysed to see if the torpedo entered the water smoothly.

I left 706 NAS the first week in September and joined my next front line squadron.

Chapter 16
824 NAS HMS Ark Royal / RNAS Culdrose. September 1971-August 1973

For the third time, I found myself serving on an aircraft carrier – the other Audacious class ship, the same as Eagle. Although Ark Royal had only come out of refit the previous year it was not in the best of condition. A lot of money had been spent on stronger aircraft arrester wires, more powerful steam catapults, water cooled jet blast deflector plates, which protected the flight deck, and an advanced aircraft landing system, all for the latest aircraft in the FAA, the Phantom F4G. The ship's steam turbines and electrical systems were showing their age and the ship spent more time in the dockyard than it did on operational duties. This is one of the reasons that we just called it the Ark! Once, when returning from the USA in bad weather, we were warned one night to standby to evacuate the aft part of the ship, as cracks had started to appear. After dressing and gathering our important documents and money, we went back to bed, thankfully, not to be disturbed as the weather improved and the sea state subsided.

A year earlier the Ark had been in collision with a Russian destroyer, which was determined to interfere with a NATO exercise. The Ark won, the destroyer didn't, but it required the Ark to go into dock again. The captain of the Ark was found not guilty of negligence as it was the destroyer that had contravened the International Collision Regulations.

The air conditioning ventilation system had been incorrectly installed (according to the engineers).

The cooling element should have been inside of the heating element, so that it would not freeze. It wasn't, so it did! In the icy cold of New York, the ship was kept warm but when we sailed south to Florida and needed the cool air conditioning, the cooling element, which had been frozen, burst in many places.

The Air Wing of Ark Royal consisted of 12 Phantoms, 14 Buccaneers, 4 AEW Fairey Gannets, 1 CoD Gannet, 6 Sea Kings and 2 SAR Wessex for Plane guard. As I have described the other aircraft earlier, I will just mention the Phantom.

The Phantoms, McDonnell Douglas F4s, were produced by the USA and were amazing aircraft for their time. They held many records. Large fighter bombers, they could fly more than twice the speed of sound. As fighters, their size was a drawback in a 'dog fight', and the latest USSR Mig aircraft (the perceived threat) could out-manoeuvre them. The acceleration was tremendous. The UK fitted Rolls Royce Spey engines and UK electronics, to further improve the aircraft. The RAF also took delivery of the Phantom, without the arrester hook etc. that the FAA (Fleet Air Arm) needed. The earlier version was sometimes called 'old smoky'. When power was applied the engines produced a plume of smoke but the British Rolls Royce engines stopped this.

It was on Ark that I found out the difference in stress levels between fixed wing and heli aircrew. After flight the aircrew gather in their respective squadron briefing room and debrief.

We heli crew would sit around drinking coffee and joke around until every heli had landed and then debrief. One night our briefing room was being used for another purpose so we used one of the fixed wings briefing rooms and afterwards flew on our 4 hour sortie. When we landed we returned to the same briefing room and had to wait until the Phantoms had landed, before our debrief. As usual we were relaxed and joking around and heard the first Phantom land. When the pilot and weapons officer came into their briefing room they just oozed tension. Not saying a word or getting a cup of coffee, they just sat down, waiting. A few minutes later the next aircraft landed and that crew silently came into the briefing room, followed at intervals by other Phantom crews. The tension was terrific and affected us all. We just sat, waiting, no more banter between us. Collectively we held our breath and listened to the aircraft roar in, hit the deck hard, then the clanging whoosh as the arrester wire was caught and pulled out. When the last Phantom had landed and the crew walked into the room it was as if a switch had been thrown. Everyone came to life, jokes and friendly insults were thrown around and coffee demanded. To fly a jet from an aircraft carrier really does take a special breed of aviators.

I joined 824 Squadron at Culdrose and the CO was Lt.Cdr. Hallett and SP Lt.Cdr. Dave Mallock, from 819 squadron. Lt.Cdr. Hallett left in November and Lt.Cdr. 'Bushy' Shrubb replaced him. We now had the 819 NAS team again.

A couple of weeks later, as duty crew, I was on a SAR to a Norwegian ship Anatina, 215 miles out into the Atlantic. This was the longest-range rescue ever in the UK at the time. There had been an explosion in the engine room and a fire. Out of the 11 people rescued, I winched 6. We also took supplies for the few crew who were left onboard to help with the subsequent salvage and tow. The weather was bad, but the size of the ship helped with winching. According to the newspapers I was an 'Officer' who was winched onboard, but I never got a pay rise!

Ark Royal had an ASW exercise in the Mediterranean but returned to the UK for Christmas, when the squadron disembarked to Culdrose. Mid-January she sailed westward to the USA and the sun.

Mid-February and we were carrying out ASW exercises off the Virgin Islands, interspersed with load lifting from supply ships and routine practices. We did have a squadron competition, flying on a NavEx around the British Virgin Islands. One task was to fly at 90 knots, 200ft and 'bomb' a target with a bag of flour. Not one of us hit the target! Another was a photographic competition for the most beautiful picture. By taking my flying boot off and photographing my big toe I won for the novelty factor.

I can remember that we had to call on VHF radio, the controlling radar station at a trials range., which was on an island hundreds of miles from land. The call sign was 'Boredom' and when we called, after a long pause a slow 'deep brown' American voice, with what sounded like a yawn, answered 'This is Boorreedom, Ooover'! It made us smile

On one exercise, in the North Sea, Ark was asked to search for a motorboat that had gone missing from its moorings. The SAR was scrambled to search and found it drifting miles from land. The SAR diver was winched down and discovered that there was an unconscious man in the cabin. He was brought back to the ship and later flown ashore. It seemed that he had stolen the boat. The local lifeboat was called to take the motorboat in tow, back to its berth. Afterwards 'Scouse', the diver, was heard to say, 'I wonder what it's like to go to sleep and wake up unconscious?'!!

During NATO exercises we were often bothered by USSR 'Spy Ships'. They deliberately got in the way during aircraft launching and recovering, obviously not having learnt the lesson from the damaged destroyer a year earlier. They were festooned in aerials and listened and recorded our radar and radio signals and were known as 'E-lint' (electronic gatherers of intelligence) trawlers. It was decided to give them something to remember us by.

In RN mess decks it is traditional to have a 'spitkid', an 18 inch, shiny, circular rubbish bin, rather like an upturned dustbin lid. Two of these were screwed at the ends of a 5ft long, 4"×4", wooden beam and the beam lashed, horizontally, to a swivel chair. This was placed in the cabin of the SAR Wessex, and the cargo door closed. The SAR heli flew to one of the E-lints, hovered alongside, slid the cargo door open and displayed the spitkid, looking very much like dish aerials. These were swivelled the length of the trawler. Whilst this was happening the Ark transmitted the national anthem, played backwards at 100 times the speed. As soon as the short burst of radio transmission stopped, the cargo door was closed and the SAR returned to 'Mother', Ark Royal. This was done frequently and afterwards, every time it happened, the Russians had their still and movie cameras out, filming everything in close-up and doubtless recording the radio noise. I wonder how many hundreds of man hours it took the Soviets, before they realised that they were being spoofed.

We were exercising with some US ships and from one of these we had an ill sailor in Ark's sickbay. After a few days he was well enough to be flown back to his ship. At the first attempt the heli went unserviceable so he did not make it. The following day the SAR was tasked with the transfer, but the US ship was too far away, so once again he returned to Ark. He did not stop complaining and annoyed everyone. For the third attempt my Sea King, which was going out on an ASW screen, was tasked to take him to his ship first and winch him down.

I suggested to the pilots that this was a chance to get our own back for his whinging. Instead of his destroyer, we came to the hover over a Russian E-lint and started to winch him down. It wasn't until he was swinging 20ft above its deck, with the Russian crew gathering to take him that he realised what was happening. I have never seen anyone trying to climb a winch cable before! I stopped winching when he was just above the deck and brought him up and took him to his ship. That gave him something to whinge about.

It was on 824 Squadron that I started to be used as a swimmer to recover our practice torpedoes. The torpedoes were electric and had their own sonar and when they detected a submarine, they would ram it and explode. To give it the best chance of detection, these needed to be dropped close to a sonar contact. To make sure that our dropping was accurate, we used practice torpedoes that had a 'Recording Head' instead of explosives. Instead of ramming, they altered course when close-by and then did another search. When the battery was flat the torpedo would float to the surface and it was recovered by a swimmer jumping into the water and hooking it onto a strop that was under the heli. The swimmer was then winched up and the torpedo taken back to the ship and the run analysed to see if it had been a successful attack. As I had been an assistant instructor on an SAR divers course, I was the obvious candidate for this job if an SAR diver was not available.

One claim to fame is that I was part of the crew of the last unit to have successfully torpedoed a British submarine – by accident!

In August '72, we had a practice torpedo dropping exercise on HM S/M Walrus (Diesel-Electric Porpoise class). This was to assess the accuracy of the drop. I was in the designated dropping heli and after the drop, I was going to jump into the sea and recover the floating torpedo, so its recording device could be analysed back on Ark Royal. Everything seemed to go well. Sonar contact was made, and we were vectored into a dropping position and released our torpedo. I had thrown a white smoke-float out of the cabin when the torpedo was dropped, to mark the position, (standard procedure on this sort of exercise) and sat in the door with my swim fins on to search for the torpedo when it surfaced and also to see the green smoke-float that the submarine had sent up when it heard the 'splash' as the torpedo hit the water. We knew that there would be at least a six minute wait as we hovered over our white smoke. From the positions of the white and green smoke it looked a good, accurate drop.

We glanced at our watches as the minutes counted down. Six minutes. Then seven;eight;nine and still no torpedo. We climbed out of the hover and started a slow circular search for the torpedo, but nothing was seen. After a few more minutes we assumed that the torpedo had failed to surface because of a defect. We were just about to call Ark to tell them we would be returning empty handed, when the submarine's radio aerial broke the surface a mile away and we were informed that they believed the torpedo had hit them and were coming to the surface to check for damage.

As Walrus surfaced, we saw that not only had the torpedo hit them, but it was stuck into their port side, jammed between the watertight pressure hull and the entry hole it had made in the outer steel casing. It was like a cartoon. Not only was the torpedo sticking out like a lance in a bull but the counter-rotating propellers were still slowly rotating as though to drive it in even further.

I was winched down to the sub and I could see that the torpedo had only missed a high-pressure air cylinder by inches. If it had hit that, or any of the attached pipes, Walrus may well be laying on the ocean floor.

The sub's captain, high up on the conning tower, shouted at me, 'Your torpedo hit me!', which I thought was an understatement. Amazed by how close to disaster they were, something that the captain had not yet realize, and wondering how to remove the torpedo from its resting place, I gave a sickly sort of grin and shrugged. 'What are you going to do about it?' shouted the irate captain. I managed a smile and replied, 'Shall I take it home with me sir?' The words he said after that were unintelligible.

I called my pilot (the CO, Bushy Shrubb) on UHF and explained that there was only one way to remove the torpedo. I told the Observer to lower the 40ft strop and lifting band and I placed the band around the torpedo as accurately as possible, the torn metal casing of the sub not allowing for a normal, vertical lift. The heli rose slightly until it just took the weight of the torpedo and then moved to port, maintaining an exact height, to pluck it from Walrus without causing any more damage to the torpedo or Walrus. It was an excellent demonstration of flying and co-ordination between the Boss and the winch operator (the observer.) When it was clear of the sub, I jumped overboard and was winched up and returned to Ark.

It was assumed that the torpedo had malfunctioned, but that was incorrect. These homing torpedoes searched in an anti-clockwise direction, and when within 200 yards of the submarine the practice torpedo turned left 45 degrees, switching its sonar off for 30 seconds or so, before going into another anticlockwise search pattern. Our torpedo was dropped on the port side of the sub. Unfortunately, the submarine had ejected a decoy air-bubble when it heard the torpedo splash into the water and altered course to port (left) increasing speed and producing a knuckle of wake at the same time. The practice torpedo, seduced by the decoy and wake, headed towards them, switching its sonar off at 200 yards and altering course to port to avoid hitting what it believed to be the submarine. The collision with the actual sub was inevitable. If it had been a live torpedo, with an explosive warhead, the tactic would have worked but the torpedo would probably have re-detected the sub on its next search if within range.

During June 1972, whilst in the North Atlantic, Buccaneers of 809 NAS stopped the invasion of British Honduras {now Belize). With a flight of 1,500 NM (2,400 Km) each way, two Buccaneers flew from Ark Royal to British Honduras, which had the Guatemalan army massed on its borders, poised to invade. The two aircraft spent 10 minutes overtop, making dummy attacks along the border, to demonstrate that the UK was ready to defend its last South American dependency. The Guatemalans had no way of knowing that the Ark Royal was over a thousand miles away, running short of fuel, or that the Buccaneers carried no weapons (because they had carried extra fuel) and had to refuel by Buccaneer tankers to get there and would require refuelling again, to return to the Ark.

The flights lasted six hours, the longest continuous flight of any jet attack aircraft ever, and required two more Buccaneers in the tanker role to refuel them twice. Just the threat of retaliation was enough to keep the peace. This was gunboat diplomacy at its best and could only be carried out by an aircraft carrier.

Phoenix Squadron by Roland White is an excellent book about the Ark Royal, R09, and the superbly executed task carried out by the ship and 809 NAS.

The last couple of weeks of August '72 in Ark and 824 we had a very busy ASW exercise off northern Scandinavia. Just before the exercise started, I had the sonar operator's dream experience. We sighted 6 Soviet Whisky class submarines on the surface, line astern, and as we approached, they dived, in formation. My voice probably raised two octaves as I reported that I had six Russian sonar contacts. They then started to move in different directions, and I was left just holding one, which was moving away at high speed. I think we were the only heli in the area and when we 'jumped' to regain contact I was unable to find the sub again.

The exercise was called Strong Express and it simulated a convoy being tracked and attacked by submarines and ships. That month I achieved almost 115 hours flying, of which over 39 were at night. Not until the Falkland's War did I get anywhere near that monthly total again.

It was the CO's brag that we had 5 helis out of 6 flying on the last day, which was true. What was not mentioned was that not one of them was really capable of detecting and prosecuting a submarine. In one, the sonar just went around in circles and two operated with much reduced power. Another heli could not transmit at all and the fifth had no auto-pilot so it was impossible to keep the sonar vertical in the rough seas. It did the Boss' reputation good that five helis were flying. Unfortunately, to achieve this, a lot of maintenance had been missed (allowed because of 'operational requirements') and for the rest of the time that I was on the squadron the heli serviceability suffered.

1973 saw Ark Royal over the pond to the USA, Florida, and flying for the rest of the time on 824 was the usual ASW; load lifting, winching etc. Most of us achieved between 30 – 40 hours a month. One important event happened that had a massive impact on the sonar aircrewmen. MOD Navy had decided that there would be an Air Crew Man branch of the FAA, and unless they opted out, all current aircrewmen (who were on a supposedly 2-year loan from their parent branch, although I had already been flying for 5 years), would form the new branch. I do not think anyone reverted to their original branch. No more 'General Service' and becoming a seaman again. It did mean that I would never get that big TASI badge, but I was extremely happy to retain the small wings on my sleeve for ever. It also meant a pay increase for flying. I considered then and still do, that being an aircrewman was the best job in the RN. We got responsibility, senior officers listened to us and often the job was exciting. Working closely with officers, we received special treatment and, to top it all, we got extra pay.

The aircraft handlers, who manoeuvre and secure the aircraft on deck had egg on their face – twice! Whilst approaching Virgin Gorda, a Buccaneer, in calm weather, slipped over the side early one morning. A few months' later a heavy tug, used for moving the aircraft, also had a 'Float Test' when it decided to join the Buccaneer. Perhaps Neptune is practicing ranging aircraft on the seabed.

Navy squadrons often had a foreign pilot and observer attached for 'cross country' training. We had a French observer. Lt. Bernard Buissont. He had a very thick Breton accent, that sometimes was hard to understand. On one sortie, shortly after take-off, he reported to the ship that 'The rudder was bent.' Ark replied and told him that he could return immediately and land and the fire crew were standing by. 'No', said Bernard, 'My rudder is bent'. 'Understand,' said the ship,' I have fire and crash crew standing by. You are cleared for an emergency landing'. 'No no' replied an agitated Bernard, 'My rudder, my rudder, it is bent.' Then a refined English voice (the pilot) said, 'He is saying that the radar is unserviceable' (code word 'Bent'). We are continuing with the sortie.'

It was on Ark that I nearly had a terminal diving accident. The ship was anchored near the Forth Bridge, Firth of Forth, Scotland, and one of the sea water inlets in the hull needed the seacock (valve) replacing. This was a routine job for the divers. We had to hammer a soft-wood plug into the inlet to seal it and then the valve could be removed and serviced. The original plan was for me to go down with a magnet and floating line, to find and mark the inlet, and then go down again to hammer in the plug. I was one of the most experienced ships' divers and I decided that I could do both jobs at once. When I jumped into the water there was a slight leak from my air bottle but as I only intended to be down for 10 minutes, I was happy to continue. I was handed the magnet and floating line, hung the loop of rope, connected to the hammer, around my wrist and another loop of rope connected to the plug (so we could pull it out when it was time to remove it) around the other wrist. I also had a lifeline attached to the back of my SABA set. I swam to Ark's side and started to descend, following a white painted gridline to help me find the correct inlet. As often happened, the facemask, in which was built the mouthpiece, started to leak. Normally these leaks can be stopped by tightening the straps of the mask but on this occasion it leaked even more. It was difficult to adjust straps when you have a heavy hammer on one wrist, a buoyant bung on the other and a magnet with a floating line in your hand. This constant leak required me to having to blow air into my mask frequently, holding the top of it to make an airtight seal (Remember the Iranian Officer? I refused to drink the Firth dry!). As the water filled the mask, I had to keep close to the ship to see the grid guideline. My magnet with floating line kept on attaching itself to the metal of the hull and when venting water from the mask, I pulled it way from the ship's side and when my mask was clear I could not see the ship at all. The Firth is not noted for its good visibility. Knowing that Ark could not be far away I swam in circles looking for it, but in vain. The wrist seal of my dry-suit had become damaged and now cold Scottish water was coming in and I was slowly becoming negatively buoyant. The turning in circles searching for the ship had wrapped my lifeline and floating magnet marker around my body, but not equally. When I twisted one way to unwind one line, I twisted the other more around myself. I had a head torch and tried to use that in the almost zero visibility but could not re-stow it when I realised it was not helping, so now that was hanging down and getting in the way. Now I was getting a bit worried. When I touched the bottom of the Firth I was surprised, and the silt I disturbed surrounded me. Now I had no visibility at all. I had so much water in my suit that I could not push myself off the bottom and swim to the surface. I was sitting on the seabed. It was time to call for assistance by giving the emergency pulls on my lifeline – that was if I could have reached it, tied to the top of my SABA set and trussed around by lines. I could not reach the release for the few weights I used.

Breathing now was becoming more difficult. I thought that this was because I was close to panicking, so I tried to calm down. I then realised that I had used up one of my two air bottles and I needed turn a valve at the back to open the other bottle. This was impossible as both my arms, one with a floating wooden bung, another with a heavy hammer, were secured with a rope, floating at one end and with a heavy magnet on the other. Using the torch, I worked out that if I could remove the line around my left wrist, I could then use that hand to untangle the right, which would allow me to open the equalising valve and jettison the weights.

I managed to reach my diving knife, strapped to my right leg, and tried to cut the lines around my wrist, but the knife was well used and not very sharp. By now I was having to suck hard for every breath. I knew that the bottle would not last another minute. I sawed franticly at the ropes with the serrated blade, but they tended to roll with the knife. I realised that I only had seconds left. I decided that my only hope was to cut my hand off; one last attempt at cutting the rope and then my wrist. I hacked and sawed viciously at the rope, not caring if I cut my wrist or not, when suddenly the rope parted and fell away, off my wrist. I slid the now loose coils off my right arm and opened my equalising valve. I could breathe again. After jettisoning my weights, I managed to swim to the surface, ropes and lines still wrapped around me. I was about 20 yards away from Ark Royal. The person who had supposed to be tending my lifeline had not noticed that it had gone slack and the diving supervisor was busy telling jokes. They just thought I was taking a long time. It turned out that the leak of air had got a lot worse and the seal of the facemask had to be replaced. If I had died it would have been because of my over confidence, and my stupidity, using defective equipment and by trying to do, in one dive, a job normally done in two. I never told the others what had really happened. I just said I lost the ship and spent the time searching. One of the less experienced divers, did the job, with two dives, in less than 10 minutes.

There was one other dive that had problems on Ark, with the same supervisor. The ship was alongside, in Hong Kong. Divers were tasked with carrying out a bottom inspection and a cocktail party was taking place on the quarterdeck, at the back of the ship. The local dignitaries were there, with their ladies dressed in their finery.

I was 'buddy' diving, with two of us attached by a line. We were inspecting the area around the screws (propellers) and a thunder-flash was thrown into the water as a signal to come to the surface. We untangled ourselves from the screws and rudders and started to ascend. I was slightly higher than my buddy, and approaching the surface, when another thunder-flash was thrown in which exploded between my buddy and me. My mask was blown off my head and I was dazed. My buddy's mask was blown down, off his face. Blood clouded the water from his ears. We surfaced at the rush and I shouted swearwords and profanities at the top of my voice to the supervisor in the diving boat. I don't think that I have ever been so angry before. When I stopped screaming at him, I realised that we were just below the quarter deck and the cocktail party, and the guests and officers had rushed to the side to see what was happening. I didn't realise I knew so many swearwords, nor did the guests and their ladies. I fully expected to be summoned to explain my disgustingly bad language, and at least make an apology, but nothing happened. My buddy had perforated eardrums, and I think that explained everything. The diving supervisor never supervised again.

Whilst I was on 824 Sqn, Flag Officer Naval Air Command (FONAC) decided that all aircrew should be trained in survival and learn about interrogation. A big exercise was arranged on Dartmoor and 'volunteers' would be interrogated when 'captured'. Whilst none of us relished this we accepted it until we were informed that we were ordered to sign a form saying that we were volunteers for interrogation. There was almost a mutiny. Ordering us to volunteer upset all the aircrew on 824 and the Boss had to give us direct orders to do so. Most of us added a written amendment such as 'I am volunteering on the direct order ...'

There must have been close to fifty pilots, observers and aircrewmen, from both fixed and rotary wing, on the exercise and we were split into groups of four, given a poncho, rucksack, ration pack, plastic sheet, compass and map and told to go to certain rendezvous (RV) positions, returning three days later. I was in the group with the Boss, Bushy Shrubb. The exercise started in the evening, each group leaving at staggered times. Most people wrapped their rucksack in the plastic sheet, and it shone in the weak moonlight like a beacon. When I pointed this out to the Boss we decided to fold our sheets and put them out of sight in our rucksacks.

Our exercise was uneventful. We checked in at the RVs and kept out of sight, away from roads, as much as possible. When we deemed it was only an hour or so before 'EndEx' (end of exercise) we crept out of our hiding place and started walking the final few miles, along the road, back to the army camp we had started from. We were ambushed by the army who put us in the back of a Land Rover and taken to the camp. We were happy with this as it saved us walking. As it was the end of the exercise, we did not get interrogated. For my group it was an easy exercise but there was trouble brewing. Quite a few of the fixed wing pilots decided that they didn't want to play at soldiers and, instead of going to the RVs, had left the area, staying in B&B and hotels. One of them sent a postcard to FONAC saying 'Wish you were here'! He was furious. All aircrew had to write a report of their actions. The outcome of this farce had long lasting effects and touched me directly, later in my career.

In August 1973 I left 824 NAS, took 2 weeks leave and re-joined 706

Chapter 17
706 NAS RNAS Culdrose September 1973 – September 1974

7 06 no longer had Wessex 3 aircraft, just Sea King Mk1 and a few Westland Wasps. Although I had flown as the observer, using the radar, many times, there had been no formal qualification for aircrewmen to do so. This changed soon after I joined the squadron, and I, after a short course at 737 NAS, Portland, was one of the first aircrewmen to be officially qualified as an AHC (Airborne Heli Controller) 3. Initially, this was during daytime only, when the weather was good, in what was known as VMC (Visual Meteorological Condition). This meant I could control my heli and other aircraft and ships. Later, when more experienced, I qualified as AHC 2 which included controlling in bad weather (IMC, Instrument Met Conditions) and at night. I could not become an AHC 1, as that entailed being able to control dropping a Nuclear Depth Bomb and, it was decided, that it was above a petty officer's paygrade.

As before on 706, I was part of the 'sausage machine' producing pilots and observers to fly on operational frontline squadrons. I was now also expected to give instructional lectures in the classrooms. Although the squadron had no formal requirement, we were sometimes required to carry out SAR.

Late one Friday evening I was called out to take vital equipment to a sinking ship off South East England. This was a five hour round trip and shortly after this it became a requirement to have a Sea King on standby for SAR 24/7. This burden was shared by crews from all frontline squadrons disembarked at Culdrose so it was generally not too onerous. When I became an AHC2, I was included in the observers roster.

On the 16th January 1974 I was the squadron duty crewman. The southern part of England was hit by a massive storm with sustained winds of over 60 knots – 70 mph, with stronger gusts. This is known as a severe storm and all flying was cancelled, as it was out of limits to start the rotors. I inspected the designated SAR standby heli and noticed that the electric control to the hydraulic rescue hoist was inoperative. This meant that it required a solenoid to be depressed by hand when using the hoist control. Also, there would be no auto stop when raising, so it would be possible to winch in too far and break the hoist wire with people suspended from it. When I reported this to the Air Engineering Officer he retorted 'It doesn't matter as we are never going to fly in this weather. It's out of limits.'

At lunch time we received a Mayday from M/V Merc Enterprise, a Danish ship, in the English Channel, saying that the cargo had shifted, the ship was about to capsize, and needed immediate assistance. Although it had never been tried before, the SAR heli was pushed behind the hanger to lessen the wind strength and we started the rotor. It bucked and fell dangerously until it reached full speed and as we lifted off and cleared the hanger the force of the wind blew us backwards even though the airspeed showed 40 knots.

The captain was Lt. Fred Hatton, and the observer Lt. Kent Flemons, both instructors, and the co-pilot, whose name I can't remember, was a senior student. We were soon in the area and discovered that the ship had capsized, and the lifeboats had overturned in the maelstrom. I could see bodies floating in

135

lifejackets and some crew still alive. We went into our standard procedure for rescuing, 40 feet above the sea, hovering over-top and touching them with the rescue strop so that they could get into it – but the standard procedure was not written for winds of that strength and waves of that height. The strop was being blown yards behind us and was submerged one minute and airborne the next. It was impossible to keep the strop by the survivor long enough for them to get into it. These conditions had never been encountered before, but I had to think of something, or they were dead men. I desperation I decided to try a completely different tactic. I explained my idea to Fred Hatton and we moved backwards, downwind of the survivor. Instead of keeping the rescue strop just above the surface, being battered by the waves, I continued lowering until it was submerged. We then moved forwards slowly above the water (with 60 knots showing on our airspeed indicator) and I aimed to try to hit the survivor with the wire. As soon as the survivor had the winch wire in hand the heli stopped its forward movement and I constantly adjusted the length of wire to allow the survivor to get into the strop and told the pilot which way to move. Doing this was still not easy and it probably took about 20 minutes to rescue three of them as it did not work first time, and each lift needed frequent attempts and constant corrections by Fred with the heli and me with the hoist wire.

After recovering three people we saw two more clinging tightly together and again we tried the same technique but this time it did not work as they were unwilling to help by letting go of each other and grasping the wire when it touched them. It was obvious that they needed more assistance and, as I was used to being in the sea, Kent Flemons took over as hoist operator and I got into the double-lift harness. Kent winched me down into the water. Initially I was dunked and swung many times by the huge waves. One minute under the water, the next swinging above the two people. Eventually I managed to grab hold of them and clung tight, determined not to lose them. Kent paid out lots of wire so that I was no longer getting airborne and got the heli into a stable position.

I discovered that one of the survivors was a woman and she seemed barely conscious. I believe they were the captain and his wife. My next problem was to get the strop around the woman, as she seemed the weakest, but that was not an easy thing to do as they were both holding each other tightly. It took ages to get the strop around her, sometimes underwater and other times being jerked by the hoist wire. They did not understand that I would have to take them separately and refused to let each other go. I signalled to Kent to winch up but still the man hung on to us and as the waves dropped below and we swung above them I realised there was only one thing to do. A size 8 flying-boot on his shoulder and he was back in the water, alone.

As we were winched up, I started to worry; did Kent remember that the electric upper limit switch was in-operative or would the wire break, sending us both falling into the sea? To remind him, as I got level with the cabin door I tapped on his helmet. According to him I hit him with a sledgehammer!

After getting the woman inside the cabin we moved backwards over the water until we were downwind of the man, and I was lowered again and dragged towards him. It took many attempts, frequently being submerged, before I managed to get hold of him and now found that, in lieu of the woman, I was now his best friend, and he wrapped his arms around me. Eventually I managed to place the rescue strop around him, with the hoist wire disappearing deep underwater to avoid being torn away by the waves.

Until that moment I was not worried about my own safety. I trusted my crew completely. This is what we were trained to do – but not in these conditions. I looked up to signal to Kent but there was no helicopter there. The sky was empty.

I felt the sea surge and heave as a huge wave lifted us skywards and I saw my heli, but it was 20 yards away and below me. I could see all of its top; I was higher than the tail rotor and that was the highest part of the heli as it was pitched nose down, to fly forward in the storm, just to keep in position. The survivor and I were on the crest of a wave whilst the heli was holding its height of 40ft over the trough. A Russian ship in the area reported waves of 70 feet – 20 meters height and I do not think that was an exaggeration. As we were winched up, I thought we were close to Plymouth as I could see the hills. They were waves.

There were no more survivors near us and we had been joined by four more Sea Kings, which were recovering the remaining survivors. We set course for Plymouth and landed at the hospital, where our five survivors were treated before being taken back to Denmark. Seven people drowned and a total of eleven rescued.

Fate had not yet finished testing us. We had scarcely left Plymouth, flying at 1,000ft en-route to Culdrose, when Fred Hatten had a cockpit warning that we were lacking in power. He diagnosed the problem as salt build up on the compressor blades of the engines. Hovering close to the rough sea for so long, the engines had sucked in salt-water spray. This was not uncommon, and the remedy was to land and have a machine do a 'compressor wash'. Unfortunately, the nearest airfield was many miles away. There was a good chance that we would not make it. Thinking 'outside the box' Fred decided to do something original and not taught. He noticed a heavy storm cloud, the sort we would normally avoid, and flew into it. The rain and hail battered the heli, we could hear it above the engine and rotor noise and we were thrown around, lifted and dropped, by the violent gusts. The torrential rain came in around the cargo door and observer's window. It was also sucked into the two Rolls Royce Gnome engines, dissolving the accretion of salt. We had an airborne compressor wash. As soon as full power was restored, we exited the rainstorm and headed back towards Culdrose. I have never heard of any other pilot doing this.

We had just landed at Culdrose when we heard two more 'Maydays'. Two of the other Sea Kings on the SAR had to carry out emergency landings in a field, in the dark, because of loss of engine power; Saltwater ingestion! They had not flown into a rain cloud. A bone of contention is that both pilots who made emergency landings received medals for the way that they handled their emergency, whilst Fred Hatton, who had the foresight not to get into trouble, did not get a mention. I think it was very unfair.

Most SAR that we do go unnoticed, but this one caught the attention of the media. Too much so. As I had rescued the most survivors, I bore the brunt of it. The novelty quickly wore off. Three of us aircrewmen were awarded the Air Force Medal from Her Majesty Queen Elizabeth, (the first time that it had been awarded to RN aircrewmen) and the Royal Medal of Reward, First Class with Crown, from Queen Margrethe of Denmark. For the rest of my time in the RN I was constantly being singled out by Admirals and Captains, asking what the unusual medals were for.

Soon after this rescue I was invited to amend heli SOPS, our standard operating procedure book, regarding wet winching in severe weather conditions, so I added a section explaining how to 'trawl' the winch wire and strop over the survivor. Hopefully, this technique has saved other lives over the years.

That February was abnormally stormy and I had a couple of SAR call outs. One was to a ship that reported that it was sinking west of the Scilly Islands in the bad weather. We were told that the crew had abandoned ship and were in lifeboats. When we got close to the reported area, I picked up a contact on radar and when close discovered the ship still afloat, with two lifeboats close by. I winched up all eight of the survivors from one of the boats and the Culdrose SAR Wessex rescued the remainder of the crew from the other boat. The first person I had rescued was the captain and his first words were 'Is there a dance tonight in Penzance'.

We did a search to make sure there were no survivors in the sea and then I asked John Teasdale, the first pilot, to circle the ship. We both agreed that it did not look as though the ship was sinking. The waterline looked normal. Half seriously, I remarked that if I was winched down to it we could claim salvage money and end up rich (but not so rich as the admiral who was safe in his office, hundreds of miles away.) As I was the only crew in the cabin with the survivors, we decided not to pursue this idea, and returned to Culdrose.

The ship did stay afloat and two days later a Dutch tug arrived and towed it into Falmouth. Perhaps I should have gone onboard!

We had two types of radio on the Sea King, a short range Line-of-Sight VHF and very long range HF. On this rescue we realised that we were out of range of our VHF to talk to Culdrose and too close to use our HF (it relies on bouncing the signal off the ionosphere, in the top layer of the atmosphere). We discovered that we could talk to Prestwick, in Scotland, and they used the telephone to pass our messages to Culdrose.

A few nights after this SAR, I spent four hours searching for the pilot of an RAF Hunter aircraft that had crashed in the sea but could not find him.

One afternoon I was informed that an extra training flight was required that night. Although it was my turn to fly, I had other commitments so I nominated another aircrewman to fly. Next morning, the BBC news said a Sea King helicopter had crashed into the cliff that night., killing all the crew. I felt awful. Had I sent someone to his death? I drove to Culdrose, breaking all speed limits and was extremely relieved that it was not one of our helis. I then found out that it was one of 824 squadron's and the crewman, Brian Sharpe, a good friend who helped me when I first started flying, had died. I remembered that on one occasion he wanted to stop flying and go back to being a seaman and I talked him out of it. Brian was a popular man and we spoke about him for years.

A notification came to the Squadron asking for volunteers to attend survival training with the RAF in the south of France. It was a two week exercise, the first week living in a hotel. This sounded like a 'Jolly', so two pilots and I decided to volunteer. The pilots received their joining instructions, but I did not. When they returned to 706 NAS they told me that it was an enjoyable fortnight and that the instructors there had asked why I had not turned up. On investigation I discovered that my joining instructions had arrived at Culdrose by post but had been sent to the wrong petty officers mess, where it languished for two months. I was upset by missing out on a 'holiday' in France and

I wrote an official Letter of Recommendation to the captain of RNAS Culdrose, suggesting that the internal mail system be more regulated. I did not expect to hear any more about it. I was wrong.

A few months later I was sent for by the CO, who informed me that the captain of Culdrose had received a directive from FONAC, stating that it had been decided that there was a requirement for a new position, of Combat Survival Instructor (CSI). These would be trained by the SAS and the first course, lasting a month, would be starting in two weeks. The course would also cover Resistance to Interrogation. Volunteers would be needed. The captain had noticed that I was keen to do survival training, therefore my name had been forwarded. A course run by the SAS – this was not my idea of career development, but I could not think of a way out of it.

Newspaper Article

Chapter 18 CSI
Combat survival instructor training
SAS

With great trepidation I arrived at Bradbury Lines, home of 22 SAS in Hereford, and found myself sharing a hut with a dozen or so other NCOs from various army, royal marine and air force units, as well as two members of the elite American SEAL Team, who had come for some cross-unit training. We were all on the CSI course. Next day we met up with the officers, including Lt. Radcliffe, a heli pilot I knew, an RN fighter pilot and two RN Safety Equipment officers, who were also on the course, as well as a dozen mean-looking, fit and quiet soldiers. It was then explained to us that this course was part of the SAS final selection test. The soldiers on the course were potential SAS men and were the few remaining who had not been RTU'd (Returned to Unit – failed). If I was nervous before, I was doubly so now. I have never considered myself a roughy-toughy. I always tried to walk away from fights and now I was on a course with potential killers!!!

John 'Lofty' Wiseman was our main Instructor, who was renown not only for his knowledge of survival, but, as I found out later, also for his leadership and bravery in stopping a massacre by the communist Addu at Mirbat, in Oman; a hero who was not known outside of the SAS. It was explained to us that combat survival was surviving and evading capture in enemy territory. No fires, no signals for help. We may well have had to escape from a POW camp. It was to be assumed that we had no weapons, so we had to be prepared to use whatever we had at hand. What I had learnt so far in the RN was that unarmed combat was used to disable your opponent. Here I was to learn CQB – Close Quarter Battle, where it was taught to kill them.

We had lectures on lock-picking, the Geneva and Hague conventions, how to conduct meetings with agents who would help us, how to navigate and travel in enemy territory and pass cordons and checkpoints as well as survival techniques (mainly in Europe but the artic and desert were also covered). We had a talk from an escapee from Colditz POW camp in Nazi Germany (I think it was Pat Reid), and told how to resist interrogation. Surprisingly, there was very little fitness training as it was assumed that we would get ourselves fit. I went for five mile runs most nights.

We had sessions in the gym learning CQB (even a screwed-up ball of paper is useful) and a visit to a herb farm at Stoke Lacy run by a woman. We were chased, and in my case bitten, by attack dogs and learnt dog evasion. We even had a butchering lesson. A sheep was hung up by its back legs and one of the RN officers was given a knife and asked to kill it. Initially he started to poke the sheep with so little force that he would have had trouble penetrating a balloon. When it was explained he was expected to cut its throat he didn't even cut its skin. I just knew what was going to happen and tried to inch to the back of the group but Lofty saw me. 'Come on PO, your go next.' I would like to brag that I bravely de-capitated the poor creature, but it did not happen. I did manage to sever its arteries, so it died fairly quickly, with only a little help from Lofty.

I was extremely surprised at how Bradbury Lines was run. No bugle calls, no parades, no marching. Soldiers were walking around carrying language and weapon books, looking very studious. In the All Ranks bar there was no bragging or boisterous behaviour. The food was excellent and put the Navy to shame. It was more like a college than a training camp for the world's most elite soldiers. I discovered that any British serviceman could volunteer for the SAS, no matter what rank, and if they were accepted became a 'Trooper', the lowest rank. They received the same pay as before but promotion was gained in the unit after experience. The SAS has been involved in covert operations throughout its history. It is the UK's secret regiment.

The first big exercise came during the third week. One afternoon we were gathered, issued with POW type clothes and a short piece of candle, then searched and told to wait by a large shed. As nothing seemed to be happening, I decided to explore the shed and found a pile of old, torn, camouflage parachutes. I realised that these might be useful, so I 'liberated' a large piece and hid it under my POW overcoat, an army greatcoat with a circle on the back. The Bedford truck arrived, and we were given a torn piece of copied map and told that we would leave the truck individually and would have to report to the RV in three days. There would be a hunter force out looking for us and, if captured, we would be interrogated. It was in March and the exercise was on the Brecon Beacons (Wales). No survival equipment. No food. No water. No hope.

I was ejected from the truck before it got dark and realised that it was not a great distance to the RV so I decided to walk during the night and find a safe laying up position (LUP) before it got light. I reasoned that if the exercise had only just started, the hunter force would not be deployed until later. I was striding along a small track when I heard voices. I saw a fallen tree and I dived underneath it, burrowing in as far as possible, until I came to the hedge the tree was laying on. I tried not to pant, breathing as quietly as I could, but it sounded loud to me. I then realised that the voices were American. It was the two yanks from the SEAL team, and they were loudly arguing. I relaxed and then heard more shouting, by English voices. The hunter team were active, and the yanks were caught that first hour. I could see the flash of torches through the branches as the search for more of us came closer. It was obvious that they would look under the tree, and I remembered the section of parachute wrapped around my body. Trying not to make any more noise than necessary, I unwound it and tried to cover myself. I could still see flashes of light through it and then I heard the crunch of footsteps by my tree and they stopped, the light of a torch shone underneath it. I held my breath and, like a child I closed my eyes, waiting for the cry that I had been found, the denouement. Nothing happened. The light went out, but I did not hear any footsteps receding. I waited and waited. Nothing heard. I knew that someone was waiting for me to move, to make a sound.

I laid there for hours, hardly breathing, not daring to move; numb with cold. I heard a rustling noise just above my head. I slowly looked up and there was a little mouse, running along the hedge. He stopped, looked at me, then scurried off, then turned around, scurrying the other way. Surely, he would not be that nonchalant if someone were waiting to ambush me?

As quietly as possible, but still, to me, making too much rustling, I slid from my hiding place and with tremendous relief, discovered that I was alone in the dark. My potential captor had not seen me had waited but then moved on.

I reverted to my plan of finding an LUP close to the finishing RV, and after observing which way the stars were moving (if they rise, it's east; setting, west; moving left to right, south and right to left, north), I cautiously trudged through field and marsh. After some hours I realised that the sky was lightening to the east, it was time to find my home for the daytime. Remembering what I had been told about laying up (nowhere obvious, such as a disused building or a small wood) I found myself on a hillside covered by blackberry bushes, so I burrowed into and under them, getting badly lacerated by the thorns, and again used the parachute to help hide me. I stayed there all day and into the following night, getting wetter and wetter as it had started to rain, and streams of water coursed their way under and around me. I could hear the hunter force crashing around, beating the bushes with sticks, and was almost stepped on by one searcher. I was feeling hungry but what I wanted most was a cup of hot tea.

By hiding under the tree so long I was further away from the RV than I intended, so around midnight I extricated myself from my spiky LUP and squelched towards the RV. I didn't know exactly where I was or how quickly I could travel. After some hours I got a good fix on my position and realised that the RV, a camp called Pontrilis, was only a mile away. The exercise was to finish at 1000 hours and I intended to arrive at that time. I was carefully navigating my way through the soggy countryside when I saw a figure close by creeping through the bushes. I was distraught, all my planning and I was going to be captured and interrogated all night until FinEx at 1000. I then realised that it was another member of the course, Mike Radcliffe, the heli pilot. I got his attention and we met up and decided to find an LUP together, until it was time to finish. There was nothing suitable in the area, although we did discover a small shed, looking like a toilet, just big enough for two of us to stand up in. The Welsh rain was beating down now, and we decided that we would probably get hypothermia if we stayed out in it, so we got into the toilet shed (for that is what it once was, now without the WC) and agreed that if we were found, being a prisoner would be better than freezing to death.

We clung together, shivering, using 'buddy warming' to try to stop the numbness of the cold. We knew that we would have to stay there for hours and longed for some heat to get back into our bodies. I think it was Mike who reminded me that we had a length of candle each but unfortunately no matches. Yes, we had! Prior to the exercise I had started to make a hidden 'escape kit'. I had cut into the instep of the sole of the bottom of one of my flying boots and made a small compartment. In there I had put a few red non-safety matches and abrasive strip and sealed it with candle wax to make it waterproof. Just maybe they had stayed dry, but I had no great faith my sealing wax had worked. With difficulty, in that confined space and with numb fingers and swollen, tightly tied boot laces, I removed my soggy boot and scrapped the mud and leaves from underneath. In the dark it was difficult to find the candle wax but with the help of a sliver of wood I dug it out and removed the shortened matches and striking pad. Using an almost dry shirt tail I wiped off as much wax as possible and then with shaking, numb, fingers, I scraped the match across the pad and it lit! It was a magic moment, seeing that flame. We lit a candle, carefully placed it in the mud on the floor between us and allowed the small amount of heat it produced to come up between us. I had dropped the remaining matches, so we had to be extremely careful that we did not knock the candle over and extinguish it. Our morale rocketed immediately, and we draped our soggy coats around us to stop any light or heat escaping through the warped timbers of the hut. Thanks to the long khaki overcoats we had been issued, the tops of our bodies were only damp, unlike our trousers which were saturated by the wet bushes, ferns and such like. When the first candle had almost burnt itself out we lit the other one. As our upper torsos were now relatively dry and no longer freezing, we decided that there was only one way to warm our lower part, so we undid our trousers and dropped them, the heat from the candle bringing some relief. We both saw the funny side of this. If the hunter force had opened the door of the hut, they would have seen the two of us, trousers down, arms around each other, trying to keep warm! It would have been exceedingly difficult to explain. The fact that we were both married would, probably, not have helped at the subsequent court martial.

Sadly, the candles burnt out before daylight, but we had survived the night and had warmed enough to continue with our plan of arriving at Pontrilis as the exercise ended. Not having watches, we were slightly early, but we were not subject to interrogation and just had to wait for the Bedford lorry to take us back to the Bradbury Lines.

Next day, at the de-brief, we were asked how many of us had smuggled items pass the search, I was hesitant in admitting that I had done so until I saw that all the SAS recruits and a couple on my course had. We got a 'Well done' for that and warned that the search for the final exercise would be much stricter. All of the SAS men and only three on my CSI course had evaded capture successfully. The two American SEALS had been released and taken back to the start, but again had been caught.

To say that I was not looking forward to the final, week-long, exercise, would be an understatement. We had the weekend free and I tried to think of reasons for not doing it, but apart from breaking a leg, nothing came to mind.

For this final exercise we were put into groups of three and again given poorly copied pieces of map. We were also given two tin cans, an empty wine bottle and a length of string. I had improved my personal escape kit by hiding a broken hacksaw blade and scalpel in my shoe arch (and renewed the matches and striker in the other) and sewn in a fishing line, a wire snare and a wire saw into my underwear. Unfortunately, there was no chance to 'borrow' a parachute. On this exercise we had to RV with three 'secret agents', exchange passwords, and were told that they would give us food. It was a much larger exercise area and there would be helicopters, a para regiment and police out looking for us. The Bedford transport, this time, had the back laced up and drove around in circles to disorientate us before we got out of it.

My group included two RN Safety Equipment Officers, and we got off the road as quickly as possible and tried to find out where we were. We had three different ideas. We eventually agreed that, keeping to the fields, we would follow the road and try to find a signpost. We very soon found a pile of empty plastic fertiliser sacks; holes were cut into them for our head and arms and we had armless raincoats. These were needed very soon.

We still had not found a signpost before it got dark, but we did come across a barn full of hay which had an open door, so we slipped in and spent the night behind hay bales. There was not a lot of loose hay to sleep in, so it was a cold night. Next morning, we got up before daylight and realised that the farmhouse was only about 200 yards away and we discovered a signpost, so we knew where we were. It was too late to leave and find another LUP before it got light, so we decided to stay in the barn. We moved deeper in the hay bales and tried to sleep as much as possible. That night we had to contact the 'Secret Agent', and the RV was about two miles away. The two officers decided that they would contact the agent and I would wait in the barn for their return. The RV was only open between midnight and 0200 and we had no watches.

About 4 hours after their departure, the officers returned saying that there was no one at the RV. That meant we had to go the next night. Or should I say I had to go by, myself, as the others were too tired. We had had no food now for 36 hours but plenty of rainwater to drink.

When I estimated the time was right that night, I left the barn and, with very little difficulty, found the RV and agent. I was helped by finding some course member returning from their meeting. I gave the password, got the correct reply and returned to the barn, only with relief, not food; only another four nights to go.

Next day we all felt quite weak, as we hadn't eaten, and the cold sapped our energy. Foolishly but luckily, we decided to move closer to the next RV before it got dark and lay up close to it. That RV was not open until the following night. We had only walked for about two hours when we suddenly came across a local man. We didn't know whether to run away or not and he smiled at us and said, 'I guess you are some of the escapees everyone is looking for'. We nodded dumbly and he said, 'I suppose you'd like some hot food then. We get a few of you every year.' We did not know what to do. Was he genuine or a plant? Was he really going to feed us or hand us in? We decided to trust him, and we were right. It seems that the local villagers always helped the SAS courses. I think it was so that no one had to resort to stealing food. We were taken in, and slept in his spare room after having a big meal. His wife and child welcomed us like family and told us we could stay for another night and if we helped him on his small holding, he would appreciate it. He was a teacher at the village school.

Next day, dressed in some of his old clothes, we did some light work on his land. We were surprised by a Land Rover turning up with soldiers but they believed us when we said we were agriculture students. I am sure it was because both officers had beards and the hunters expected to find clean shaven soldiers on the exercise.

The second night there, the RV was open, and I found myself volunteered to go and contact the agent. The officers said that they would go to the final one. It was only a distance of a mile but there were roads around. One way to avoid detection is by 'assuming an identity'. If you see a man with a ladder and bucket, you assume he is a window cleaner. I asked the schoolteacher if he had a shotgun I could borrow. He said no, but he did have a broken air rifle. I was going to be a poacher!

With the benefit of knowing the time, I left the house and intended to be at the RV early, so that I could check that it was not compromised before contact was made. I had scarcely gone 200 yards down the road when half a dozen figures jumped out of the hedges and grabbed hold of me. 'Keep still! Who are you? What are you doing out?', screamed English voices. I was petrified but managed to get my wits together and, in an atrocious Welsh accent, swore at them and told them this was my land and I could go where I liked when I liked, and no English bastard was going to stop me. This took them by surprise and they saw the gun I was carrying. One of them knelt down and felt my shoelaces and said, 'He's OK' and let me go. I was obviously a Welsh poacher. Later I realised why my shoelaces were felt.

Soldiers lace their shoes criss-crossed, but mine, like all sailors, go straight across, so we can cut them off if we fall overboard. Lucky for me, they did not know this.

There was only one route to approach the RV without being seen and I took it. I was surprised when I saw the dark figure of the agent already there. But there was nothing else suspicious, so I approached the agent and gave him the password. It was Lofty Wiseman, our instructor. 'Hello Jacko', He said. 'The Bedford's just down the bottom. Get in and we will all go for some hot scran (food). You must be famished.' I gave the password again and Lofty said, 'That's alright, get into the lorry'. He did not give me the password reply. I told him OK and went in the direction he indicated and as soon as I was out of sight, altered direction and started to make my way back to the house. I soon saw other course members and warned them that Lofty had not given me the correct reply and I believed he was a 'Double Agent'.

At the course de-brief, Lofty told us that his role in the exercise was to pick us up, unseen by the hunters, and then take us to the interrogation centre. When Lofty got back to the Bedford he jumped in the cab and had only gone a mile before he was stopped by the hunters and challenged. He said he was a farmer out looking for his sheep, but they insisted on checking the back, which, unbeknown to Lofty, was empty. He was rather surprised, and relieved not to be 'captured'. He was allowed to continue and thought everyone was hiding on the canvas roof of the truck. When he stopped later and called out 'Well done Lads, you can get down now,' and nobody answered he realised that he had been 'Bubbled' which is SAS slang for found out, exposed.

The next night was to be the last RV, so my trio decided to move closer to it when it was dark. I was moving some posts for the teacher during the afternoon and suddenly came face to face with our course officer and an instructor, who recognised me instantly. After Lofty's failure to bring us in the previous night, it had been decided to send out our instructors to look for us, as, unlike the hunters, they knew the RVs and our likely area and movement. They were also told by the hunters of a suspicious couple of chaps with beards, the two officers. I told them I was on my own and had lost the other pair nights ago. I was put in the back of the Land Rover and taken to the interrogation centre. I was to be a prisoner for the next three days and interrogated.

Unlike the films, interrogation does not start as soon as you are caught or by torture. Pavlov, between experimenting with his dogs, said that 'Any unusual event engenders into man the need to communicate'. This need can be exacerbated by 'Conditioning'. Evading, then being captured, is pretty unusual for most people. Prisoners are then disoriented, blindfolded, given confusing, contradictory orders, and put in stress positions. All this is done to heighten the need to get into the warmth, to sit in a chair, hope for a promised hot drink, and extend that relief by talking. The most reliable information is obtained by good questioning, not by force. The veracity of information obtained by torture is unreliable. Most people will admit anything the interrogator wants when in pain, but it may not be the truth.

I was blindfolded and made to squat in the mud, in the March rain, for hours. The muscles in my legs seized up and my body shook with cold. Eventually, in silence, hands pulled me to my feet and half dragged me, to face an unseen wall. My arms were extended, hands against the wall and feet kicked back and apart until my body weight was taken by my arms. After the long period of squatting my legs were weak and had trouble keeping me up. Soon, my arms and shoulders developed cramps. It is impossible to say how long I was in that position, but it seemed like hours, and eventually silent hands pulled me upright and, still blindfolded, I was taken through doors, along assumed passages, turning left and right until I lost all sense of direction and location. I thought that any moment now I would be taken into a room and sat in a chair. I was determined not to say anything except 'The Big Four' – Name; Rank; Number; Date of Birth. But that was not their plan. Once again, I was pushed to a wall, arms extended, and legs apart. It seemed hours later, my arms refusing to hold my weight and my head touching the wall, when silent hands grabbed my hair and pulled my head and body back away from that wall, my arms having to take the weight again.

In these exercises, a 'Prisoner' can call for an umpire and ask to be released. You know that you can do this at any time. It is a test of will power and moral fibre not to do so. It is so easy to say 'Umpire, I want out'. It is sheer bloody mindedness that stops you doing so.

I really can't say how long I was wall standing, until once again silent hands took me away and, after another staggering walk, I was pushed onto a chair. I must confess that, apart from unresponsive muscles and coldness, I was not feeling too bad. This probably was because of the food I had with the schoolteacher and a warm room to sleep in, but I was not going to let the interrogator know this. I slumped in the chair, trying to look more exhausted than I felt. 'Mustn't overdo it', I wanted sympathy, not contempt for being weak.

As expected, I was told that I just had to answer a few unimportant questions, coffee was on its way, and, afterwards, there would be a bed waiting for me. I truthfully answered the 'Big Four' and every other question with, 'I cannot answer that question.' It was a great temptation to start telling lies to prolong the questioning and the time I could sit in the chair. Maybe there was a cup of coffee coming... It was not easy, but I managed. The reason for not lying is that it is too easy to get caught out. The interrogator is alert, you are tired.

I was held for interrogation for almost three days and interrogated three times. I know that during one bout of wall standing I fell asleep. My muscles started twitching violently and I thought I was getting electric shocks, but it was only muscle spasms. When the silent hands led me away from the wall for the fourth time I assumed it was for another interrogation but it was to be taken away, blindfold removed and an umpire telling me that the exercise, for me, had finished. I didn't believe him. It had to be a trick, lulling me to believe that I was to be released then they would take me again to the holding pen. Even as I was having a hot meal I expected those silent hands to grasp me. This feeling lasted until I returned to my hut and met the rest of the course. Although I felt exhausted, I did not sleep well for many nights. Ten days after my return to Culdrose I played squash and I was abysmal. I then realised that I could not raise my arms above my shoulders. No pain, just no strength. It took another week to get to my normal flexibility.

The two American SEAL team who were on course had once again left a legacy. They had been captured early in the exercise and had attacked the guards in the holding pen and tried to escape. As they had no idea where they were, instead of getting out they got further in; right into where the guards were resting. They ended up by being 'Subdued' by a dozen or so irate Brit soldiers. I don't think we saw them again.

Did I enjoy the CSI course? No! Would I volunteer to do it again? No!! Am I glad that I had done it Yes!!! It taught me so much about myself, that I was stronger than I thought. I realised that most men would not have completed the course, even those that brag about their abilities. One of my course members was an RN fighter pilot and a bob-sleigher. In the bar, prior to the exercises, he told me that he was not worried about it. He opted out of the exercise. I am very proud that I was the first RN NCO to have completed the course, where many more senior people hadn't.

When I arrived back at 706 Sqd I was quizzed in great detail about the course but I always gave a bland description, if anyone was interested they could do the course themselves. As I was now Culdrose's CSI I found that I was required to give lectures to the different squadrons and also organise short survival training courses, some overnight and once for three days.

September '74 saw my last flight with the Squadron and I was drafted to 820 NAS, which was attached to HMS Blake.

Chapter 19
820 NAS. HMS Blake/RNAS Culdrose September 1974 - April 1976

Blake was designed and had commenced being built in WW2 as a Tiger class Cruiser with 6 inch guns, but was laid up in Gareloch, Scotland as soon as she was launched in 1945. She stayed there until modernised with the latest, semi-automatic armament from 1954-61. She was only in commission for two years, and in 1965 was again modernised and converted into a helicopter carrier, being completed in 1969. The aft 6 inch and 3 inch gun mounts were removed and a hanger and flight deck installed. When I joined, with 820 Sqd, she was almost 30 years old and had served only seven years total in commission, millions having been spent on conversions and needing a crew far larger than a modern ship.

Blake's pennant (side number) was C99. We replenished at sea (RAS) from a USN tanker, whose pennant number was A2. The first time we did this, as we broke away, after refuelling, they displayed the Avis, car-hire company, slogan 'We are number 2 and try harder' A week later we had another RAS with them and again they showed the Avis slogan. We then showed ours 'We are 99 and feel it'.

An unusual event happened before I joined. A 'special weapon' (Nuclear Depth Bomb) had disappeared. It had been loaded onto a heli and, after flight, off loaded and sent down the weapon lift to the armoury, in the bowels of the ship. Five minutes later, the armoury chief phoned the flight deck and asked where the weapon was and said that the lift had come down but was empty. No NDB. It had disappeared. On further investigation it was seen jammed halfway down the weapon lift shaft. It had not been secured properly and as the ship had turned it had rolled off the cradle and was suspended in the shaft. I understand that there was pandemonium onboard as there had never been a plan to deal with this situation. Anti-flash gear and tin hats were put on, but I really don't think they would have done much good in a nuclear explosion. Eventually the lift was raised, the weapon secured properly and lowered to the magazine.

The UK has a good system of handling nuclear weapons. There are more practice weapons than real ones but every one of them is treated the same. When they are transported or fitted to aircraft or other delivery systems, all are treated as live nuclear devices. Even the operator (such as the aircrew) is not told if it is a dummy or real weapon. On a ship only the captain and the weapons' officer know which is which. I don't think that even the squadron CO is aware of it. Later I found out that it was a live NDB!

820 had four Sea King Mk 1s and, unusually, the CO was an observer, not a pilot. Lt.Cdr.'George' Brown. The senior pilot, Lt.Cdr. Holt, disagreed with this and there were tensions in the hierarchy which filtered down to the rest of us. George Brown was relieved by Lt.Cdr. Craig Robertson, a pilot, in July 1975.

Blake and 820 did ASW and other exercises as we steamed south towards Gibraltar and Cape Town, which was our first and second port of the deployment. These exercises continued for the next ten months until our return to the UK in June. For the first time I was involved in Naval Gunfire spotting. A target was dropped into the sea and from about six miles away the ship would fire at it and we would photograph the fall of shot and give corrections. It was amazingly accurate. As usual, the helis, apart from ASW casexs, were required to transport underslung loads, transfer pax (passengers) from ship to ship and ashore, casevacs, and firing a machine gun at a target in the water (not easy if the aircraft is twisting and turning, whilst flying at 60 knots). I was also jumping in the water and recovering our practice torpedoes. Luckily, HM S/M Warspite, which accompanied us on the first part of this deployment, was never hit.

The act of 'Streaking' (running naked) was renown at the time, and we had a young pilot, Lt. Paris, on the squadron, and at a wardroom mess dinner he decided to 'Streak'. To avoid the wrath of our notoriously strict commander, he decided to hide his identity by wearing his flying helmet with the visor down. He entered by one door and ran the length of the wardroom almost making it to the other door, when the deafening shouts from the commander of 'Lt. Paris! Stand still!' stopped him in mid stride. Paris turned to the Commander and asked in a surprised voice, 'How do you know it was me sir?' The answer was, 'Your name is on the back of your helmet!' Lt. Paris's name was also very prominent on the duty OOWs list for a couple of months after that.

We visited Gibraltar, Karachi, Hong Kong, Seychelles, Mombasa, Singapore, Manila, Kota Kinabalu in Malaysia, and Gibraltar again on our return.

In Singapore, whilst disembarked to Singapore Armed Forces ((SAF) Tengah airfield, I did another jungle survival course, one run by the Gurkhas. With me was our senior observer, (Sobs) and a couple of the other crewmen. Sobs and I had a strained relationship before this course. He was very much a book man and knew chapter and verse. After Hereford, and the jungle course I had done years before, I knew what to expect and how to set traps etc. but it did not mean that the course was easy. I had forgotten how tenacious leeches were and how cold it got when you were wearing wet tropical flying suits. I did make my mark when turning up late one morning for a fishing demonstration by the instructor. I had set a night line, with multiple hooks the previous evening and I then arrived carrying four fish. After that survival course, Sobs and I got on together very well.

At Kota Kinabalu a group of us from the ship ascended Mount Kinabalu. We had transport up to about 10,000 feet and started walking from there. Not knowing what to expect, we had sturdy boots and clothing, and carried ropes. It was not quite the climb we expected. The path was up thousands of steps, made by roots of rain forest trees. Very tiring and in the thin air, we soon were panting and needed frequent stops. During one of these stops, whilst we were catching our breath, we heard the giggling and chattering of girls and women. Very soon, up the path we had just travelled, trotted a large group of young females. On their heads were bags of cement, sand and tools and some had large balks of timber. Obviously something was being built. When the work party reached us and saw that the fighting fit men of the Royal Navy were fighting for breath, they giggled even more and very quickly disappeared up the path. To rub things in even more, they were wearing flip flops!

We spent the night camping on a plateau about 1,000ft below the peak, which is 13,500ft above sea level. None of us had suitable clothing and we were freezing. We sat around a large fire which was constrained by a ring of stones. We had tents and sleeping bags but they were not designed for negative temperature and I knew that it would be a sleepless night. I put off turning in (Jacktalk for going to bed) as long as possible and then had an idea that might help me to keep warm. I took one of the hot rocks that had held the fire and placed it into my sleeping bag. It worked a treat; I had my solid 'hot water bottle'. A pity it had burnt a hole in the sleeping bag.

Next morning we were up before dawn and had a wonderful view of the sunrise. The descent used different muscles and we were glad to embark on the busses waiting for us when we arrived back down at the road.

As I mentioned, there was a lot of tension between the CO and the Senior Pilot. I once flew with Splot to Gan, to pick up mail and stores, and throughout the outbound trip he was complaining and deriding the CO. The tension in the heli was very uncomfortable and the observer, Mike Norman, was getting very upset but saying nothing. When we landed, it was obvious that the load was much larger and heavier than we expected. I explained to Splot that we could not fit everything in the cabin and secure it properly and we would probably be outside of our centre of gravity. I was ordered to load it. I loaded as much as I could restrain with the cargo net and reported that the rest could not be carried. Again I was told to get the remaining stores onboard. I had to obey and eventually all the cargo was fitted inside but it covered my seat, and Mike Norman, the observer, was jammed in. I then told Splot that it was all onboard but I was not going to fly back with him, it was too dangerous and not allowed. He would have to come back and pick me up later. Splot went crazy, almost foaming at the mouth, screaming at me, and gave me a direct order to get into the heli. I had to obey a direct order and climbed on top of the mountain of stores and mail, not secured at all. If we had ditched both of us in the cabin would probably have died. Not a word was said on the return trip, no crew debrief, which usually happened, took place. Next morning Sobs approached me and asked why I had refused to get into the heli. For once I held my tongue and asked if he had spoken to Lt. Norman. When he said yes, I said that he, Sobs, must know what had happened, and I had nothing further to add. Sobs nodded and walked away. I never heard anything more about it.

Whilst we were in the Far East, the civil war in Cambodia was drawing to an end. We received a signal asking us to evacuate people from the British Embassy. It seemed that the Americans had not been able to fly in fixed-wing aircraft because of gun and rocket fire. Union Jacks were painted on the underneath of our dark blue helis. We fitted folding troop seats and then the largest of our aircrewmen, Benny Goodman, was given a pickaxe handle to control the crowds and protect the four helis. The brief, given the night before we were due to fly, was that we would formation fly at 500ft, following roads, and land in the embassy compound and take 11 pax each. I was stunned by the incompetence and stupidity of this plan. Normally at a briefing 'Any Questions' was asked but not at this one. Afterwards I was impertinent enough to ask why we had an aiming mark (the Union Jack) on the bottom and was told that was to show we were not Americans; why were we flying in formation along roads, which was where the guns and rockets would be; it would be safe as we had Union Jacks painted; and what good would Benny Goodman do, armed with a stick, if many people rushed the helis; the embassy soldiers would control them. Thank goodness the Americans managed to send in their helis and our mission was cancelled. If we were not shot down before we reached the landing site and the hundreds of people wanting to save their lives had not rushed in and overloaded the helis then we would have been destroyed on the way back. I have since seen video of USA helis being rushed by scared evacuees and live ammunition having to be used to stop them. Benny and his stick would not have stood a chance.

We may have been excellent at hunting and destroying submarines but in land-based warfare we were extremely inept, stupid and naive. The Fleet Air Arm does have a military wing of helis but there had been very little cross training. Things had improved a bit when the Falklands War started, but not a lot. There, it was on job training.

Frequently, we were briefing and flying over lunch time and initially took 'Bag Meals', consisting of sandwiches with us, but by the time we reached the Indian Ocean we were upgraded to a proper packed lunch, prepared by the Officer's Wardroom chefs. These came in neat containers, like aircraft meals. We even had dessert.

We often had a problem with our radar overheating in the tropical sun, and the remedy was to climb to 10,000ft to allow the aircraft to cool down. This provided us with the perfect excuse to have our lunch in comfort. During a quiet period during an exercise, we would take it in turn to report that our radar was overheating, climb to 10,000ft, engage the autopilot, and eat our wardroom lunch in comfort and in cool conditions. Being aircrew has its perks. This ploy did seem to reduce the number of occasions when the radar overheated.

Blake was in Hong Kong for Christmas and the squadron was detached to Kia Tak airport. This was the one that was built starting in the city and ending in the sea. The approach to land was between tower blocks, which stretched above the glide slope; very unnerving. On the 23rd December I was in the mess at lunch time, talking to the RAF crew of a passenger aircraft that was returning to the UK that afternoon. When I said that I wished I was on it, I was told, come then, it's empty. With no real expectations, I applied for ten days local leave and got it. I just managed to board the plane and arrived, unannounced, at my home in Cornwall. I would never do this again. All Christmas I was worried about getting back to Hong Kong before Blake sailed. When I applied to get a (free) ticket back I was told the aircraft was fully booked. A commercial ticket was £1000, which was far in excess of my pocket. I went to Culdrose and they wrote that I was a priority, but that only got me a standby ticket. I arrived at RAF Brize Norton early and was told that there were no cancellations. Waiting until all the passengers had checked in, I asked again was told that there were still no empty seats. I had to get back, but I could not work out how to do it. Then there was a call for priority standby passengers. A relief crew had intended flying out, but they had cancelled. There were now seven empty seats! I promised myself that never again would I take a one-way flight.

Apart from torpedo recovery I also had to keep up my diving minutes and in the Seychelles it was a pleasure – except for just before we left to go towards Rio. The chief 'stoker' (engineer) of

Warspite decided to go scuba diving one afternoon by himself. He was not an RN diver. Unfortunately, he never surfaced. The following day Blake's divers searched for him and after finding his body we took it to Blake. I can't remember the results of the inquiry into his death.

A few days later I joined Warspite for five days of the submerged passage. When I arrived onboard, I was told that I was lucky as there was an empty bunk now that the chief stoker had left DD (Discharged, Dead). I didn't think it prudent to mention that I had torpedoed Walrus! I had been on submarines before but only for a day, and never a nuclear one. After being on the old diesel electric submarines, I was surprised as to how much room there was. As I did not have a job onboard, it was a rather boring. I kept a few watches in the sonar room but there was nothing for me to do as I knew nothing about the 2001 sonar that was fitted. HMS Verulam may have been the trials ship 10 years before but the ship's company was not allowed anywhere near the secret sonar. What I did find interesting was when Blake kept a steady course and speed and we passed underneath her, photographing the complete bottom through the periscope. We surfaced when we met up with another task force for an exercise which included the Brazilian Navy. I was winched off and commenced ASW exercises again, trying to find and attack my home of five days.

After a week exploring Copacabana beach at Rio de Janeiro, We sailed for more ASW exercises en-route to Gibraltar. When the exercise had finished a 'Sods Opera' was arranged in the hanger. This is the RN version of 'The RN has Talent' – or lack of it. I did a 'Fill in' between acts. Getting a junior ratings uniform I pretended to serve the admiral and captain with drinks (advising them not to drink it, as it was cold tea). Whenever there was a pause, as performers 'got their acts together', I trotted out to serve the pair, appearing more drunk each time, ending up staggering around and drinking the booze (tea) myself. It went down very well with the audience and got a lot of laughs and cheers. In Gibraltar, a PO came up to me and asked if I had got into trouble for being drunk. I asked him what he meant, and he said, 'on the night of the Sods Opera'. He had trouble believing that I was acting and completely sober.

1 and two other aircrewmen, PO Dave Fowles and Leading aircrewman 'Taffy' Williams, had been awarded the Air Force Medal (AFM) for the Merc Enterprise rescue, so I had to fly from Gibraltar to the UK, by RAF BAC1-11 passenger aircraft, to go to Buckingham Palace to be invested by Her Majesty Queen Elizabeth 2. As I was early for the flight, I walked the upper road to North Front airfield, and looked down onto Shephard's Marine, admiring the yachts moored there. I remember thinking how beautiful they looked and wished I owned one of them, knowing it would never be possible. 20 years later I sailed my own catamaran into Shepherd's Marina, and it was the biggest sailing boat moored there. T. E. Lawrence was right when he wrote, 'All men dream: but not equally. Those who dream by night in the dusty recesses of their minds wake in the day to find that it was vanity: but the dreamers of the day are dangerous men, for they may act their dreams with open eyes, to make it possible.'

Christmas leave, 1975. We had double call out on the 29th of December. The first was in the morning. A WW2 mine had been seen floating in the English Channel between Plymouth and Land's End. A smoke float had been dropped by another aircraft to mark the position for the Bomb and Mine disposal ship that was on its way from Plymouth, but that would be burnt out by time they arrived. Our task was to mark the position until they came. For reasons which will be obvious, I will not name the heli's captain, a young Sub Lieutenant, but will call him P1 – the first pilot.

We found the mine quickly and hovered close to it for 15 minutes before getting bored, (after all, we should be at home playing with the kids Christmas toys) so we then did circuits around it until we were bored again.

P1 had seen a ship steaming eastwards from Land's End, so it was decided the crew would appreciate us saying 'Happy Christmas' to them. We dropped a 60 minute (burning time) smoke float and flew off to see the ship, full of Christmas cheer. We had no radio contact with the vessel as we used UHF radio and did not have marine band VHF. After circling the ship, a cargo vessel of about 10,000 tons, we gave the crew a wave before returning to orbit our still burning smoke, feeling good with ourselves.

I was sat in the cargo door way, strapped into my despatchers harness to stop me falling out, when I realised that the ship had altered course towards us – and the floating mine.

When I told P1 he was initially surprised but then remembered that the international signal from an aircraft to a ship to 'follow me' was to circle it and depart over the bows – which are what we had done.

I was told to get the little Aldis signalling lamp and flash Morse code 'U 'at the ship, which means 'You are standing into danger', I plugged in the lamp and signalled' dah dah dit', and very soon the ship altered course away from us and directly towards the mine!

Nobody spoke in the Heli, we did not know what we could to do, as we watched the mine rose on the bow wave of the ship, only yards clear. The ship's crew had now seen the mine and were pointing at it, as the mine bobbed up and down as the ship passed it. Collectively, we expelled the breaths we had been holding, as the ship steamed away from the mine.

It was a very subdued crew who guided the Mine Disposal vessel to the mine, some time later. It was an extremely quiet crew who flew back to Culdrose and that incident was never, ever, mentioned. Our stupidity could have sent a ship to the bottom of the sea and killed sailors.

I was adding to my tally, first we had hit a submarine with a torpedo and now almost sunk a ship with a mine, and we were not yet at war!

Shortly before Mid-night the same day, we had another call, this time to Tug Boat Royston. This was to bring a casualty from Royston to Culdrose medical centre. We made sure that we did everything by the book this time and it was an uneventful night winching task, not very easy to a small, pitching deck at night but well within our capabilities. I was back home in bed by 0300.

The next day (still on Christmas leave) we had another call out but this time on a trial for a secret device. I got back home in time to say 'Good night' to my 3 boys.

31st March 1976, I was submarine hunting on a routine casex in the Portland exercise areas. Lt. Sid Drain was the first pilot and my observer was Lt. 'Doc' Omerod, We had been on exercise searching for the 'enemy' submarine for almost an hour, without getting any contact. The Sea King, like all helis, vibrates quite a bit, but whilst in the hover, with the sonar lowered deep in the water sending out its 7.5 kHz 'Ping', we remarked to Sid that the heli was remarkably smooth. After another fruitless sonar search I raised the sonar and Doc Omerod gave the pilots a heading to 'jump' us to a new position, for another search. The heli accelerated and started to climb away from the hover. The routine call, of 100 feet, 100 knots, had just come from the cockpit, when a tremendous vibration continuously shook the aircraft. We were violently thrown around in all directions and Sid just had time to say, 'Mayday Mayday Mayday' and for me to lock my five point seat harness, when we hit the water, still moving forward very fast. The impact sheared the tail off, at the back of the cabin, and the heli rolled to starboard and steadied upside down, the sear rushing in and quickly covering our heads. Initially I was frozen, hanging upside down in my seat, thinking that it could not be happening to me, but as the water surged around my head I suddenly thought 'this is just like the Dunker' (heli escape trainer, which we had to do every 2 years) and all the years of training and practice kicked in. I slid my seat right back, put my left arm behind Doc Omorod and waited for the cabin to fill with seawater. Doc was then going to jettison his window and escape and I would follow him out. I don't know if Doc had jettisoned his window early or it had become displaced on impact, but water was already rushing in. Doc released himself and tried to get through the window and got stuck. He was struggling and kicking and I got a painful pounding from his flying boots. Doc was a big strong chap! I had been submerged for what seemed minutes and realised that I would not be unable to hold my breath much longer.

From my very first time in the Dunker I have always thought, what would I do if I could not escape through the observer's window? The next nearest escape route was through the window of the cargo door, on the starboard side. I had never practised this, but I decided that I would go for it. I released my harness but then was completely taken aback, when the air in my immersion suit turned me 180 degrees, head to the surface, and the sea, still rushing in, swept me to the very back of the cabin. This had never happened in the Dunker! In every drill I had done in the Dunker I had worn immersion suits, life jackets and backpack life rafts that were already soaked from previous drills, and had not worn bulky clothes, to keep warm, underneath them. I was now very buoyant, and it was impossible to swim underwater to an emergency exit window. I was disorientated, in an upside down heli that was still filling with water and possibly sinking to the bottom of the English Channel.

Getting very close to not being able to hold my breath any longer, I saw daylight. The force of the crash had forced the bottom of the sliding cargo door (which was now the upper side) off its runner and it was only just below the surface. As the waves dropped away into a trough, I could see the surface and managed to gasp a quick breath of fresh air. I tried to slide the cargo door open, but it was jammed. I put my arm through the gap at the bottom (now top) of the door and started to bend the door outwards, making the gap bigger and, somehow, I eventually bent it enough to get out. It is amazing how strong we can be, if we have to. I kicked myself away from the Sea King and as I did so, Doc Omerod forced his way through the same gap, having been unable to escape through his window. Both of the pilots had escaped successfully and all four of us were rescued by another of our helis that was on the Casex, with no serious injury.

After the crash, there was the usual inquiry as to the cause, but nothing was really determined. Possibly it was a bird strike and a rotor blade breaking. I wrote a report which was published in the Navy News, about the problems I had being buoyant and suggested that Dunker drills should be carried out using dry, buoyant kit. This was approved and thereafter was applied. I think that will have saved lives.

Whilst we were disembarked to Culdrose, we were often called on to ferry the Prime Minister, Harold Wilson, to The Scilly Islands, where he had a holiday home. He was never on time, sometimes hours late, sometimes not turning up at all. It was a duty we all dreaded as it often meant staying at the squadron in evenings, at weekends and during leave periods. Invariably he was accompanied by his secretary Marsha and a yappy little lap dog. On one occasion, after waiting four hours on a Friday, when he didn't turn up, and then called in again the following day I decided I would inconvenience him. I bought some Exlax (laxative chocolate) and when almost at the Scillys, fed half a bar to the dog. I only hoped that he pooed on Harold Wilson all weekend. The PM had spoilt mine.

After announcing swinging cuts to the RN and FAA, Harold W was not well liked and when he made an official visit to Culdrose and a special dinner was arranged in the wardroom, everyone intended to boycott it. It required a direct order from the captain that made sure enough officers would attend.

⸻⊷◅▻⊶⸻

Chapter 20
RN Foreign Training Unit,
April – November 1976

The British Westland version of the Sea King was very successful and it was sold too many countries around the world and the training of the crews and engineers was at Culdrose. One of these countries was Belgium, who wanted an SAR version for the North Sea, the Mk 48. We had an ad hoc unit for their training. The CO was Lt.Cdr Mike Pitt – not only a first class pilot but an excellent Boss who made sure that all aircrew, including Wally Sanger and myself (the only two aircrewmen), were invited to all the official and social events. SObs was Lt.Cdr 'Kron' Ronaldson, who was well known as an RN boxer.

When the Belgians arrived, with their personal luggage, many of them had brought bicycles. What they had not taken into consideration was that Cornwall is a county of hills and valleys, not at all like their homeland, and they had very little use.

It seems that Belgian squadrons have a tradition of having a Friday lunch, with wine, for the aircrew. The RN instructional staff enthusiastically endorsed this ritual. A hotel in Helston, which specialised in continental cuisine, was booked every Friday afternoon. Any ideas that we had about Belgians being a boring race were swiftly dispelled It was a very happy unit and we regretted that it was only for six months.

Others, at different times at Culdrose, included the Indians and Egyptians. Dave Mallock was the SP of 706 Sqd at the time and late one Friday afternoon he received a telephone call and a man with a very pronounced accent asked, 'How long will it take a Pakistani to fly a Sea King?' Dave Mallock, thinking he recognised the voice of one of his instructors, who was 'winding him up', replied, 'Normally six months but for a thick bastard like you, ten years'. There was a spluttering sound at the other end of the phone and the voice said 'This is the Pakistani Ambassador', and it was! Letters of apology were required from Dave and the captain of Culdrose and they must have worked as the Pakistan unit was formed later. Later, the RAFTU was formed and the RAF also had the non-sonar version of the Sea King for SAR and troop lifting.

Chapter 21
706 NAS Culdrose, November 1976-August 1977

Shortly after joining 706 I had a motorbike accident and was 'grounded' for 3 months. To keep me occupied I was tasked with updating Helisops, our operating procedure book. Remembering past experiences, I worked my way through the manual and made a few slight amendments, such as landing in clearings with long grass the crewman should not step out of the heli but be winched down. This was because a few years before, Norman Anning, a senior crewman, had jumped out when hovering just over the grass and discovered it was almost 2 meters tall, and ended up with a broken leg. I discovered in Helisops a rescue procedure that had been invented many years earlier which had been forgotten about when helicopters had longer rescue winch wires. It was called a Hi-line and I realised that with certain modifications it would be invaluable with modern helis. We were now carrying out rescues in conditions that were unthinkable 15 years earlier and we were doing them at night. The concept of a Hi-line was that helis with short winch wires could not hover above the tall masts of ships, so they would lower a rope, attached to the winch, and then move clear, to the side of the vessel winching out the wire with a strop on. Sea Kings had very long winch wires and could hover well above masts but at night and in bad weather it was difficult to winch safely, especially if there were wires holding the mast up. I suggested that we should lower a line first and if it got tangled, throw it away and have another one ready for a second attempt. I liaised with the Safety Equipment section and a valise with two Hi-lines, ready for use, was made. After trials it was accepted that the Hi-line would be the standard rescue method if there was any doubt of safety for ships and yachts. I was very pleased with that.

Nearly all my sorties were standard pilot training flights. I had two unsuccessful searches for crashed aircraft in the sea and two casevacs (casualty evacuations) to the same ship, HMS Matapan, within three weeks, for the same problem. Sailors had dropped the ring pull from their beer cans and then swallowed them. It's hard to believe that people can be so stupid.

June '77 was the Queen's silver jubilee and I had my navigational skills really tested. There was going to be a flypast of the FAA aircraft at the Spithead Fleet review. The helis and the fixed wing aircraft had to co-ordinate to pass over-head with split second timing. 706 had sent 3 helis, I think, and I was the lead navigator. We flew from RNAS Yeovilton in Somerset and had to rendezvous with the rest of the display and slip into a gap left for us. The timing was critical and I was extremely pleased when it happened as planned.

I think that this was the year that I was a participant in the diving display at RNAS Culdrose Air Day, an annual event. We had a large tank with a glass side and divers in it. The divers wore a communication system and there was a diver with a microphone outside. We asked the youngsters what they would like the divers to do, such as take their masks off or stand on their heads and suchlike. The favourite was to sing 'I'm forever blowing bubbles' with their masks off. It was a popular side show and I enjoyed participating in it every year that I was at Culdrose for Air Day.

Having been 'On the wrong side of the law', metaphorically speaking, on my combat survival course, I thought that I ought to change sides and become a 'Good Guy'. I had learnt how to withstand interrogation so now, I decided, would be a good time to learn how to interrogate. I attended two courses at the Joint Services Intelligence Wing (JSIW) at Ashford, in Kent. The first was a Prisoner Handling and Tactical Questioning course, where I learnt the best way to treat prisoners prior to the first round of interrogation, which was called Tactical Questioning (TQ). The information that is required is of immediate concern. Which unit he is in; what the task was; what are the immediate, future plan ? etc. Despite popular belief, as I said before, torture is counter-productive. Putting pressure on someone by torturing or killing a friend can be also. Maybe you have chosen the wrong person. What is needed is a way to prolong the initial shock of capture and the need to communicate, and a good start to this is 'Dislocation of Expectations'. The prisoner is expecting to be treated in a certain way and if it doesn't happen they are confused. An example of this happened with me on an exercise a year or so later, when two of us were tasked with questioning a 'captured PoW'. Normally the interrogator is sat in the room, behind a desk, before the prisoner is brought in blindfolded. We had decided to do the 'Mut and Jeff', or 'Good guy, Bad guy' routine, which can be successful. On this occasion, the prisoner had already been brought outside the interrogation room and his blindfold removed before we got there. This was unusual and required a quick rethink of how to treat him.

He had no reason to know that we were the interrogators, so we asked how he was, being very friendly with him, and reminded him that when he went in to be interrogated he must only give Name, Rank, Number and Date of Birth. We told him that the interrogator that was waiting for him was a sneaky so-and-so and he had to be very careful and polite to him. He was very grateful for this advice and then answered all our questions voluntary and truthfully, as he trusted us, his new best friends, and did not realise that he was being interrogated. Later that day, when he was next questioned by another interrogator, in the normal fashion, he only gave the 'Big 4', Name, Rank, Number, Date of birth.

Interrogation is the gathering of long term information, confirmation of other prisoner's stories, information about units and individuals, and often snippets of gossip which he may think unimportant. It could be as trivial as the name and colour of someone's dog – that can be used to persuade the dog owner that we know all about him. Interrogation is a long term process and can take months.

On completion of these two courses I was often called on to participate in exercises, as there were very few interrogators in the RN and I was the first Non Commissioned Officer to become one. Most of the others were retired officers.

As summer finished in Cornwall, so was I. It was time for me to leave my second line squadron and join 826 NAS, a 'front line', operational one.

⚬⚬◄❮▶►⚬⚬

Chapter 22
826 NAS. HMS Tiger, September 1977-April 1979

HMS Tiger, C20, was the sister ship to Blake and the lead ship name of the three WW2 built Cruisers, the other one being HMS Lion. Lion had also been laid up as soon as she had been built and only served in the RN for 6 years before being laid up for good and used as spares for her sister ships (so much of her was used on Tiger, that Tiger was often call Liger by the crew) and eventually scrapped.

Tiger became famous in 1966, as the last ship to open fire on a Royal Naval Dockyard. Whilst undergoing maintenance in Devonport dockyard the Artificers were carrying out a check on the 6 inch forward guns and had inadvertently loaded a live cartridge to test the system. When the firing circuit was made there was a tremendous explosion, smoke and flame belched out of a gun barrel and a heavy (luckily an inert dummy) shell screamed across the dockyard, somehow missing other ships and buildings, and crashed into the dockyard wall, demolishing a section and hurling bricks and masonry onto the main road. Amazingly, no one was hurt, or other property or cars damaged.

826 NAS had 4 Sea King HAS 2 helicopters and just a couple of weeks after I joined the squadron we embarked onboard and sailed for the Far East. The CO was Lt.Cdr Harvey and the Sobs, Lt.Cdr Dick Just. In October the Commanding Officer changed and Lt.Cdr 'Jock' English, who had been the SObs on 819 Squadron 7 years earlier took over the position. This was an unpleasant surprise to me and to another one of my PO aircrewmen, Tudor Davies, who also was on 819 at the same time. Neither of us had got on with Jock, so little so, that Tudor was thinking of requesting to leave the squadron when he heard that Jock was going to be our CO. We were both mistaken. Lt.Cdr English turned out to be one of the best COs that I served under. He respected my judgment and allowed me to flourish. When my B13 promotion order, to Chief Petty Officer, came through, he threw a champagne party for me in the briefing room and all the aircrew attended. Although Jock was an observer, there was none of the acrimony and bickering that had taken place on 820 squadron four years earlier. He also impressed me when he gave me the Royal Medal of Reward, 1st Class, with Crown, awarded to me by the Queen of Denmark for the Merc Enterprise rescue, at a special squadron parade and read out the citation in fluent French, which is still the official Court language.

As usual with these task forces (we were part of a small fleet), our first stop was Gibraltar and then through the Med to Athens. Not only did we do ASW exercises with our tame submarine, HM S/M Dreadnought, but we also practised my newly re-discovered Hi-Line rescue and it became the standard method of winching from the confined area of submarine's conning tower (fin).

We exercised with NATO forces in the Med, participating in Exercise Display Determination. Amongst the forces were Greek and Turkish ships. During these exercise it was normal practice that the command of the exercise would change every few day so that every country could practice being in command. When the

Turkish admiral became the commander, the Greek ships were unexpectedly recalled to Greece and when the Greek admiral took control, the Turkish ships were recalled! Until then, I did not realise the depth of the animosity that existed between the two countries. The Greeks remembering that for centuries the Turks ruled Greece, whilst the Turks recalled that the Greeks had invaded the Turkish heartland of Anatolia after WW1. Also Cyprus was remembered for the way that the Greeks had tried to remove the Muslim, Turkish Cypriots from the island and that the Turkish army had sent troops and defeated the Greeks, with a heavy hand, and still had a garrison on Northern Cyprus. This ill feeling is still strong between the two countries today, but there is a difference in the ill-will. The Greeks are taught to hate the Turks, whilst the Turks are told never to trust the Greeks. As usual, these feeling are exacerbated and used by the respective governments to unite their countries, whilst the mass of each population are tolerant of each other and are prepared to work together, with the aim of self-advancement and business.

Tiger visited Istanbul on an official visit at the end of the exercise, having visited Athens before the start. As usual, on these visit, as a public relations exercise, the ship hosted a party for the orphaned and underprivileged children. The cooks made cakes, desserts, jellies etc. and we dressed up as pirates, intending to entertain the kids and give them a good time. Shortly before the party the mayor of Istanbul decided that there were no orphans or underprivileged children in the city! The Turks do not like losing face. It was too late then to cancel the party, so the over privileged offspring of western embassies were invited instead. Although we worked hard and gave them a good time, our hearts were not in it.

After Istanbul, Tiger and the Task Group sailed for the Suez Canal and the Far East. HM S/M Dreadnought had a problem, so she did not transit the Suez Canal with the rest of us. I don't think we saw her again until our return to the UK. This resulted in a shortage of UK ASW exercises afterwards, with only international ones, but we had no shortage of other tasks. There was transfer of stores and pax to ships and land, GPMG (General Purpose Machine Gun) firing at stationary and towed targets, in-flight refuelling from small ships and torpedo recovery. On one recovery I saw a large shark just before I jumped in the water but thankfully the noise of the heli scared it away. That was one of the quickest recoveries I had ever done.

Tiger also practised firing her 6 inch guns. A target was made and dropped in the sea many miles away. Tiger would detect the target by radar and open fire on it. On one occasion I was in the spotting heli. Because of the poor radar echo of the target, our task was to hover over the target to give a good 'echo' and then, when Tiger had aligned its twin gun on our contact, we would move a few hundred yards away and say 'Shoot' to the ship. The photographer on the heli would then photograph the fall of the shot for evidence of accuracy. The first shoot went well and I was impressed with just how accurate the gunners were. The second shoot did not go as planned. We hovered over the target and the ship said that they were 'Locked on' when suddenly hot oil from the main rotor gearbox poured into the cabin and the pilot's warning caption came on showing loss of oil pressure.

With a cry of 'Shit!' S.Lt Fox, the pilot, landed the heli on the water next to the target. The Sea King is designed to land on the water and also has buoyancy bags but it is never practiced, as the electronic equipment in the hull is ruined. As soon as the rotors had stopped turning, both pilots evacuated the cockpit whilst I inflated the large multi seat life raft we carried for passengers and my two pax and I stepped into it and paddled as far away as possible from the target. I was worried that the expletive shouted by the pilot may have been interpreted as 'Shoot' by the ship!

Tiger, picking up our distress radios, realised what had happened and rushed to our assistance and lowered a seaboat, when close, and rescued us. The next task was to recover the heli by crane.

As I was the diver of the squadron, once onboard I changed into my diving suit and, with the correct spanner, jumped into the sea and swam to the heli close by. Climbing up to the rotor head and removing the 'Beany' cover, so that the special lifting sling, now hanging from the ship's crane, could be attached was, in theory, a simple job. Once in position a large pin was inserted through the rotor head and the heli could be lifted. Easy on dry land or a deck but with the ship (and crane) and the heli both rising and falling, rocking and rolling in the swell and waves, I could not align the pin to go through the two tight fitting, holes of the sling and the two holes of the rotor head. In my frustration I managed to crush my hand and had to relinquish the job to one of the squadron engineers. The heli never flew again from Tiger but when we returned to the UK, it was taken to Westland in Yeovil and refurbished. Surprisingly, I had no broken bones but the skin of my hand had burst which caused pain for some weeks.

For the third time in my life I went to Karachi. In 1960, on Albion, I thought it was such an overpopulated, dirty, city that, being a Muslim country and allowed no alcohol, I promised myself I would never go ashore there again. When I later went there on Blake, four years earlier, I amazed my messmates by refusing to go ashore. After the visit most of them agreed with my decision. A talking point was about the bus that had killed a pedestrian on the jetty. The driver had run away, so the fare collecting conductor was arrested and taken to jail instead.

Again, I said that I would not go ashore, but decided to accept an invitation to enter a sailing regatta hosted by the local sailing club. We used bosun dinghies and I and my crew were allocated a sad looking craft. After a reasonable start we ended up trailing the fleet. I was rather surprised at my abysmal performance but when it came to pulling the boat up the beach, at the end of the race, all became clear. The integral buoyancy chamber was full of water and it took 15 minutes of draining, before it was light enough to wheel up the ramp. Amends were made in the clubhouse when an English industrialist, who worked in Karachi, invited us to his villa for dinner and real refreshments (soft drinks only in the sailing club). After a superb curry dinner and varied refreshments, we were given a bed for the night. I got some strange looks from my messmates when I returned the next morning as I was the only person to have been ashore all night, and refused to comment when asked 'Was she pretty?' Keep them guessing is my motto.

Later we visited Mumbai, my first time in India. That was an interesting experience, big luxury hotels and around them people living in huge, uninstalled, sewage pipe, in the middle of large roundabouts. At least we could buy a beer. I was surprised at how popular the Brits were in India. People went out of their way to be friendly.

During none of my 25 years in the RN did I ever come across any intentional racial or religious abuse. Looking back perhaps we were naive to think that racial comments would not be taken as they were intended, as a joke. Don Nelson, a very well-liked black medic, would always be reminded to smile and show his teeth when the ship was darkened. He would remind us that if it snowed he would be the first to be rescued. We joked about each other's personal qualities and features. On one ship the nickname of one chap was Gonzo, after his likeness to the Spitting image puppet. It was never meant in an offensive manner. One evening, on Tiger, a friend was looking and acting depressed. When I asked him what the matter was he said people did not like him because he was a Jew. I was amazed, I never knew he was a Jew and, when I asked around, nor did any other person. It just did not matter to us what religion or race they were, we judged on abilities and nature.

Tiger spent Christmas in Sydney, Australia, and a week after arriving, 824 Squadron flew to RAAF Nowra, an Australian Airforce airfield to the south. There we met up with various Australian aircrew whom we had previously known in the UK when they were doing courses there. We didn't do a lot of flying, just a lot of partying and fishing. Whilst Tiger was in Sydney I had arranged with the city hospital that the aircrewmen, who were all trained in first aid, would, on a voluntary basis, help out there. It was very successful. Not only did we learn a lot and help them with the usual manpower shortage, but it enabled the unmarried men to find solace over the Christmas period with the nurses. I had done the same thing when on 706 NAS at Culdrose and working a shift at Trelisk hospital in Truro was popular. In Sydney I was showered in blood during an operation on a road traffic accident patient who had a crushed spleen. Unfortunately he died during the op. The doctor wrote a letter to the captain, thanking him for allowing us to assist the hospital. I think it was the first that the captain had heard of it.

Before we entered the river where Bangkok is situated, I was surprised that the ship stopped out at sea and the divers had to place large strainer baskets over all the inlets and take lines from each to the upper deck, with a label showing which inlet it covered. I had never had to do this before but soon found out the reason. Every day in harbour we had a duty watch of divers and every day we were required to unblock at least one strainer. I have never dived in such dirty water. Visibility was a brown zero as soon as I left the surface and if I let go of the line I would have been swept away and unable to find my way back. I don't know how it was possible, as the mouthpiece was built into the mask and I had a nose clip on, but I could smell the sewage stench. I had a sack with me and when I felt that I had reached the strainer, I grasped handful of plastic, vegetable and animal remains that were clogging it. I am glad that I could not see, as it was impossible to know if it was animal or human remains there. It was a case of dragging it off and stuffing it into the sack, which was sealed as soon as I got to the surface. Despite washing thoroughly, the diving suits and sets smelt for ages and we required long, hot, showers and lots of after shave.

Before returning via the Suez Canal, Tiger went into Aqabar, Jordan. King Hussein, the ruler, visited the ship and flew in one of our Sea Kings. The ship had been given permission to have a camping expedition in the desert, near the magnificent archaeological site of Petra. With me on 826 was a pilot whose name I believe was Lt. Craven, who had recently completed the CSI at Hereford. We volunteered to go to the proposed camping site a couple of days early and practise desert survival and then remain as instructors to the campers.

This was our first time in the desert and we reread our notes about it carefully. Although we were warned, we were both surprised at how cold it got at night. We collected dead shrub wood and made a fire but it soon burnt out. Initially, it was a pleasure to see the morning sun but as the temperature climbed to into the 40s we longed for the night again. We had a jerrican of water and our water bottles with us but decided to dig solar stills. These are holes dug in the sand, a container placed in the bottom and the hole covered in sagging plastic that we had bought with us. It was difficult to dig with our hands and I recommend to anyone that some form of shovel is used. The air gets very hot under the plastic and absorbs moisture from the surrounding sand. This moisture condenses on the plastic and drips into the container. We were amazed that although the sand seemed very dry, every container had some water in it. Each person would need about a dozen holes to survive but it can be done. The next night we urinated in the holes and that produced more water. It tasted fine but the hole was smelly.

We fruitlessly looked for animal tracks but only found a few faint reptile marks. For practice and demonstration of traps and snares we set a few, knowing that we wouldn't catch anything. We also decided to have a trek in the desert, for the experience. As we came around a sand dune we were met by an Arab with his camel. He greeted us and, copying his gestures, we tried to reply. He beckoned me to get on the camel and led us to his tent, about half a mile away. There, we were offered 'kave', Arabic coffee. We knew that it was impolite to hold the cup in the wrong hand but neither of us knew the correct one. We looked at each other, then the Arab, realising our predicament, moved the little cup towards our right hand. We were also offered dates and fruit. This was my first taste of Arabic hospitality and it made its mark on me. The tent was pleasantly cool and it was with regret that we left and headed back to our camping site.

After heating up our ration pack supper, we discussed how we could keep warm that coming night. We decided that we would only light a small fire and would sleep either side and close to it. By our head we each had a small pile of brushwood and, when cold, threw a handful onto the fire. This worked quite well and the small fire was kept burning for most of the night.

Next day, the main party of campers arrived with camping equipment, and it was with great pleasure when we snuggled into sleeping bags that night. Even though we had seen the stars and planets frequently, at sea, the moisture free and non-light polluted atmosphere allowed us to see millions more and everyone was amazed and enjoyed it. There was disbelief about getting water from dry sand and there was a cautious up-take when it was offered to them – especially from the smelly holes!

Tiger returned to the UK mid '78 and apart from a couple of photographic exercises using the squadron's Hasselblad, it was routine flying from Culdrose. In July the squadron again embarked on Tiger and we headed to the north for a NATO exercise called Northern Wedding.

I believe that Northern Wedding included landing troops in Norway, but we were not involved in that side of it. As usual, before the exercise, all aircrew and ships' officers attended a briefing given by the admiral's staff and attended by the admiral. At the briefing I realised that a big mistake had been made. When nuclear weapons can be used (such as the 'special weapon' NDB), the area was colour coded. Area Green was the area where the weapon could be used with no danger to us, Orange where it could be used but could do some damage to friendly forces and area Red, where it could not be used as it would destroy our forces. The admiral's staff had the colours wrong. According to them we could drop nuclear weapons on ourselves but not the enemy. At the end of the briefing the usual 'Any Questions?' came, and I expected a senior officer to challenge the colours, but no one did. At the end, when the final 'Any more questions?' was asked I put my hand up and asked for confirmation that the colours were correct, which was answered in the affirmative. When no one else wanted to ask another question I again put my hand up and, trying to be diplomatic, asked for confirmation that area Green was based over our forces. The admiral's staff officer glared at me and, tight lipped, said 'Yes Petty Officer'. I had one more try and asked 'So area Red is over the enemy?' With clenched teeth and a snarl the reply was 'Yes! Briefing finished'. The admiral, captain and senior officers left the briefing room, followed by the CO and squadron officers and aircrewmen. Outside, the CO, Jock English, was waiting for me. He came close and hissed 'Don't you ever tell the admiral that he is wrong again' and I could not stop myself saying 'But he is, Sir'. When I saw the colour of Jock's face go bright red I realised that I had better get away quickly. Two days later the colours on the board in the briefing room had been changed and nothing more was said.

I have always enjoyed reading, especially anything historical, based on true stories. During Northern Wedding we had the usual trouble with Soviet Elint ships. There were two very similar ships but the information they collected was different. One was code name Moma, the other Mirma. The main way to distinguish the two was by counting the windows of the deckhouse. One had six windows, the other seven. I was crew with Splot, Lt.Cdr Kirby, the first pilot, and was sent out one night on an ASW screen to positively identify one of these Elints, which was in our sector, about 50 miles away. Remembering the DidTac trial that 819 had carried out many years before, I realised that it would be no easy task at night. To count windows, we had to be close, and we needed light.

We picked up the ship on radar and decided to run in, pass the contact, at 100 yards and at 50ft height. I got the little Aldis signalling lamp, plugged it into the socket by the starboard cargo door, sat in the doorway and we approached at about 60 knots. As soon as I saw the stern of the vessel I turned on my lamp and then we were blinded by a large searchlight from the Elint. Lt.Cdr Kirby immediately climbed to avoid crashing and it took a few seconds to gather our wits. Again, we tried the same tactic, flying down the other side of the ship but with the same result. We were blinded by the powerful light. You might now be asking, 'What is this to do with reading books?'

In the days of wooden men-of-war and cannons, because of the manpower required to fire the guns, only cannons on one side could be manned at a time. To use the other guns required the gun crews to rush over to the other side. I remembered from a book, that the captain of a ship acted as if he was going to attack the enemy on one side by displaying his guns, but altered course at the last moment and passed on the other, where his gun crews, unseen, were ready to open fire. Years earlier, when I was a seaman, keeping my watch from the ship's bridge, I knew that there was a signalling lamp on both sides but only one signalman. The connection was obvious.

I explained my plan and it was accepted. We approached as before, but slightly slower. Before reaching the ship, from the stern, I flashed my little signalling lamp out of the starboard cargo door, as though testing it, then, unplugging the lamp from the cargo door connection, rushed forward, connected it to the socket by the pilots, and opened the top of the crew door on the port side. We altered course, just as we reached the stern, and flew up the starboard side of the vessel. It worked perfectly. We saw the signalman rushing from the port search light to the starboard, but he was too late; we had counted the windows. We climbed away, with the searchlight belatedly shining behind us and carried on with our submarine hunting; a successful mission. In wartime this would not have worked, we would have been shot down, but this was the Cold War; guns not allowed.

After one of the most enjoyable 18 months in the Navy, it was time for me to leave the squadron, which disbanded. HMS Tiger was decommissioned and once again laid up, and eventually scrapped.

HMS Tiger

Sea King Mk 2

Chapter 23
Sea King Advisory Team Egypt
(SKATE), June – October 1979

T he Egyptians had purchased the ASW version of the Sea King some years earlier and had been trained by the Foreign Training Unit (FTU) at Culdrose. They had now requested further, long term, training in Egypt. It was a small team consisting of two pilots, an observer, an aircrewman and two radar specialists from General Service, the ship navy. The Boss was Lt.Cdr Kron Ronaldson (my SObs from the Belgian FTU). It was envisaged that the training would take about 18 months, so it was a 'Married Accompanied' draft, which meant that I could take my family with me. The last time that happened was when I was drafted to 819 Sqd in Northern Ireland, 10 years before.

In London we had a meeting and briefing at MoD (N) (the Admiralty) and found out that we would not be wearing uniform, we would be in private accommodation, and families would be allowed a maid. We would also be supplied with transport. This was a big step up for me. There would be an advance party of Kron and I, with our families, to arrange things. Crated luggage would be sent by merchant ship and the remainder of the unit would join a month later. It seemed that I was set for the high-life; there would even be a private school for our children. Although I had transited the Suez Canal a few times, I had never visited Egypt and knew nothing about the country. I tried to get a language book but no shop in Truro had a book for learning Egyptian – which was not surprising as the language is Arabic!

We flew out as planned, by British Airways, and landed at Cairo. As we walked from the aircraft to the terminal building we were surrounded by boys and youths who grabbed our baggage and carried them halfway before dropping them, holding out their hand and demanding 'faloos' (money). We had no Egyptian money and only a handful of UK small change. As soon as they had the coins they ran away and another group carried our bags for another 50 yards before trying the same trick. As we were penniless and piastreless, they were very upset when they received nothing and left us to carry the bags ourselves the last 50 yards.

The journey from Cairo to Alexandria, by Egyptian Airforce Jeeps, was a new experience for us. If anyone asks which side of the road they drive on in Egypt, the answer either, and sometimes the pavement. Kron was so incensed, that he made the driver stop and then, after throwing him in the back drove the last half himself.

My family had a newly built flat. Well, the flat was newly built but the rest of the block, both above and below, had not been finished. It was decorated and furnished in a style which can only be described as 'Louis Faruk'. Large chandeliers were everywhere, Imposing looking, plush covered, upright chairs that were impossible to sit on and plywood cupboards with ornate carvings, looking like an exam piece for a GCSE (failed) one handed woodwork student. We were not the first residents; a tribe of rats had squatted first. Kron had a villa about 10 miles away, on the beach. A lovely looking bungalow with sea views – and a million cockroaches over 2 inches long, that covered the ceiling and did aerial attacks when displaced by their brethren.

We had no TV and no English speaking radio stations. We loved it there. My sons insisted going to the Corniche every night and, looking over the sea wall, watched the thousands of rats scampering and fighting. They were enrolled in the Schuts American School. I used to take them every day. To get there meant climbing over a 2 meter high pile of rubbish that blocked the road. After about a month it was cleared away but within a week it reappeared in embryo form and steadily grew to its original size. My wife was followed constantly by two suited men for the first month but was told by everyone that they were 'Secret Police'. Or perhaps they were not so Secret Police.

The Sea Kings were based at an Egyptian Air Force base at Alexandria, named Dakhalia. Kron and I were made welcome there, and we were told that anything we required would be arranged. We asked to see the class room and found a dingy store room full of furniture. *Lays hasnak aa Muskila*, (No problem) it would be ready *Bukrah, Insh'alla* (tomorrow, Allah willing.) Eventually, I used the local aircrewmen and moved things out ourselves. I asked for an overhead projector and was promised *Bukrah, Insh'allah*. Next when I asked where it was I was told that the man with the key would open the cupboard *Bukrah, Insh'allah*. The day after, I was told that he was on leave but would open the cupboard on Monday. On Monday it turned out that his leave was extended but he would be back the following Monday, *Insh'allah*. Then he lost the key; a new key had to be cut; it didn't fit. Another new key; wrong cupboard; man with key on leave. Does it remind you of the song 'There's a hole in my bucket'…? Eventually I borrowed an OHP from the British Council and kept it at home. The Egyptians were very friendly but would not tell us when things could not be done or they did not have what we needed. That would have caused them to lose face. We decided that Egypt was an IMB country. The answer to most problems was *Insh'alla* (God willing), *Bukrah* (tomorrow) or *Ma'lesh* (I'm sorry, it doesn't matter, it's not my fault anyway!) I saw a pedestrian knocked down by a car and the driver got out and, realising that the pedestrian was dead, dragged him to the side, saying '*Ma'lesh*', and drove off.

We received a telex (no fax or internet in those days) saying that our crates had arrived at Alexandria Harbour. It was my task to get them to the squadron. After being kept waiting at the dock gate I was directed where to go inside the port. I went to the indicated warehouse, to be told that first I must go to an office in town, which was now closed. Next morning I arrived early at the office, to find that not only was I not the first but other people pushed in and were welcomed whilst I had to wait 6 hours. Eventually forms were given to me to fill in and I was told to come back the next day. To fill the forms I had to find a customs agent. He invited my family and me to dinner and explained that my problem arose because I was not giving *Baksheesh* (back-handers). Armed with the filled-in forms and a few Egyptian pound notes, I got my permission to collect our boxes. This time I was stopped at the dock gate. No, I could not enter as I did not have a pass. 'Where do I get a pass?' I asked. 'At the office inside the docks' was the answer. 'But you won't let me inside the docks!' I got a shrug from the guard. I asked him to look at my form again and this time folded it around a pound note. He passed the form, minus the money, back to me and directed me to the Pass Office. I thought that I had cracked the system and at the office I was given a form to enter and leave the docks. Work had now stopped for the day and I had spent the whole week getting permission to enter and leave the docks and notification that I could collect our sea boxes. Next Monday, I reasoned, I will get transport from the air force and collect our gear. If only it was that simple.

On Monday I spoke to the CO of the Sea King squadron, asking if I could have transport and was told that it was no problem. I just had to call him when it was required. Entry to the docks was easy with *baksheesh* and, armed with my papers, I trudged to the assigned warehouse. A gift was given. A long time waited. The boxes were not there. I had to go to another warehouse, and then another. Eventually I was approached by a man who said he was an agent and for two pounds he would help me. He got two pounds; I got very hot and sweaty in the midsummer heat and nothing else. My 'agent' told me how stupid the dock offices were and told me to come back tomorrow and he would definitely, *Insh'allah*, be able to help me, for another two pounds and the *baksheesh* he would have to give the officials.

I was past the frustrated stage now. If that was the way they wanted to play it, I realised, I must go by their rules. Next day a small gift got me into the docks, and I started the search for the missing boxes again by myself, as no agent had turned up. Very soon, a youth approached me, shook my hand and told me he had seen me wandering around for days, and asked what my problem was. I explained things to him and showed him my papers. After a short walk he said 'This is the warehouse you want sir' and took me into the office. With a gift attached I gave the papers to the clerk and he asked me to follow him and identify the crates. I could hardly believe it. I turned to the youth and tried to thank him with high value paper but he refused to accept it: 'You are a guest in my country and I am pleased to help you.'

I would like to say that was the end of the saga of our sea boxes but of course, the airforce lorry had to be booked a week in advance; they could not send one right then. It just so happened that the clerk had a good friend who had a truck... Unfortunately he did not have a pass to get into the airforce base... Another day later I finally unpacked our sea freight.

Corruption was rife in Egypt but occasionally, as in the dockyard, I was surprised how some people went out of their way to help. I was driving the unit's car in Cairo, after a long drive through the desert from Alexandria. At a junction, a policeman stopped me and told me that I would have to pay a fine as my car was dirty with desert dust. I protested and a man walking past stopped and started arguing with and ended up shouting at the policeman. The policeman backed down and the man came to me and apologised for the policeman's behaviour. Another time, I got the car stuck in the sand and dozens of children came from nowhere, pointing and laughing, asking for *filose* (money). Then an elderly man appeared and organised the children and got me dug out of the sand. I was very happy to pay for the help but the man chased the kids away and said that it was their duty to help visitors. I said that I wanted to pay something, but he refused, telling me that he was a Coptic Christian. I then asked if I could give money to the Monastery. He refused to accept anything but said that if I wanted to, I could drive back to the Monastery (which is why I had been in the desert) and put something in the offering box, which I did with grateful pleasure.

That year, the Holy Month of Ramadan fell in July – August. Nothing must be swallowed or their fast would be broken. This meant that coughing and spitting phlegm was prevalent. During the midsummer heat of the day it was impossible to have a drink of water. I needed to see a dentist but he was only open after 2200 hours. Strict Muslim countries should be avoided during Ramadan.

At Dakhalia I was told that one of the Sea Kings had a problem that they could not solve. When the sonar was lowered onto the sea, the heli would not auto hover over the cable, and the sonar was constantly being tilted and unusable. This was a common problem and the usual cause was that there were two spring loaded rollers that pressed against the cable and their movement fed into the autopilot to auto hover, and these rollers sometimes seized, due to salt build up. I was assured that this had been checked, but when I got into the heli's cabin I found that I was right, the rollers had seized. I pointed this out to the Engineering Officer and was told that I was wrong and this was normal. Next day it was reported that they had fixed the problem and the heli was going on a check test flight. I watched as the Sea King took off and headed south, into the Sahara, instead of north, towards where they could lower the sonar into the Mediterranean. An hour later the Sea King returned and I was told that the check test flight was successful. When I climbed into the cabin to check, the rollers were still seized and, by the absence of salt spray from winching in a wet sonar cable, it was obvious they had not lowered the sonar into the sea. There was no secret lake in the desert and the pilots had just flown on a 'jolly' to wave at their families.

I tell this story to explain how the Egyptian Airforce and Navy cooperated, or rather how they didn't. The Airforce Sea King's crew consisted of two Egyptian Airforce pilots, an Egyptian Navy, observer and a sailor sonar operator, Although the Sea King squadron's costing came out of the Airforce budget the Airforce did not think it was their job to hunt submarines, which they considered was the Navy's task. The 'superior' Airforce pilots refused to talk to the 'inferior' Navy observer unless necessary, and nobody spoke to the 'lowly' sonar operator except to shout at him to do exactly what he was told. He could not venture an opinion on anything, including any submarine contact; that was the observer's right.

We could have lived, and dealt with, this attitude, but it became much more serious. Egypt's defence budget came from Saudi Arabia and when Israel and Egypt signed a peace accord between the two countries, Saudi Arabia was so against it, the money was cut off. As far as the Airforce was concerned, they didn't want to find submarines, they wanted spend the money on missiles, fighters and bomber aircraft. This came to a head when, a few weeks after the rest of the team arrived, we were not allowed on to the airfield. As before, the Egyptians did not want to tell us the reason we were banned (because they had run out of money,) but that we had to have passes to enter, despite not needing them before. Unfortunately, the man with the passes...

It ended up that we had 4 months paid holiday in Egypt, meeting once a week in the Boss's house for a brief on progress (none!). I managed to get as far as Luxor and a three day donkey ride to visit the Valley of the Kings and, even more impressive, the Valley of the Workers.

There was one incident that upset me, and that was initiated by one of the RN pilots. He approached me to ask if I would put my name on a letter complaining about Kron. The letter was to blame the Boss for the breakdown in communications with the Egyptians. Whilst it was true that Kron could be rather brusque at times, I believe that had no bearing with our situation and I refused to add my signature. To me it smacked of mutiny. I don't know if the letter ever got written or sent.

There was another, personal, incident that could have had a serious effect on my family. My youngest son became very ill with a pain in his wrist. I took him to the local hospital and was told that he needed an operation immediately. I was unwilling to leave him at the hospital (which future events proved very wise) and after telling the Boss, who advised me to do whatever was necessary, I contacted the Military Attaché at the British Embassy, who arranged a flight to the UK for my son and wife, within hours, I then lost contact with them, not knowing what was wrong or where they were. Telexes were sent but no answer forthcoming. A few days after they left, we were told that the Egyptian Government wanted us out of the country within a week. We were allowed into Dakhalia for one day, to pack up our equipment and arrange for it to be sent back to the UK. I also had to pack up everything at the flat and prepare my two remaining sons for the return.

Apart from 'mislaying' my wife and one son, I did not know where I was going to in the UK. Before we had left, almost four months before, I had alterations made to my house and instructed a local estate agent to rent the house out until my return, supposedly 18 months later. Apart from two threatening letters from the Inland Revenue, we had no post, so I did not know if my house had been rented or not.

The day we left Egypt, I was given flight tickets from Cairo and £50 to get us from Alexandria to Cairo by train and from

Heathrow to Culdrose, in Cornwall. Landing at night and having been travelling all day with two boys, I realised that we would have to spend the night in a hotel, and the train, underground and hotel took almost all of the £50. These were the days before bank cards and it was on a Sunday so no banks were open. I had no money and did not know where my wife and son were. I was very worried and did not know what to do. Telephoning Culdrose on a Sunday would have been a waste of time. I then remembered that there was a Royal Navy Patrol HQ at one of the railway stations (can't remember which one) so I asked if they could help. Help they did, I was impressed with their efficiency. They discovered where my wife and son where and arranged for us to go to see them at the RN hospital, Haslar, near Portsmouth. Rail tickets were provided there and onwards to Cornwall and I was given another £50 out of the emergency fund for any expenses. In common with most sailors, I had very little respect for the regulating (police) branch of the RN, but I could not have wished for better service. At Haslar hospital, I found that my son was recovering from an operation for osteomyelitis, an infection of his bone marrow, and my wife had been allocated accommodation there. He would be discharged in a few days. When I arrived at my house in Cornwall it had not been rented because the builder had not finished, so we had a home to go to.

Thus ended the short lived SKATE. The sad thing was that at least half of the training programme could have been saved. The Egyptians had already paid half the money up front, and if they had told our Ministry of Defence the problem, instead of hiding it, we could have worked, instructing, for at least nine of the planned 18 months. Saving face cost them a lot of money and resulted in a very inefficient ASW squadron, which had trouble telling the difference between sea and sand. I learnt patience, which I never had before, and that lesson has stood me in good stead during the following years.

Chapter 24
706 NAS RNAS Culdrose
November 1979-May 82

O nce more I was serving on my home base squadron, flying an average of 20 hours a month. This was a big difference from my last 5 months, when I had a total of 40 minutes, consisting of one area familiarisation trip at Alexandria. As before, 706 NAS was still training pilots for Advance and Operational Flying Training (AFT and OFT) but now only using the Sea King helicopter. RFA (Royal Fleet Axillary) Engadin, a purpose built helicopter carrying ship, was used during every OFT course, to teach ship-borne operations. Sometimes we were based onboard her for a few days, sometimes for more than a week. Landing on a moving ship, by day and night, was a big step from landing on a large area of concrete. We were also now training observers, as well as pilots, on OFT.

As we were the base Sea King squadron for RNAS Culdrose, we were required to supply a heli 24/7 for SAR. There were many call-outs, day and night. The Wessex heli, on Culdrose's

SAR flight, did the short range work, 706 did the long range and bad weather rescues, with our bigger, twin engine, Sea Kings. I was called to fly twice during the Christmas leave period of 1979. Once to rescue six people from a sinking tug and the next day to take firefighting equipment to a ship called Butesis. A few weeks later it was to take a pump to a sinking Dutch fishing boat.

One difficult SAR was to the 5,000 ton cargo ship MV Penta, 160 nautical miles, (184 miles), from Land's End. The wind was reported at 75 knots, (86 mph), and waves of 60 ft. A sailor had been injured in the storm. The cabin of the ASW version of the Sea King is very cramped. The radar, sonar electronics and winch with 300 ft of cable, take up much of the forward part, whilst the sonar and radar displays and operators seats take a good portion of the back. There is just room for a lightweight stretcher at the back. We only carry the stretcher when we are likely to need it, such as on this casualty evacuation (Casevac). We also had on a doctor from Culdrose, who I think was Lt Waugh. The first pilot, Lt Thompson, had his work cut out trying to maintain a steady position as the ship steamed slowly into the mountainous seas, with the wind on its port (left) bow. Not only was it pitching half out of the water one moment and then dropping its bows deep into a trough the next, with spray being thrown into the air and half obliterating the ship, it was also corkscrewing from side to side. The only technique to use in these conditions was to use the Hi-line. We hovered ahead of the ship at about 100 feet of height and I lowered the Hi-line's weighted end. It was instantly blown back and to starboard by the storm. More by luck than judgment, a crewman on the ship managed to grab hold of the weight as it gyrated in the turbulence, one moment 50 feet above the deck, the next just touching it. As soon as he had hold of the Hi-line weight, I paid out the rest and checked that the upper end was attached to the winch hook, then 'conned' the heli back and left until the pilot could see the ship again and we were adjacent to a clear area of deck, which I intend to winch the doc down to. We descended to a height of 40 feet above the waves and, with the doc now in the rescue strop and also connected to the winch hook, I winched him out and down until he was just clear of the waves. As I 'conned' the heli to starboard, towards the ship, winching out, and the crewman on deck pulling on the Hi-line, I instructed the pilot to slowly climb. This was to keep the doc at a safe height above the sea, so he would not have too far to fall if the rescue winch cable broke. The next bit was the hardest and most dangerous for the doctor. I had to judge when to place him on the deck. If the ship was rising in the extremely high waves as I winched down, he could have broken his legs or even worse. My pilot was excellent, he managed to keep an almost constant height above the ship as it pitched and pirouetted in 60 foot seas, a very difficult task, even for a pilot instructor such as him. As soon as the doc touched the deck he was grabbed by the crewman and he slipped out of the strop and went to tend the injured man. We climbed to about 100 feet, and after pulling in the Hi-line, we hovered clear above the storm torn sea spray just behind the ship, and I prepared the stretcher for lowering. Unfortunately the sailor was dead when we arrived and the stretcher was not needed as the body was to be left onboard the ship. All we had to do now was to recover the doctor. Once again I used the Hi-line, as the last thing we needed was for the winch hook to attach itself, as the storm flung it around, to the ships rigging. When the rescue strop was in hand on the ship and placed around the doc, I winched in and as soon as he was clear of the deck, instructed 'Up 10 feet', to lift the doc clear the ship quickly, then winched in as we moved to port, and descended, keeping him at a safe height above the waves. This was our Standard Operating Procedure (SOP) for using the Hi-line but I had never before used it in such extreme conditions.

Whilst practising an Hi-line on a small launch, in Falmouth Bay, there was a dangerous incident. There was a thunderstorm, miles to the west, over Land's End but only light winds where we were operating. For practise, we decided that we would do it very high, at 150ft I winched down my crewman, Tom Holden, starting at 40ft above the sea, and climbing to 150ft. It is very hard to judge the height to lower a person gently onto a small deck, which was why we were practising. When Tom was over the deck I lowered him onto it. He collapsed as soon as he touched it, I thought because I had lowered too quickly. The crew on the launch tried to get Tom out of the rescue strop but for some reason could not do so. I was perplexed, as to what was the problem was. It was difficult to see exactly what was happening, 150ft above him. I then realised that the crew seemed afraid of the strop and Tom. Eventually I guessed what was happening, something I had never experienced or had heard about before. He was being electrocuted. It was fairly common, because of static electricity, to get a small jolt when first touching the deck, but that was only just as you landed, not continuously. In an attempt to 'earth' the winch cable, I winched out more, laying it on the deck, but it did not seem to help, probably because of layers of paint insulating it. I did not want to winch Tom back up again, in case he needed more support than I could give. I then tried a different idea. I 'conned' the heli to port a few yards, away from the launch, so that the winch wire was touching the bare metal of the launch's guard-rail and that did the trick. The crew managed to remove the strop and Tom was carried into the wheelhouse. We called Culdrose and asked for the duty doctor to be brought out to the launch and we returned to base and the heli shut down and thoroughly inspected for defects. Nothing was found wrong with the Sea King. The SAR Wessex heli had flown the doc out to the launch and in the normal 20ft hover, winched him onto the deck with no problem. Tom was now conscious and the SAR flew him to Trelisk hospital in Truro, where he spent three days in intensive care before being discharged.

There seemed to be no explanation for this incident and I was tasked with researching why it had happened. I had access to all the literature Culdrose had on static electric discharge from helis and within a couple of days I discovered the cause. Eclectically charged ionised air from a large Cu-nimb (cumulonimbus, a very tall, towering cloud that has violent air currents and produces thunder and lightning) can extend dozens of miles downwind of the cloud. There was a strong thunderstorm, about 20 miles away, that day. We were practising an Hi-line and had 150ft of winch wire, which is 150ft of aerial to attract the static. The SAR Wessex was hovering much lower, at 20ft when it winched the doc and Tom. A voltage of 250,000 volts could have been attracted by our cable, luckily at small amperage.

The next problem was how to stop this happening again, as rescues are carried out in thunderstorms. I liaised with the Safety Equipment Section and they produced a prototype winching suit with an embedded cable, which would earth the static electricity in the winch wire without going through the crewman. I expect that they are still used today, doubtlessly modified many times. Another night I winched up an injured seaman and 10 minutes after landing was called out again. That second flight was recalled after 15 minutes. There were searches for crashed aircraft and people lost overboard, usually unsuccessful.

One man-overboard search that was partially successful was for a lighthouse keeper of the 7 Stones Lighthouse, off Land's end. After allowing for currents we found his floating body. As soon as I was in the water, passing the rescue strop around him, I realised that he was dead, but decided to attempt resuscitation. I continued for the entire flight back to Culdrose, thumping his chest as hard as I could and giving mouth to mouth but there was no sign of life. A few weeks later the inquest was held at Penzance, I arrived late, and was told to sit in an empty chair next to a young woman and wait to be called by the coroner. When asked by the coroner what had happened, I explained and said that he was dead when we had recovered his body. I was asked how I knew he was dead, as I was not a doctor. I agreed that I was not, and that was the reason I tried to resuscitate him continuously until the doctor at Culdrose confirmed it. After the inquest the woman next to me gave me a hug and said 'Thank you for what you did to my husband'. I had no idea that she was the widow, and was relieved that I had tried to revive her husband for so long.

Whilst operating from RFA Engadin I was required to go on a search for a lost sailor. I was crewman and a student was the observer. After about 10 minutes the student asked me to take over as he was confused. I took over as Scene of SAR Commander and I was in control of 3 ships and a Nimrod aircraft. I gave them search plans and instructions for over two hours. Little did all those senior officers realise that a petty officer was telling them what to do. I would like to brag that the body was found, but unfortunately it was not. When we arrived back onboard Engadin the Sub Lieutenant Observer was complimented and I did not get a mention! In a way that was a compliment. Although it was not in the aircrewmen job specs, it was understood that I was as capable as any fully trained officer observer. My attempt at landing on a train was a long time in the past.

An embarrassing moment came when I was doing a drop of a new, secret, torpedo on Porthkerris range, just south of the Helford River. Cameras had been set up ashore and the drop was to be photographed and filmed by multiple cameras to check that the torpedo left the heli cleanly, the attached mini parachute worked and entry into the sea was at the correct speed and angle. The cameras were adjusted and correctly lined up as we did two 'dummy' runs and then I was told that the next run was 'live' and filmed. I was told 'Stand by' and I made the correct switches. With only a few seconds to go I was told 'This will now be a dummy run', which I acknowledged. When we reached the correct position and heard 'Drop drop drop', I could not stop my finger going up to the 'Drop' button and the torpedo fell from the heli. I felt such an idiot. The torpedo development had cost millions of pounds and I had inadvertently dropped it. When we landed and arrived back at the squadron building I was extremely relieved to be told that, despite being a dummy run, the cameras were all rolling and had filmed a successful drop. I did hear rumours that my new nickname was to be 'Dummy' but thankfully it never came to pass.

Apart from flying, occasionally I got a message from the captain of Culdrose saying that he had received a signal telling him that it was 'requested' that I be released to go on a restricted operation. This meant that I was being used as an interrogator, usually at Hereford. The captain was never given any details. I am very happy to say that it was extremely unusual for any of my team to get info out of the SAS recruits. They are very well trained in resistance to interrogation. One of my 'SAS prisoners' is now a well-known author.

When programmed to go on a training sortie, I was once asked if I would scatter the ashes of an old sailor, who had wanted them cast into the English Channel. I was given an ornate tin box with them in and, when we were in the hover over Falmouth Bay, I removed the lid of the box and tipped out the ashes. What I did not realise was that the high pressure air of our rotor downwash would immediately blow them back into the heli, and the cabin and I ended up covered in fine ash. I even got a crunchy mouthful! On return to the squadron crew room I put down the box, not knowing what to do with it. A few hours later I went into our kitchen area to get a cup of coffee when I noticed that the box was in there, but now it was full of biscuits. When I left the RN, a couple of years later, 706 squadron was still using it. As a biscuit tin.

One of our students was HRH Prince Andrew. Unlike every other student, he had a personal instructor, Lt Phil Shaw. Normally a student flies with many different instructors to stop any bias in training. Andrew was known as 'H' (His Highness) by all on the squadron. The students traditionally make coffee and snacks for their instructor. Phil Shaw once asked for coffee and poached egg on toast but H, never having received any domestic training, was stuck after the coffee making and asked me how to poach an egg – he had learnt how to use the toaster. So I am pleased to brag that I am a cookery instructor 'By Appointment to the Royal Family'. As the Chief Aircrewman (promoted at last), I did a lot of flying with him. At the end of flying training, there is always a celebration, normally in a pub. H's course improved on that. We had a meal in a hotel and a stripper had been hired as after dinner entertainment. H, very kindly, made sure that I had a seat in the front row!

H did have a sense of humour. One of my Leading Aircrewmen was a cockney ex-stoker, called 'Ginge' Tyler. Ginge tended to march to his own tune. 706 had a 'families' day when wives and lovers (not at the same time!) and family were invited to see how the squadron operated. Ginge sidled up to H and asked, 'Is yer mum cummin' Aitch?' Andrew looked down on him and said 'Well actually I think her Majesty is rather busy with Affairs of State' Whereon Tyler says 'Well, fank Gawd for that, we don't want those corgis shitin' everywhere!' A few weeks later there was a newspaper article about an RAF Sergeant that had been awarded a medal for a rescue and this brought on a tirade from Ginge along the lines of 'Cor blimy, I did much more than that and I got nuffink for it. It ain't bleedin' right.' H had heard this, and some time, later said 'Tyler, you were on the (so and so) rescue weren't you.' 'Yeh,' said Ginge, ''ow do yer know that?' 'Well', said H, 'You were recommended for an award you know.' 'An award! I didn't get nuttin', did I.' 'Well Tyler, when there are recommendations for awards Her Majesty, Prince Phillip and myself, peruse them at the breakfast table and I remember that your name came up and we thought that it merited attention. Unfortunately, one of Her Majesty's corgis jumped up on the table and upset the coffee all over it so we threw it away!' 'Aitch, you've been bleedin windin' me up, ain't yer!' And of course he had.

I was a Combat Survival Instructor; a Resistance to Interrogation Instructor; had done a (self-taught) desert survival course and two jungle survival courses. The only gap was a winter survival course and when there was memo circulated asking for volunteers to attend I did not hesitate, especially when I heard that two weeks of the three week course was living in a hotel. It is a strange twist of fate that starts with winter survival training and leads to teaching desert survival to Arabs, but unforeseeable things, of seemingly inconsequent actions, do seem to be my forte.

In early February 1981, I joined number 4 course, at an RAF base in Germany. We were only there for 24 hours before travelling to a hotel at Bad Kohlgrub in the Austrian Alps. I instantly made friends with another student, Flt. Sgt Gary Seaward , who was an RAF Load Master Instructor (teaching non-pilot aircrew) at RAF Brize Norton. We arranged to go into town together that evening and when I went into his room to meet him, he had many large sheets of paper, covered with hatched lines, spread over his table. When asked what they were, he explained that they were completed C130 Hercules trim-sheets, which he was marking for his students back in the UK. I remarked that I had never seen anything like them before and Gary showed me how they worked. His instruction was so clear that I quickly understood the whys and wherefores. Very soon he finished the marking and explanation and we, in naval jargon, had a good 'run ashore', with a headache the next morning to prove it.

For the next two weeks the winter survival training consisted of a hearty breakfast in the hotel, ski training in the morning and afternoon and with lectures and demonstrations during the middle period. I had never skied before so I was in the beginners group, learning first how to wear skis and walk sideways up a slope in them and how to stop by 'snow-ploughing'. I am not a sporty person so I was surprised that I picked things up fairly quickly. 'Follow in my tracks' was soon learnt from our Austrian ski instructor. I did not realise how tiring skiing twice a day could be and after a week was extremely happy to snuggle down under a goose down duvet at night. Maybe the large dinner with lots of beer, wine and schnapps every evening may have had a part to play also. At the end of the course we had a race and I am proud to report that I managed to beat most people in the intermediate group, who had skied before. Honesty will also make me tell of the very strange words I heard when I was skiing fast down-hill and, when I saw an old lady and her daughter crossing the slope, was unable to stop. I managed to hit both of them and all three of us ended up sprawled in the snow and sliding down hill. I was very surprised that German ladies used such language. I managed to hide from them for the next few days. The first two ways of stopping, when learning skiing, is the plough stop and the pine tree stop. The second is not recommended unless you have a high pain threshold. Also the Frau stop should be avoided.

The first survival exercise was one when we had to be on our own, with no sleeping bag or tent. We did have a rubber poncho cape each and were dressed in appropriate clothing for travelling. The temperature in the area was about -17°C. I found a fallen tree with very little snow under it and after collecting lots of fir branches to lie on and cover me, made a reasonable bed for the night.

Next day I navigated to the main camp area and met up with the rest of the course, none the worse for wear. Gary and I teamed up and, by lashing our two ponchos together, made a reasonable little two man tent. The directing staff (instructors) were kind enough to issue us all with sleeping bags. Unfortunately they were not winter ones. The first couple of nights were very uncomfortable and cold. During the evening we had a fire for cooking and warmth and this fire offered a good chance to dry our boots, as walking in the snow doing various exercise, left them sodden. We did not wear our boots in our sleeping bags and in the morning the boots had frozen solid. Not a good start to the day. I looked around for some rocks to heat, as I had when climbing Mt. Kinabalu, but, if there were any, they were underneath three feet of snow. On the third night I started to use my brain. Whilst drying my boots I arranged to get them as hot as possible by removing them and placing them upturned on sticks, close to the fire. Then, keeping my socks on, I warmed my feet and dried my socks. At sleep o'clock it was off socks, grab boots, run to our poncho tent, place hot socks on feet, put hot boots into the sleeping bag and turn in. The boots were almost as good as a hot-water bottle for much of the night. The boots may not have been hot in the morning but they were not frozen solid either. I strongly recommend this technique in cold weather. The directing staff had not seen it before and were impressed. They, of course, slept in proper tents with camp-beds and artic sleeping-bags.

The final exercise was an 'escape and evasion' with an interrogation phase at the end. I was exempt the last phase, because of my qualifications. I was happy about this as I did not fancy a long conditioning period in the cold, but it would have been fun pitting my wits against the interrogator. The exercise was a 30 hour navigation exercise with hunters from the British army and local police force. Traveling during the night, I ended up separated from Gary in an ambush (I believe he got caught) and although the rule were to give ourselves up if alone, I decided to continue by myself to the final RV. In the excitement of escaping the ambush I mistook my position (OK, I got lost!) and managed to pass the RV position. I decided not to retrace my steps but find somewhere to lay-up for a few hours until the end of the exercise. When the time was up I saw what looked like an army camp and walked into it. It was the interrogation centre! I think they were a bit peeved when they realised that I was exempt from interrogation.

I was soon taken back to the hotel with other students, around 0500, and was told that everyone was returning and there would be a bus ready for us at 1000 to take us to a sauna. I told the staff that after five days living in the snow, the last thing that I wanted was to get up early and go to a sauna. It was then mentioned that it would be a mixed sauna...

Next morning the bus was full and I had my first Austrian sauna, including rolling in the snow naked. Yes it was a mixed sauna! I enjoyed that course and had discovered what fun skiing was. The reason we skied was because it was our fitness training and acclimation to the cold. I wish all my courses had been run from hotels.

I was due to leave the navy in a few years so I decided to advance my education by becoming a teacher in Further Education, City and Guilds 720. It was a year's course at Camborne College. I had to attend one afternoon a week, which the RN allowed me off, and one evening. Once qualified, I was paid for teaching fitness training and taking students out for day sailing on my 30ft trimaran.

The last time I was on 706 squadron I had bought a small, 24ft, (7m.) yacht. This was little more than a dinghy with a cabin, 2 bunks, one gas ring and a toilet bucket. It had a history, being built of wood in 1928 and owned by the ambassador to Austria and later by the sailmaker/racer, Bowker, who one year, won the Junior Offshore group class V championship in it, The boat was named *Dante*. It had a trailer and during the winter, when I was away on 826 squadron, was kept outside of my house. I was known, in my village of Frogpool, as the sailor with a boat in his garden as well as in his bath. I had never thought that I would be able to afford a yacht but when a friend of a friend decided to sell his, I could not refuse the £500 asking price, especially as it came with a mooring in Restroguet Creek, off the River Fal.

I now had saved up enough money to have a small extension added to my house. That was until I saw an advert in the local weekly newspaper, offering a 30ft (9m) trimaran for £1,500. It was obviously a misprint so I was loth to reply to it until my wife urged me to do so. It was not a misprint but the owner had to have the money in three days. The exact amount I had saved for my house extension. The owner offered to pick me up and show me the boat the next morning and, on the journey, he mentioned that two other men had shown interest and would be waiting for us when we arrived. He confided that maybe he had under-priced the yacht but would accept the first offer. When we reached the boat the other two prospective purchasers were there and rushed towards the car. I instantly grasped and shook the owner's hand and said I would buy it for cash. So an ex-council house boy now owned two yachts!

Things were not yet 'plane sailing'. The trimaran had no engine and the wooden mast, made by the owner, broke whilst sailing across the river Fal to my mooring. I obtained a tall alloy mast that was broken and made a replacement the correct size. I knew nothing about mast making but the public library did; no internet in those days. I also contacted the original designer, builder and owner of the boat, Jim Ditchfield, who had moved to

Australia. He had built it for the transatlantic race but became ill and decided to move to Australia. He had sold the mast and rigging separately. For those interested, it was a triple diagonal, cold moulded plywood sloop. Dagger boards (lifting keels) were in the two 'outriggers' and accommodation was in the centre hull. He called the design 'Skua'. By the time I found that out (by Pidgeon mail to Australia) I had already chosen a new name: *Tallata Du*. *Tallata* is Arabic for three and *Du* Cornish for black as it was coated in black epoxy sheathing. She was a very fast boat and would beat all local boats and catamarans.

My wife enjoyed sailing and our first cruise was our honeymoon on the Norfolk Broads. We had charted a two berth sailing boat for the week and were rather miffed when discovering that there were two single berths on shelves, with very little headroom. Ah well, on a honeymoon love will always find a way. I can really recommend a week on the Broads as a way of getting to know each other and learning to work together.

Before I bought *Dante*, a friend who had a 29ft (9m) *Golden Hind*, use to encourage me to crew for him and allowed me to use the boat when I wanted. The first time my wife and I sailed to the Scillies was an overnight trip on the *Golden Hind*. We were sailing past Penzance, heading westward in the dark and I showed her how to get the boat on a compass heading and how to use a star to maintain it. These were the days before GPS and we had to take compass fixes all the time. I was plotting a fix at the chart table when I felt the boat's movement change. I asked if the wind had changed and was told no. I then asked if we were still on course. This time it was an affirmative answer. When I went on deck, I found that we were heading north, directly into Penzance. I asked my wife why she had altered course and was told she hadn't. I made some remark that as far as I knew Penzance was a stationary piece of land and was sharply told that she was doing exactly what I had told her to, and she was keeping the rigging steady on a star. 'Which star? I asked tersely. 'That one', she replied and pointed at a flashing satellite on its orbit around the earth!

Talata Du

Chapter 25
825 NAS. MV Atlantic Causeway, San Carlos settlement, Falkland Islands.

The first week of April 1982, General Gailtieri, the head of the Argentinian Junta, sent his navy and troops to occupy the island of South Georgia and the Falkland Islands. Like most people in the UK, I had never heard of South Georgia or the Falkland Islands. Initially I thought that they were somewhere off Scotland, not thousands of miles away in the South Atlantic. The second week of April, I was on a re-settlement course, in preparation for leaving the navy, after practicing being at war for 24 years and never having had to fight in a real one. After all, what country would declare war after witnessing the carnage of WW1 and WW2?

On returning from my course I was told that the UK was assembling an invasion force to retake the islands and 706 NAS and other RN squadrons would be supplying helicopters and aircrew to commission a new squadron, 825 NAS. The First Pilots (P1) would be the Qualified Helicopter Instructors (QHI) of 706, the second pilots (P2) senior students of 706, and the navigators and crewmen from 706 and other squadrons. The senior aircrewman of the new squadron was going to be a senior Petty Officer of mine, Gary Callow, whilst I was going to stay on 706 as the senior Aircrewman Instructor, but I was not going to allow that to happen. I immediately remind Gary that he was starting an Officers course in a few months and would miss it and then informed the CO, who re-arranged the draft, naming me as the senior aircrewman. As one of my leading hands reminded me later, I said that I had been practising for this war for 24 years and I was going!

After a brief re-commissioning ceremony on the 3rd of May we were ready for war. There had been a previous 825 NAS, the first in 1934 with American Wildcat aircraft. Flying in Swordfish aircraft, 825 Sqd. aircrew had helped sink the Bismarck and also attacked Scharnhorst, Gneisenau and Prinz Eugen with torpedoes, unfortunately losing all six aircraft, without damaging the ships. It also flew in the Korean War. In 1960, for a couple of years, it re-commissioned again, this time with Wessex helicopters. After de-commissioning on the completion of the Falklands War, 825 was re-commissioned in 2014; once again with aircraft called Wildcats, but this time the Wildcats were helicopters.

After six days of refresher training, including confined and sloping landing areas, load lifting, winching, low level navigation and ship transfers (deck winching), we were ready to embark for the South Atlantic. Surprisingly, our training did not include mounting the GPMG (general purpose machine gun).

On the 13th of May eight Sea Kings took off from Culdrose to embark on the Ro-Ro (Roll on, Roll off) container ship Atlantic Causeway, which, in a matter of weeks, had been converted into a helicopter carrying ship. A sister ship, Atlantic Conveyer, had left a few days earlier, loaded with Wessex 5 troop carrying helis and 5 RAF Chinook helis. When close to the Falklands, Atlantic Conveyer was hit by two Exocet missiles and the ship sank, losing most of the aircraft.

For the flight from Culdrose to Atlantic Causeway, sailing past Cornwall on passage, I was nominated as second pilot. I was extremely thankful that I wasn't asked to land on its confined deck; I had enough trouble landing on an airfield!

The remaining two Sea Kings of the Squadron were to embark on the liner QE2. We were rather surprised that the two pilots accompanying them were the Commanding Officer and the Senior Pilot. They arrived in the Falklands a week after the rest of the squadron, after travelling in luxury. Not what generally is called, 'leading from the front'.

We managed some day and night deck landing practice on the first few days and nights as we sailed south to the Falklands, via Ascension Island, but most of the time we had various lectures from a Royal Marine sergeant, who was our military adviser. I also prepared my personal 'escape kit' as learnt at Hereford, This included matches, hacksaw and scalpel hidden in boots, mini compass disguised as a button, fishing line sewn into a string vest and £5 notes folded and ironed flat hidden in clothing labels.

29th of May saw us about 400 miles from the Falklands and after the destruction of the Atlantic Conveyor, it was decided that we would dis-embark from a distance in two groups, the first on the 29th and the second a day later. The plan for my group, the first, was to land on HMS Hermes, an aircraft carrier, get the latest sitrep (situation report), refuel and then fly low level (below the radar beam on the Falklands) without using our radar or radio, to avoid detection. We even had our flashing anti-collision lights switched off. For some reason that I still can't fathom out, I was the lead navigator of the first group, despite having an Observer in one of the following helis.

I used a technique which I had often used in sailing, called 'off-set navigation'. This was a method where, instead of heading directly towards a point, you aimed at one side and then you knew for sure which way to turn if you could not see it. In those days there was no GPS and hundreds of miles flying over sea with no landmarks and being affected by an estimated wind can easily produce errors of miles. Much to my (and doubtless everyone else's) relief, the plan worked and we approached our landing destination at San Carlos shortly before darkness fell.

We found a suitable field to land and, not being shot at by the Argentineans, decided it was friendly territory. Erecting tents in the falling gloom showed a massive gap in our training; how did all the brown canvas, poles and string fit together? We eventually managed and after heating our rations over little Hexamine solid fuel stoves it was decided to 'turn in' and take turns in keeping sentry duty.

I was awoken for sentry duty at midnight and, after putting on as many layers of clothing as possible to combat the cold, grabbed my .762 machine gun and relieved the previous sentry. After he had departed I realised that I didn't know what I was supposed to be guarding. Did I stay close to the tents to protect the aircrew or did I go past the helis, a hundred yards away, and protect a much larger area? I decided to go to the perimeter and protect the helis and found a little hollow by a low stone wall which I settled into. I could see over a 180 degree arc and was protected by the wall. After some time I thought I heard something. I strained my ears and then was certain that I had. There was a rustling ahead of me and it was not a solitary sound, it was coming from a large area. It was obvious to me that a large section of the Argentinian army was creeping up through the grass, preparing to destroy the aircraft and kill us. I did not know what the best course of action should be. If I fired my gun, I would be an instant target and killed. Maybe I should creep back to the tents and wake everybody up and there would be a fire fight, but then the helis would be destroyed and eventually us also. As I was deciding the pros and cons of each plan I saw a movement ahead of me. Something was creeping towards me in the dark. Not just one thing either, but many. Now there was no time to run back to the tents. I would have to shoot as many as I could, keeping below the wall and hoping the noise would wake up my comrades.

I pulled the stock of the gun close to my shoulder, so that the recoil wouldn't hurt me. Trying to control my fast breathing, I laid the barrel on the wall and, as quietly as I could, pulled back the cocking lever. The 'snick' of metal on metal sounded loud but there was no reaction from the enemy. I chose a target to the left side (I knew the gun jumped to the right when fired) and, looking down the open sights, squeezed the trigger.

Nothing happed. I squeezed the trigger again and again; the target I had chosen was now only a dozen yards away and still approaching. I then realised that I had not taken the safety catch off and, unfamiliar with the machine gun, I could not find it without lifting the gun up. There were now at least 20 targets within yards of me, and suddenly one of them farted and said 'Baa'. The flock of sheep that had narrowly escaped a massacre carried on munching.

Needless to say, I did not mention anything to the others except to say that there were sheep grazing around.

Next morning we started lifting stores and supplies from the ships anchored in San Carlos water and later we were joined by the remaining four helis of our Atlantic Causeway detachment and ended the day with all of us landing in a farmer's field at San Carlos Settlement, which was to be our base for the rest of the war. Some of the second battalion of Para troops (2 Para) was already camped there. They told us that their OC had been killed when he mistakenly thought that all of the enemy had surrendered. We were also warned of snipers that had killed someone the previous day. We were joined there on the 1st of June by the two helis from the QE2, with our Commanding Officer and Senior Pilot, their luxury cruise to the Falklands finished.

After a couple of days living in tents, with nights interrupted with air-raid warnings, most of the aircrew were invited to stay in the farmhouse. We ate in the mess tent and slept inside the farm house, which was appreciated as it was freezing most nights. The ground-crew, still living in tents, had to spend hours in the morning darkness de-icing the helis before we could fly, as well as working in the cold and dark, fixing any snags with the helis and carrying out routine maintenance. We slept and they worked. We worked and they still worked, on any unserviceable helis, providing sentries and producing a hot meal for our return. I think the ground crew had drawn the short straw and they excelled in producing serviceable aircraft for us, despite the difficulties. We seldom managed to get airborne before 1200 hours. I think we kept to Greenwich Mean Time.

Against this background, what I consider a gross act of misconduct happened. Every morning, each aircraft was given a packed lunch for the crew, made up from military ration packs and whatever fresh food was available. The ground crew were able to heat their lunch but had the same food. We were flying from first light until nightfall and usually refuelled from ships, where we were also given sandwiches, hot drinks and often a hot meal. One day I flew with the CO, and when he inspected his packed lunch, the normal bar of chocolate was missing. He was furious and on return to base at lunch time, (because of cancelled tasking), told the ground crew that in future, as punishment for not giving him a chocolate bar, they were not allowed to heat their midday lunch. As far as most of us were concerned it was a disgusting display of temper and ungentlemanly conduct. It was an action not becoming any officer, never mind a Commanding Officer.

That same day, the 8th June, is one I will never forget. The paras were 'yomping' over the hills towards Stanley, because the sinking of Atlantic Conveyer with the Wessex and Chinook helis had left us short of transport, and the Welsh Guards were aboard the two landing ships, Sir Tristen and Sir Galahad that had anchored the previous night in Fitzroy inlet. The reason that we had returned after only 30 minutes was that our task to off load the Welsh Guard was cancelled. We were soon tasked to again fly to Fitzroy and get tasking from the command centre that had been set up on the shore.

When we arrived at Fitzroy we saw the two landing ships, massed with troops, anchored less than 200 yards from the shore. We were told on the radio that tasking was being arranged, so the CO decided to land by the command tent and hurry things along. The CO and I went into the command tent and asked why our task of disembarkation of the Welsh Guard troops was cancelled, when we could see that they were all ready to go ashore. The answer was that the Guards CO had refused, saying that his troop would disembark by landing craft as they had not been trained in helicopter disembarkation. We just could not believe this and said that they did not need training and every heli would only take minutes to fly a dozen troops ashore on each flight. The offer was again refused.

I wandered out of the tent and was offered a 'brew' of tea, which I accepted with gratitude in the cold. I had taken just one sip when I heard the air raid alarm, followed, in seconds, by three Argentinian Sky Hawks screaming up the inlet. I was level with Sir Galahad and I saw a bomb drop and bounce off the sea and enter the side of Sir Galahad, exploding. All told, she was hit by three 500 lb bombs and immediately caught fire and ammunition started to explode. A missile fired by the troops ashore chased after the Sky Hawks but it was much too late and ended its life crashing into the mountain.

We rushed to our Sea King and got airborne ASAP and saw that two helis of 825 were already rescuing survivors, one flown by Lt Steve Isacke and crewman Bob Harris winching from the raised bow, with ammunition exploding around them and another winching survivors from the water. Arriving after the others, I could see that the heli winching from the sea was, unfortunately, blowing other survivors back towards the blazing Sir Galahad with its downwash.

Once again, my avaricious appetite for reading reminded me of a book which I had read called *'Angels without Wings'* when I started my aircrewman's course many years before. It was written about the RAF SAR helicopters, and told of an event where the SAR heli blew swimmers towards the beach and safety. I told the CO of the problem and the solution and he agreed with me and broadcasted that all helis winching from the sea were to blow survivors away from the ship first. Because we were operating from the aft, downwind, section of the ship, this required us to fly very close to the ship and to disappear into the dense black smoke that was pouring out of Sir Galahad. The P2 (second pilot,) Sub.Lt. Evans, who was sitting in the port pilots seat, had his work cut out, verbally conning the heli as close as possible to the ship, because of the lack of visibility in the dense smoke. Too far left, we would hit the ship or be caught by the exploding ammunition; not far enough and the men jumping overboard would be blown back. As we were very close to land, as soon as I had winched up a couple of people we flew them to the shore to get medical treatment quickly and then returned and blew and rescued another couple. All told I winched up 10 casualties. They were all blackened by the fire and most were badly burnt. It was difficult to see if they were Welsh Guardsmen or Asian crewmen.

I was rather surprised when the CO said that we were returning to base as he wanted to land before it got dark. Steve Isacke, rescuing from the bow, amidst exploding ammunition, arrived back an hour after nightfall, and two other helis shortly before him.

That night, listening to the BBC World Service, we were amazed that our task had been reported by the media. Our action of disappearing and reappearing in and out of the smoke had been filmed by the BBC and became an iconic photograph. When we returned to the UK, an official painting was commissioned, which hangs in RNAS Culdrose wardroom and I have a print of it.

During a rescue the adrenalin tends to blind one to the horrors, it is later, when the chemical wears off, that memories emerge. My memories are re-enforced by the following day's tasking. Much of it was carrying badly burnt survivors from Fitzroy to, I believe, Goose Green, where Surgeon Cdr Rick Jolly had set up his field hospital. Apart from the visual impact of the blistered, bandaged, burnt, casualties, the thing I remember most is the cloying smell of charred flesh. The heli smelt of it for days afterwards. I awoke in the middle of the night, smelling it, for weeks afterwards.

One of our tasks was to carry large black rubber balls full of both aviation and vehicle fuel,. These were carried under-slung, on 30ft wire strops. On one occasion, soon after we had arrived, we were flying low level along a valley carrying two of these when a Argentinian Pucara turbo prop attack aircraft screamed close overhead from behind us. The valley confined our manoeuvrability, as did the heavy under-slung load. We quickly descended and landed the two fuel balls. Lt Boughton, the pilot, immediately landed the Sea King, shut down the engines and we then all jumped out and hid amongst the rocks. The Pucara must have seen us and we expected him to come back and attack us. We knew that the Pucara carried rockets and machine guns and we had no chance of evading, we were an easy target, with no weapons to fight him. After 10 minutes and no sign of enemy aircraft, we got airborne again and carried on with our tasking. After that close call, I had the Perspex windows removed from the cabin, as they obstructed our vision to port. Live cowards are more useful then dead heroes.

825 squadron's job was to move troops, food, ammunition, 105 mm guns and transport wherever they were needed. We found a broken down military truck, loaded with army motor cycles in the mountains. After a few days we realised that it and its cargo had been abandoned so we air lifted two motorcycles back to base and used them as recreational vehicles. Tug Wilson, one of my aircrewmen got quite skilful at dirt bike scrambling.

When lifting guns and other loads to a certain unit of 2 Para, I noticed that when the under-slung load was at head height above the ground, one of the soldiers would always take a flying leap, kick the load, and then fall to the ground. After transporting a few more loads, we landed the heli and I asked the soldier, covered in mud, why he was doing so. He replied, 'Static electric Sir, it goes back up into the chopper'. I told him that it did not quite work that way and all he had to do was wait until the load had touched the ground, earthing itself, before unhooking it. My advice did not sink in and every time we supplied that unit he continued with flying kicks.

A frequent task we had was transporting prisoners. We started by putting them in seats with seat-belts but as we were only able to transport 11 at a time, we soon didn't bother with seats, and just made them lay face down on the floor, jamming them in so they could not move and attack the guards or crew. The standard load then went up to 22. They never caused any trouble and seemed happy that, for them, the war was over. I never saw any ill treatment; most of them were youth conscripts and we felt sorry for them. It seemed that most of the professional soldiers were in the capital, Stanley, in comfortable billets. Many of the PoWs thought that the Falklands were very close to Argentina, not almost 1200 miles away.

825 Squadron ended the Falkland war a day earlier than expected – by accident. Normally the crewman or captain navigated, but towards the middle of June, on one sortie the second pilot (P2) was given the job. The task was to land Gurkhas on a hill prior to attacking the penultimate hill before Mount Longdon, the last Argentinian defensive position before the capital, Stanley. P2, a student of 706 NAS, who had yet to qualify as a helicopter pilot, managed to navigate the heli to a mountain beyond the tasked position. Seeing a group of soldiers at the assumed position, the Sea King landed and dis-embarked the Gurkhas. Everyone was surprised when the 'reception party' of troops on the ground turned tail and fled down the mountain. They were Argentinians. It is insane to attack a stronghold by sending in a small squad of troops in one helicopter, so the

Argentinian troops on the ground were sure that another dozen or so helis must be on the way very, very, soon, and that they had better escape whilst they could. Because of this error in navigation, the attack on Mount Longdon was advanced by 24 hours and so the war ended early, on the 14th of June.

There were many rumours circulating about the war and some of them, it appeared later, were true. There were SAS men flown into Argentina by heli who attacked aircraft on the ground and who then escaped via Chile. SAS men had entered Stanley, undetected, and spent days hiding in drains and other places, spotting and plotting. They noticed that every day at a certain time the senior officers would meet in a certain room in town and the SAS then directed a helicopter to fire a rocket into the room through the window.

After the British 3rd battalion paratroopers had taken Mount Longdon, tasking was light so two other aircrewmen and I decided to see what it was like. There were surprisingly few dead bodies and no Para left there at all. I found an HF single sideband transceiver and a Vary type signal pistol, both of which would be useful on my boat in England. One of our Sea Kings had dropped us off and said that they would pick us up later, but it did not turn up. After waiting an hour and realising that it was getting dark, we were preparing to walk down a path to Stanley, which was some miles away. At the last moment, I noticed a Sea King in the distance and called it on my emergency radio. It turned towards us and landed. The P2 was Prince Andrew and we exchanged greetings and three grateful aircrewmen were flown to 825 San Carlos Settlement base. We did not immediately realise just how lucky we were and it was some time later that we discovered that the path down the mountain to Stanley had been mined. Avoiding mines and booby traps had not been included in the ASW aircrewman curricula!

My liking for books again helped, when an Argentinian Iroquois helicopter was found at Stanley. All the pilots of 825 wanted to fly it, but the instructions and instruments were in

Spanish. No one spoke Spanish but I had brought with me a Spanish dictionary and that was sufficient to fly the heli. We brought the Iroquois back to Culdrose and it is now in the Fleet Air Arm museum at RNAS Yeovilton.

The day of the Argentinian surrender, the CO of 825 decided to have a 'flypast' of Stanley, with all the squadron and flying the UK flag. This may have gone down well with the press and Islanders but the feeling in the military was somewhat different, as troops were on the mountains in the middle of winter with wounded soldiers and no tents or supplies. It can be summed up by a radio call from 'Sunray', the overall commander of UK forces 'Big Blue Job leader (our call sign), very pretty, now how about doing something useful! Out.'

With the war finished, tasking became lighter and it was realised that the village school at San Carlos had not had a teacher for months. I was asked to run the school, as I was now a civilian qualified teacher, albeit in Further Education. There were only about a dozen students, aged between about 7–13 years. There was no curriculum available and all the students were in one class. A peripatetic teacher used to come to the school from Stanley every week or so, before the invasion. During the weekends I flew both days, to allow my crewmen time off.

On the 13th July 1982, we flew seven helis to Atlantic Causeway and they were shipped back to the UK. The aircrew returned home by RAF C130 Hercules aircraft, carrying out inflight refuelling and when we landed at RAF Brize Norton in the UK we discovered that our wives (only one each!) and families had been brought up from Culdrose to meet us and we were transported back together. Some of us were hard to recognise, as we were in battle dress and often beards had been grown. For us the war was over and I am proud to be associated with it. It was a short, professional and effective campaign, 8,000 miles away from the UK. It won Margret Thatcher a landslide victory at the next election, cost almost 300 British and Asian lives, introduced new weapons and equipment to the armed forces years ahead of schedule, and it still costs millions of pounds to garrison and protect the Falklands today. It also hastened the removal of the thuggish government of the Argentinian Junta, freeing the population from a regime of terror. In retrospect it would have been much more cost effective, for the UK, to give every person on the Falklands £1,000,000 and bring them back to the UK.

The town of Helston, near Culdrose, had a 'Freedom of the City' ceremony and I was very proud to lead the squadron as we marched through the town.

The South Atlantic Medal was awarded to all who were involved in the war, and other awards were also given. 825 NAS Commanding Officer was awarded the Distinguished Service Cross for his work. 825 was the only combat unit where no other member received an award. Not even Lt. Steve Isacke and his crew, who hovered over exploding ammunition for hours, returning in the dark to an unlit field or the Air Engineering Officer who had ensured that the aircraft were nearly always serviceable, in extreme conditions in the semi frozen mud of a field. They had not been nominated by the Commanding Officer. They did not even get a bar of chocolate.

Chapter 26
706 NAS, RNAS Culdrose September 82 –April 83

After the Falkland's war, returning to the routine flying on a training squadron was a let-down. Back to the 'sausage machine' of churning out new aircrew was boring. I knew that 706 would be my last squadron before leaving the RN, on my 40th birthday, in February. I thought it was an absurd decision of the MOD to make sailors leave on that anniversary. I was at the height of my capabilities and doubt if any other person in the Fleet Air Arm was as competent or as highly trained as I, and also the aircrewman branch was undermanned. There once was an option to stay a further five years but that had recently been stopped because of defence cuts. At least the Falklands had given me the satisfaction and justification of the money that the UK had spent on training me for all the years. I reasoned, based on the peace of the last 20 years, there would probably be no more conflicts for another 20 years so leaving the RN and becoming a civilian was for the best. I just could not think of what to do when I left.

I had an appointment with the station re-settlement officer and was told that I was free to do anything I wished and civilian firms were crying out for good SNCOs but could not actually suggest anything. The visit was not a complete waste of time because, as I was waiting to go in to see him, I found an advert in a magazine seeking aircrewmen and Air Load Masters to join the Sultan of Oman's Air Force. I wrote to the recruiters, Airworks, at Bournemouth, and had an interview but was told 'Don't call us we will call you'.

In preparation for leaving I was allowed to do a month's re-settlement training course, on any subject I wanted. My trimaran had recently sat on my mooring block, at low tide, and had been holed, half filling with water, and was now in Restronguet boatyard for repair. I decided that repairing my boat could be called a boat maintenance course and it was accepted.

When I first returned to 706, I was told that one of the aircrewmen who had remained on the squadron had proved quite a star. His professionalism and coolness in emergencies had been outstanding and that he had been recommended for officer. This made me extremely happy as I had nurtured this young man and he had come to my home at weekends, as he was an orphan and had no siblings. I was also nominated as his next of kin.

This lad did seem to be rather unlucky when he was flying, as he had many emergency landings but his actions were always beyond reproach and coolly executed. Emergency radio calls were word perfect and emergency landing sites quickly identified. A common problem was a smell of burning in the heli, or cockpit warning lights would illuminate. Most times, the engineers could not find the cause of the problem and were at a loss to explain them. Whilst flying one night on a sonar dunking training sortie, he reported that the sonar body was in the water and he could not raise it. I was in an adjacent training area, also dunking, so I went through the emergency check list with him and he reported that nothing worked, not even by winching it up by hand. Rather than cut the cable and lose tens of thousands of pounds of equipment, it was decided to fly 20 miles back to Culdrose, in the dark, with the sonar body hanging100 feet below the heli. My heli escorted him back to Culdrose. He then had to 'con' the aircraft and land the body on mattresses that had been placed on the airfield, a very difficult job in the dark. He did it magnificently and again I was very proud of him.

We landed alongside him and I jumped out of my heli and walked over to the other one to see if I could determine what the problem was. A visual inspection showed nothing obvious so I attempted to raise (wind in) the body using the normal electro hydraulic handle and it came in perfectly. That night the engineers stripped the system down and could find no reason why it had not worked.

Next day there was the usual banter of someone being a Jonah and I decided to do some investigation of my own. I went to the hanger and asked if it was possible for an aircrewman to initiate these problems, especially the cockpit warning lights. The Chief Aircraft Artificer initially said 'No' but then said he would double check with the Electrical Artificer. Later that day he came to see me and told me he had something to show me. We went to a Sea King and he removed a section of soundproofing just above the radar and exposed a hidden electrical junction box. 'Look at this.' he said and showed me some scratches on the terminals, made by something sharp. 'These are terminals for the cockpit warning lights. If they are shorted out, the lights come on.' I felt sick. All aircrewman carry steel dividers for navigating on charts and these could be used to short out wires and would leave scratches similar to those I saw. I was sure there was some other explanation and I asked him not to say anything.

Collecting the personal documents of my aircrewman from the Staff Office, I went through his previous history. I was shocked by what I read. Before becoming an aircrewman he had been a ship's electrician. He had discovered a fire on a ship and was recommended for his actions and later he was discovered lighting another one. When disciplined he said he did it because, after discovering the first fire, he enjoyed the praise he received. How he was ever accepted into the aircrew branch is a complete mystery to me. He had the skill and knowledge to short out terminals, the smell of burning could easily be manufactured by setting light to paper in a tin and then, replacing the lid, putting it in his pocket. Also there had been no problem found with the sonar winch. It was a classic case of 'Munchausen by proxy', when problems or physical harm is manufactured, to receive praise and award.

I had just finished reading his personal file when we had an SAR call out and the duty aircrewman was my suspect. A second aircrewman was also required for this call out, as it meant being winched down to a ship and tradition said that the duty aircrewman did the winching. Much to the chagrin of the rest of the aircrewmen (we all liked to be involved in a SAR) I said that I was going. This resulted in mutterings about the Chief wanting another medal before he retired. I, of course, was worried for their safety when being winched. If anyone did the winching it would be me. In the event, the SAR was cancelled shortly after take-off.

On return, I presented my findings to the CO (the same one from 825 NAS) and he completely over reacted. There was no hard evidence of the sabotage, just circumstantial. Instead of laying a trap, using a camera, he immediately called the RN Special Investigation Branch and banned the aircrewman from going to any squadron aircraft or building. Nothing could be proven against him. The tin with burnt paper was found but it was explained that it was a cigarette tin, for illegal smokes. His recommendation for officer was rescinded and as his enlistment was expiring in a couple of months he left the navy with no record of any criminal act. Sometime later I heard that he was working in a hospital as a porter. I have often wondered if I should have said something. I really liked the lad but it would have been too dangerous not to report him.

Towards the end of 1982 a senior aircrewman, Fleet Chief Pete Matthews, who was attached to a RAF trials unit died. He was to be buried at Portland and I asked the Senior Pilot (the CO was away) if the non-flying aircrewmen of 706 could be flown to Portland by a squadron aircraft, tasking the flight as a continuation training navigation exercise. This was commonly done for meetings etc. I was refused on the excuse that we were too busy and, when I tried to prove that we were not on that day, was dismissed. When I went to the RAF Training Unit and asked the same question I was told, 'Of course, it is no problem. How many people do you want to take?' I asked the other squadrons who would like to go, and got about 10 passengers. When I rang up the motor transport section of HMS Osprey, Portland, I was told that all transport had to be booked a week in advance. I replied that yes, it was very inconsiderate of Pete to die without giving a weeks' notice, and he wouldn't do it again. Please could we have transport for 10 people? Refused. Give a week's notice.

After informing the duty officer of 706 squadron that three of 706 aircrewmen would be absent on official business, no one missed us when we flew to Portland, In true RN fashion we all went to the pub for a pint and a pie, intending ordering taxis to take us to the church. In the pub we met a dozen RAF aircrew, from Pete's unit, including the OC (the RAF have OC, the RN CO). They had driven for hours, coming from the middle of England, in an RAF bus, to attend the funeral and we were offered a lift to and from the church, which we gladly accepted. The RAF Sea King was waiting for us at the airstrip on our return.

The RN has a monthly newspaper, Navy News, which accepts articles from all serving sailors. I checked with the Public Relations Officer of Culdrose if I needed to go through official channels or could write directly to the Navy News. I knew the answer, directly, but wanted confirmation, which was given. I wrote an article about what had happened and headed my article 'Thank you RAF'. I had to smile as I knew that it would not be published until March and I was leaving the RN in February.

Shortly before I left 706, I received a message from the Safety Equipment Officer (who was my indirect boss for giving survival related lectures and courses) asking me if I could give a Resistance to Interrogation (RtoI) lecture to aircrew. This was routine for me and required no extra preparation. I would turn up at the nominated squadron on a non-flying day and give my spiel in their briefing room. A week later, I was asked if everything was ready and that Culdrose's theatre/cinema had been booked. I asked why the theatre was being used and was told that it was a station 'Stand Down' day and it was dedicated to flight safety and survival training. All available personnel would be present. I realised that my normal lecture, when given in a theatre, would not be sufficient, so I decided to add a little interrogation scenario.

36 hours before the lecture I was told that it would start at 1000 as the Admiral, Flag Officer Naval Air Command, would be landing at 0930. The Admiral! Nobody had mentioned that the Admiral would be flying from RNAS Yeovilton (the FAA headquarters) and would be attending. I was surprised that the Admiral knew I existed, never mind that I was also trained in unusual skills.

His attendance meant that I would have to do a drastic re-think of my lecture technique. I spent all night writing out a script and designing a presentation suitable for FONAC. Next day I recruited my aircrewman and a newly qualified RtoI instructor from another squadron and rehearsed my presentation. It lacked the oomph that I wanted and I realised that it would need to be more dramatic. A visit to the armoury and the film library gave me what I need. Early next morning we had another rehearsal, this time with sound effects from a BBC sound tape. It went well but I kept my biggest oomph a secret.

Everyone in the auditorium stood up as the Admiral and staff officers, accompanied by the Captain of Culdrose, arrived and sat down in the front row. The lights were dimmed and from the loudspeakers came the hum of aircraft engines, getting louder. The sound started at the rear and then crossed from side to side, at full volume. There was then the crack and explosion of anti-aircraft fire, whilst lights flashed on and off all around the theatre, followed by the scream of an aircraft engines as it crash dived towards the ground. There then was silence. I was sitting just behind the Admiral and had placed a dustbin in the isle. As soon as there was silence, as surreptitiously as possible, I lit the thunder-flash I had got from the armoury, put it in the bin and replaced the lid.

It is quite amazing how a thunder-flash exploding in the dark wakes people up – and also how high a dustbin lid flies. I thought for one moment it was going to hit FONAC but it just missed him and then rolled at speed and crashed into the stage with a loud clang. I can safely say I had grasped everyone's attention.

The next act was on the stage as a dishevelled aircrewman staggered on, only to be set-on by 'enemy soldiers' who started to beat him with their rifles. It looked extremely realistic, even to me. An 'enemy officer' then rescued him and escorted him to an 'interrogation room' at the other side of the room and he was subjected to various types of interrogation. Apart from saying 'I'm sorry, I did not hear that', 'Yes' and 'No', he said exactly what he should have said, which is 'I cannot answer that question'.

After that little play, I explained what had happened. When first captured by untrained troops expect harsh treatment. Later, when handed over to trained troops and interrogation, treatment will be better. I then described the techniques used during interrogation. We then had a question and answer session, which lasted for over 30 minutes. I think I satisfied every one. I then asked the audience a question – 'Who has read a copy of the Haig Convention or the Geneva Convention for the conduct pertaining to a prisoner of war?'. Not one person answered. When it was time to end, I had the PoW brought onto the stage again and complimented him for obeying the rules and when the audience started to nod in agreement I said 'But did he?' I played the same trick I had played years earlier but this time not with a signature on a piece of paper. Over the sound system came the March 'Colonel Bogey', and the voice of the interrogator and the prisoner. After giving his name, rank and number, the prisoner, when asked if he had dropped biological bombs on Porthleven (a little village near Culdrose) said 'Yes'. When asked how he felt he answered 'I'm sorry'. Did he denounce the imperialistic action against the peace loving villagers? 'Yes'. Words were taken from his interrogation and a 'confession' concocted.

I was very happy how the presentation went and it was beers all round for my cast. The admiral also enjoyed it and I was forgiven for almost decapitating him with a dustbin lid. Sadly, none of my squadron's senior officers had bothered to attend.

It was almost the day of starting my terminal leave when I was asked if I would consider staying longer in the RN. It had at last been realised that we were short of aircrewmen, especially ones that were qualified airborne radar controllers. I said that I was interested if it was for five years but was told that was still not allowed but they could offer me two years. The new aircraft carrier HMS Ark Royal had just been completed and was going on a world cruise, showing the flag. I said that if I was going to be the senior aircrewman on her, I would be interested. A world cruise would be a fitting end to my career, but it was not to be

I was offered a squadron that, in the summer, would be going to the Falklands, returning after six months and then six months later returning to the Falklands for another six months. Summer in the northern hemisphere is winter in the southern. I had already had three consecutive winters and the navy was offering me four more! It was a no-brainer and I refused the offer. A day later I was again asked to stay, this time for three months until 22nd April. My first response was to refuse but then realised that the RN pension year started on 1st of April, and if I left after that date my pension would be slightly higher, so I accepted. There was one thing that I had forgotten about. That was my letter to the Navy News.

Two days before I was due to report to HMS Drake, the shore base in Devonport, for release, I was summoned to the CO's office. There, I was confronted by a white-faced Splot and incandescent CO. On his desk was an open copy of the latest Navy News and big headlines proclaimed, **THANK YOU RAF.** My article had been published. It seemed that FONAC had also read it and had personally telephoned the CO, asking him to explain what it was all about and the Admiral was not in a happy mood. The CO demanded to know why I had written it and that I was not allowed to write to the Navy News without his permission. How I loved watching him squirm! I had great trouble keeping a straight face because we both knew that I was right and he could do nothing about it. I was homeward bound, just days from being a civilian.

The aircrewmen at Culdrose gave me a good send-off party but, for some reason, I was not surprised when the CO did not congratulate me. I knew that I would never see him again – but isn't fate funny

Chapter 27
CIVVY STREET, 1983-85

After spending a month or so re-decorating my home in Cornwall and getting in my wife's way, I started seriously looking for a job. I did a trial month on a diving boat, running from Falmouth, as a trainee skipper. I had no trouble with the skippering but the partying every night with the holiday divers and the supposedly day off when the boat had to be cleaned and re-victualed, was more than I wanted, so I turned the job down.

I was only offered one other job, painting the men's toilets on Penryn but my pride made me refuse that also. I was not that hungry. Instead, I answered an advert and became a hot foil printer, producing fancy business cards and advertising items, working from home. I enjoyed starting a business from scratch and for the first time in my life took control of my own future. It got so successful that I was thinking of renting a small industrial unit.

That summer, of 1984, I had plenty of time to enjoy my hobby of sailing and also did some yacht deliveries.

I was crew on a delivery of a Catalac catamaran from Poole to London. The Skipper was Clive Phillips, a larger than life character, who was a Yacht Master Instructor. I had no formal yacht qualifications although I had my own boat and had spent nine years as a seaman in the RN with many hours of watch keeping on the bridge of warship and now was a dayboat (sailing dinghy) instructor.

It was around midnight and we had had just entered the Solent with a good SW wind on our starboard quarter, trundling along at a steady 6 knots or so. I was on watch, Clive was fully dressed, dozing below and our third hand turned in and asleep. I noted a faint white light about 20 degrees to starboard and decided it was probably the stern light of a crossed vessel. A Mars Bar later the light seemed brighter, which I thought was because the night was darker. Just to be sure I took a compass bearing of it and checked around for any other traffic.

Next time I checked to starboard the light was definitely brighter and higher, still on the same bearing. No other Navigation lights visible. I called Clive and he came up and he called me a 'Silly B****r' and told me it was the stern light of a vessel which had crossed. I stoutly denied this and asked him to check again. The bearing was steady and now the bulk of a ship could be faintly seen. Clive grabbed the helm from me and altered course to starboard, towards the light. Very soon we were bathed in the green glow of the vessel's starboard navigation light, surmounted by two steaming lights, as it passed down our port side. A ship was crossing the Solent backwards!

After a long discussion, nursing cups of hot chocolate, our only logical explanation was that the ship was a 'double-ended' Isle of Wight ferry, which had not changed its navigation lights for the return trip to the mainland. The lessons I learnt was that all a light tells you is that something is there, always take a compass bearing and be prepared to make decisions based on facts, not suppositions or rote.

In February, 1985, out of the blue, I received a letter from Oman, asking me to come to the Sultanate as soon as possible to be an instructor. It was a two year contract and renewable. I had closed my mind to ever flying again but as soon as I received that letter I realised I missed the excitement, the smell of jet aviation fuel and the fun. I had no trouble selling my business and after a couple of months I found myself sweating in the four hour queue waiting to pass through Muscat airport immigration. I would gladly have waited all day if it meant flying again, even if the temperature was 40°C outside.

Chapter 28
Muscat, Salalah, Sultanate of Oman. 1985 -94

Oman is a long narrow country on the eastern side of Arabia. Once, the Sultanate included Zanzibar and all the countries that now form the United Arab Emirates (UAE). The UAE was also known as the Trucial States, so called as there were many Arab pirates operating from there until the British had enforced a truce from the involved Sultans. An unusual fact about Oman is that the northern part (Khasab), jutting out at the entrance of the Persian Gulf, is separated from the bulk of Oman by the UAE.

The Indian Ocean coast, which runs the length of the country, was pristine and teemed with life. Most of the year the sun shines, except for the southern part, which receives 4 months of Khareef (monsoon), a seasonal wet southerly wind, which is cool and brings welcomed moisture to the land. Mid-summer brings temperatures of up to 50°C in the desert areas but the cooling winds along the coast means it seldom reaches 40°C.

I found the Omanis very friendly and prepared to work, unlike the Arabs in most of the Arab countries. That is not to say there were no expatriate workers from Pakistan, Baluchistan, India, and Philippines etc. Sultan Qaboos bin Saied, the ruler, made it a rule that if an Omani could be trained to do a job, they would do it. At the time, this was unique in the Arab world. Also, unusually, the Sultan was very popular with his subjects. Women were allowed to drive, alcohol was available (with some restrictions) and there was no 'baksheesh', bribery.

Joining the Sultan of Oman's Air Force (SOAF) was impressive. My uniform consisted of RAF style blue serge jacket and trousers for cool climates, and in Oman, cotton light brown shirt and trousers, desert camouflage shirt, trousers and a shamag, a cloth covering for the head that is wrapped around and tucked in tightly. All of these, except for the shamag, were made to measure, and took just one day to produce by the Asian tailors.

On the second day I went to see the Commander of SOAF, Aqueed (Colonel) Erik Bennett, who has been knighted and awarded the CVO KBE CB. He was a man small in stature but great in power. He greeted me by my first name, which was not navy fashion, and told me that I was to be the Air Load Master (ALM) and Helicopter Crewman Instructor and would be teaching C130 Hercules, BAC1-11 and Skyvan ALMs as well as 205, 212 and 214 Augusta Bell helicopter aircrewmen. I was completely taken aback. What did I know about fixed wing aircraft? I had trouble spelling C130! I thought that I would be returning to helicopter flying.

Now I can return to a comment I made about fate, when I described my winter survival course. I remembered that first night of the winter survival course in Germany, when Gary Seaward talked me through the intricacies of the herringboned hatched trim (loading balance) sheet. I realised then, that with more familiarity, I could teach that subject. As for the actual aircraft, well, I would have access to all the manuals that I required and would undertake on job training. I started breathing again. Yes, I could do the job, even the requirement to teach desert survival. The threads of fate had woven and given me the mantle, now it was up to me to wear it.

A week later I went south to a SOAF airfield at Salalah, which was originally built by the RAF 50 years earlier, and there I was introduced to Augusta Bell 205, 206, 212, and 214 helicopters, and Skyvan. I arrived just before the wet Khareef started. The temperature was perfect, day and night, and, after the Khareef arrived, the stony desert and mountains became colourful with grass and flowers, almost a Scottish landscape, for 3 months. Not much rain falls during the Khareef, it is mainly a damp mist that blows in from the sea and shrouds the land. Netting, suspended over long troughs, collects condensation, allowing it to drip into the troughs, and this water is collected in tanks for use later in the year. Streams trickle down the mountains and village water cisterns are filled. Close to Salalah are the remains of the Queen of Sheba's palace and picturesque springs called Ains. For those interested in SAS and Oman's history, the fort at Mirbat is also near-by.

The NCOs' mess garden had a knurled incense tree that was reputed to be the oldest in Arabia. It is a sad fact that in 1990, when the mess was handed over to the Omanis, they cut it down.

There was great comradery at Salalah. The first question that 3 squadron OC, Tim Seebrook, asked me,was if I played an instrument and would I like to join his jazz band. Unfortunately the answer was no to both. I would have been very happy staying at Salalah but the Trade Training Institute (TTI), for which I had been recruited, was at Muscat, so after 2 months I had to say good-by and fly back north.

I now had four months to get qualified on the fixed wing aircraft and to produce a four month course for ALMs and aircrewmen. Skyvan qualification only took half a dozen flights as it is a simple aircraft but the C130 Hercules, being more sophisticated, took more. I did manage to get a sortie taking helis to Singapore for refurbishment and returning with completed ones. It was planned as a three day trip but ended up as six because of unserviceability. Living in a hotel and visiting the places that I used to know so well and with all expenses paid by the Sultan was no hardship.

The subjects and periods for the TTI course had been approved in advance but there was no guidance to course content. This was the first time that I had been tasked with constructing a course and I decided to do it navy fashion, by achieving aims and building further aims on top of them. It seemed to work well and I had good feedback from the squadrons. I was kept very busy all working hours (which was from 0800 – 1300).

Apart from the usual aircrew subjects, which included desert and sea survival, the syllabus included swimming and logic. The last subject caused me a lot of thought; what was required and how do I teach it? My students were bright Omanis but very few were completely fluent in English. Eventually I obtained a Postman Pat wooden jigsaw, for children up to 4 years old. It consisted of 20 large pieces and on the back of each one I put a letter for its row and a number for its position. I carried the puzzle into the classroom, emptied the pieces into a desk and placed the box lid, with the picture on, where it could be seen. With no more instructions, I told them it was a picture and they had to connect the pieces together. They had never seen a jigsaw puzzle before and not once, in four years, was it completed by the class. I stopped them working after 25 minutes to ask them what the jigsaw picture was and none realised that the box lid picture was showing them the finished picture. When shown, it still took the whole class 10 minutes to complete it.

The next Logic period I again brought in the jigsaw and told them to complete the picture by looking at the back (where letters and numbers had been written). Until I pointed this out to them they did not connect this with completing the puzzle. This Postman Pat jigsaw became my way of getting them to look around and garner information before making a decision.

It also was my introduction to Grid Reference and Latitude and Longitude.

It was not because of any lack of intelligence that the Omanis had difficulty but because the education system, run by Asians, only taught the answer to exam questions, and did not require any thinking, just a good memory. I gave a test at the end of each subject and initially most of the students did poorly when working with figures, with a frequent complaint of 'You did not teach us that Sir.' When I showed them it was in their books I was told that the numbers were different!

The majority of my students were recruits but occasionally it was a serving ALM or crewman that was either selected for advancement or need extra tuition. One of these was an aircrewman called Saied. The senior pilot of the squadron he had been serving on for 2 years, informed me that he was useless and wanted him to be failed by me so that they could get rid of him. I strongly objected to this and said that I was employed to pass people, not to fail them. After a week on the course, I realised that Saied had a problem with understanding anything; I understood the squadron's problem and knew that Saied would not pass the final exam. When asked a question he would look blankly at me, with his lop-sided face, although frequently, later, he would come up with an answer. As he was already a qualified aircrewman I looked back at some old course reports and was surprised at what I read and saw. He had done well on the course and his photograph showed a handsome, straight-faced man.

I called him into my offices and asked how he felt and did he have any problems. It was hard to get an answer from him so I asked if he had been in an accident, perhaps a car crash. The answer was 'No'. In desperation I asked if he had ever banged his head and he denied it, but then told me he had been suffering from headaches for years. He had been getting Ibuprofen tablets from his friend in the medical centre but that had not worked. I told him that he was not allowed to see his friend if he was unwell. Because he was aircrew he had to see the Senior

Medical Officer (SMO) only. I took him to the medical centre and spoke to the SMO and explained my worries and showed her (yes, a lady SMO) his old photograph. Within minutes of talking to him she diagnosed that there was a problem with blood getting to his brain and prescribed tablets. Within a week I noticed improvements to Saied. I am extremely happy to report that Saied did pass the course with an average mark. When he returned to his squadron they could not believe the difference in his performance or looks. A few years later he was promoted. When I asked why no one had noticed the change in his face during his time on the squadron there were shrugs. Perhaps it was because the change was very slow, that no one had noticed it.

Another one of my students, a corporal who needed upgrading for promotion, became very quiet and withdrawn. I spoke to him and asked what the problem was. He explained that he was getting married at the weekend. This surprised me as I knew that he already had two wives and a corporal's pay was very low. Eventually, he told me that he did not want to get married; in fact he only wanted his first wife. I was puzzled about this until he explained that his brother had died and he was forced into marrying the widow, with two children and now his uncle had died in a car crash and he had to marry again and look after his family. It seems that he came from a poor village and he, on a corporal's pay, was earning the most. In Oman in those days there was no National Assistance. Traditionally this was so throughout the Muslim world and that is why the Prophet Mohamad permitted up to four wives, providing that each one can be supported equally.

Flying around Oman is spectacular. There are large areas of sand desert in the north (Sharqiya Sands) and south (Rub al Qa'li –the Empty Quarter). Along the northern and southern coasts it is mainly fertile plains but separating it all are the mountains, which are riven with valleys (waddis) in which are hidden villages and plantations. Water is carried from high springs by hundreds of aqueducts cut into the mountain sides or by underground canals, collectively called falaj that go for dozens of miles underneath stony deserts. The falaj have access wells, looking like bomb bursts from the air, along their length. When the falaj comes to a village it is used for drinking, hygiene and irrigation. Irrigation for individual plots is controlled by placing or removing rocks and there is a trusted villager whose job it is to do this and who times things by a post in the ground casting a shadow on rocks or stakes.

There were only two prohibited flying areas in Oman, The Royal Palaces, (one in Muscat in the north and another in Salalah, south) and the Royal zoos, again north and south. Otherwise we had freedom to fly where we liked when clear of normal airfield restricted areas.

Apart from continuation training, most of the flying in the south was transporting the Rural Health Service to villages hidden in the mountains. We would take a doctor and nurse with their box of medicine (mainly Ibuprofen) and land at a small helipad, often a very confined one with no space for a mistake. We would 'shut down' the heli and wait for the doctor to finish examining his patients before flying to the next village, taking with us any person needing hospital treatment. We were always given coffee, dates, wild bee honey, (which was eaten with mini chapattis) or oranges at these villages and in one village the Sheik (village elder) always opened a box of Scottish shortbread biscuits for us.

The coffee in Oman is very special and brewing it an important ritual to the Omanis. It is lightly roasted with cardamom seeds and brewed in a typical Arabic coffee pot, with a long spout and served in very small glasses. I was told that it was important to always drink three glasses. On my first tasting of Omani coffee I thought it was disgusting, and extremely thankful that the glass was small. As instructed, I held out my glass for a refill and then realised that it was not quite as foul as I had thought. Filling my glass for the third time I discovered that I really liked the taste, it was very refreshing, and then accepted another refill. I love cardamom coffee now.

One of the villages we visited was controlled very firmly by the Sheik. Whenever we landed, the villagers would run towards the heli en-mass but here, the Sheik would push them in line, using his cane if someone was slow in obeying. After greeting us, he would escort the doctor along the line and decide who was ill enough to see the doctor. If the Sheik decided they were not ill, the villager would acquiesce and walk away. He knew the malingerer and everybody respected him.

Another village we regularly visited required descending over 5,000ft into a sheer valley. This took about 10 minutes. We had to circle as we descended because of the danger of re-circulating from our rotor downwash being sucked back up. If this had happened we would have fallen very fast, out of control. This effect is called 'vortex ring' and deadly in confined areas.

Descending to one village I noticed many grape vines and jokingly remarked that they must make good wine. The Sheik (a Muslim of course) replied that it was 'Haram' (forbidden), but then with a smile said 'We do make medicine'. I am sure that he and the villagers will live to a healthy old age!

At the majority of villages, we were greeted by men and boys, the females hiding indoors, whilst the boys brought out refreshments, but in one village, in Jebel Akdhar (Green Mountain), in the north, it was women and girls who formed the reception party and they did not cover their faces or hair.

The island of Masirah is about a dozen miles off the eastern coast of Oman and was an ignored place by the Omani government until Sultan Qaboos became the ruler. His father, Sultan Saied bin Taimur, after finding out that the islanders had killed the crew of a British ship, (SS Barron Innerdale), which was wrecked there in 1904, destroyed all the buildings and forbade them from rebuilding for 100 years. He said that if they acted like animals, they could live like animals. The only buildings for most of the 20th century were those built for the

RAF at the air field. Sultan Qaboos lifted this ban. The women there wear a very distinctive Burka. Imagine a thick black cloth thrown over the head and shoulders, with slits cut for eyes and the cloth over the nose sewn to make a solid, rectangular, rudder like appendage. Whilst it is haram to see the face, the babies are breastfed in public.

The freedom from most of the normal flying restrictions, unfortunately, meant that some pilots exceeded the common sense boundary. I was flying as P2 in a 205 heli going from Thumrait in the south to Seeb, Muscat, in the north. P1, an ex-army pilot decided to fly low level along the desert road linking the two. He flew so low that a lorry heading south drove off the road into the desert as the driver thought we were going to hit him. The same pilot, on another sortie, managed to hit a navy ship with his rotor tip. His contract was terminated after that incident.

After starting ALM courses at TTI, my flying only took place when I had no course, so my flying hours were low, but did include many types of aircraft. Apart from a couple of Casevacs the rest of my flying in Oman was routine supply, continuation training or passenger flights.

The ALM syllabus included desert survival. I was rather worried about this phase. It seemed rather far-fetched that a sailor could teach Arabs anything about the desert. On day one of the first survival course, one of my students told me that his village was only 10 miles away. I then remarked that he must know this area of desert. He looked at me in surprise, saying 'Why would I go into the desert?' He had a point, if you live near a swamp or a motorway we tell our kids not to go near them. When the Bedu travelled for hundreds of miles leading camels, they spent weeks fattening their livestock, interviewing other travellers and planning their route. They did not just go on an extended stroll.

These days, camels are mainly used for racing or milk. The Sultan has given every family group 4×4 Toyota pick-up trucks.

It was not uncommon to see one of these pick-ups speeding to the market, along a sandy road with an expanding dust cloud behind it. In the open back were women and children, covered in dust whilst in the air-condition backseat of the cab would be jammed half a dozen goats. Happy goats are more valuable than happy wives.

It was a surprise to my students that we could eat snake and once shown how to catch snakes it was difficult to stop them. Also they were extremely surprised that I could divine water, they had never seen it before. Actually, most people can, it just needs two L shaped metal rods. When it was decided to construct a swimming pool for the sergeants mess, the public works department could not find the water mains, their map was wrong, but with my two bent wires I quickly discovered it for them.

My desert survival courses had good feed-back and I had a member of the Omani Royal Family on one course and he bragged about it.

After four years there was a pause in training and I was moved to the SOAF Headquarters in MAM (Muaskar al Murtafa, being the camp in the foothills), Muscat. For the first time in my life I became an office worker. I was SO2, Training (second in charge). I did not enjoy a sedentary office job, my nickname being Action Jackson. After a few months I got to grips with it and had a budget of £9,000,000. My boss, SO1 Training, was an Omani and he had a habit of promising to arrange courses but forgetting to write them down or inform me. I frequently sat around the office all morning and just before it was time to close up shop, there would be a frantic phone call asking about a course abroad that was supposed to start in a few days of which I knew nothing about. I suppose SO1 was happy with me as he begged me to stay and come back to work with him when he discovered that I was leaving Oman.

I heard that there was a new unit being set up, a Standardisation Flight. It was to comprise of the senior pilots, flight engineers and ALM instructors. On a whim, I wrote a memo saying that RAFO (Royal Air Force of Oman, as SOAF had changed its name to) did not have a survival and rescue officer and the job could be combined with the ALM instructor. I was asked to write out the job specifications and when it was agreed upon, asked if there was anyone in RAFO who was qualified. It may not come as a surprise that there was only one person in Oman that had all the required qualifications that I had recommended; desert survival, winter survival, jungle survival, sea survival and combat survival, resistance to interrogation and also a City and Guilds Qualification as a teacher. Me!

So the Standardisation Unit of RAFO then had a Survival and Rescue Officer. It was a dream job. I could fly on any RAFO aircraft to check out the cabin crew and I also travelled to all RAFO airfields and carried out desert survival training, abandon aircraft drills, parachutes dis-entanglement exercises and sea survival training. I was my own boss. It was, for me, the best job in the world. It was made even better as I had met a beautiful Danish nurse and we had a villa together.

Life was not without its embarrassing incidents. I was running sea survival training and had used a 16 squadron Land Rover that had very expensive radio equipment, to tow the recovery boat and trailer. The OC of 16 squadron had insisted that I launched from a certain beach, not one I would have normally used. When the training was finished, whilst towing the trailer and boat up the beach, the Land Rover got bogged down in the sand and the tide was coming in. I sent one of my sergeants to get a recovery truck from the motor transport section 10 miles away (no mobile phones in the 90s). Unfortunately when it arrived, three hours later, the sea level was covering the bonnet of the Land Rover and $25,000 of radio equipment was written off. The vehicle was only valued at $2,500. The bonnet made a good diving platform!

My life outside of the air force was very busy – and not just with Danish girlfriends.

During the cooler months many of us would go 'Waddi Bashing' which meant driving our 4 wheel drive vehicles to a remote location and camping for the weekend. I saw many isolated villages whilst flying and would try to find them again by driving. I don't say by road as once you left the main highway there were no black roads, just tracks which would disappear beneath the sands in strong winds. My friends and I visited some beautiful villages, hidden by rocky walls and who had not been visited by a 'white eye', as westerners were known as, for many years. The hospitality was amazing. In some villages every house brought us food and drinks. I felt very embarrassed when I thought of how a foreigner would be welcomed in most English villages.

A waddi is a dried up riverbed but when it rains it becomes a raging torrent. A week after I left Oman, two people were killed in a waddi that I had traversed weeks before and before I left Oman an Austrian friend had her legs crushed in another flash flood which moved large rocks. Some of these waddis were very long with no road and had to be trekked on foot. We would travel in separate vehicles, parking at either end and when we met in the middle of the waddi would exchange car keys.

Running on the 'Hash' was also very popular. The Hash, which is short for the Hash House Harriers, H3, is a club for extraverts who drink but have a running problem. It was started in Malaya before WW2 by a group of expats who met every week at a restaurant called the Hash House and who decided that they could drink more if they had a run first. There are rituals which go back years and there is a Grand Master at its head and on the Muscat Hash we also had a Grand Mattress as a female deputy. Rude names are usually given. There are positions to be filled, such as Hash Cash (treasurer), Hash Trash (person who cleans up after the post run wining and dining), Hash Flash (barbeque provider), Hash Hares,(who laid the flour trail that we followed and the Hash Quack, (doctor). I produced a weekly A5 broad sheet and was known as Big Ed.

As I mentioned, you had to be an extrovert and some of the rituals are strange to say the least. To join, you pour beer over your head and any infringement of rules, even those that had not been passed before, is subject to a Hash-Shit. An example was when a Norwegian doctor, Nils, and I wore new running shoes and bragged about them. When the run of 10 miles over mountains and desert had finished, the new rule of no new shoes was announced and Nils and I had to fill our sweaty, sandy shoes with beer and drink it.

I had only run on the Hash once and knew very few of the members, when a few nights later there was a 'punks, perverts and prostitutes' party. I had grown a beard and decided to shave it off, just leaving half a Hitler moustache. The shaven half of my face was 'made up' by the visiting daughter of a colleague, who also gave me an old dress and shoes. The other side of my face, with the moustache, was starkly pale after shaving off the beard and looked very odd against the suntan of the rest of my face.

Not being known by the majority of the Hashers, they did not know what to make of me and the men were distinctly embarrassed if I spoke to them, backing away to escape. But the women were the opposite. I was pinched where no lady had pinched me before and they all insisted on dancing with me. It was an exhausting and fun night.

Even before the party, my fancy dress gave me laughs. The dress was too large at the bust for the recommended socks, so I decided to buy a bra in the local town of Ruwi. The Indian manning the shop was surprised when he asked 'What size is your good lady' and I replied that it was for me and I was a 38 chest. He quickly threw a box on the counter and said 'Eight rials.' He then said 'Just one minute Sir.' climbed a step ladder to a high shelf and removed another box and, placing it on the counter, he said 'You have this one Sir, it is 18 rials'. 'Why is this one so expensive?' I enquired. 'This one you can wear many, many times Sir!' If anyone is interested in a size 38 bra, only worn once, please contact me...

Another pass time which took up a lot of my spare time was the Muscat Amateur Theatre. I appeared in quite a few productions, including a life size Punch and Judy, which we performed in the in the local shopping centre. The Omanis had never seen anything like it before and were quite bemused at the crazy 'white-eyes'. Our director for most of the plays was Judith Razek, who was later made an MBE for her varied work in media in Oman.

We also put on a production at the magnificent Al Bustan Hotel, which was built to house the Sultan's guests as well as being a hotel. The production was Alan Ayckbourn's *A Chorus of Disapproval*. One of the scenes involved a couple moving around the (huge) stage and was very complicated for lighting. It took two days of rehearsals for our lights specialists, Bernard and Sally Perry, to set up the lights for this scene and as normal practice, marked the positions by putting masking tape on the stage floor. The dress rehearsal went well and we were surprised when the director decided to have another run through just before the first performance. It was a good job he insisted, as the hotel's Asian cleaners had decided to have a good clean up and had removed all the tape that marked the lighting positions! The full-house audience had to wait over 30 minutes before we were ready but everyone agreed it was worth the wait.

Fate had once again pulled the strings and one of the main characters of the play was a newcomer to Oman – my last CO from the Falklands 825 squadron and 706 squadron, who I had never expected to meet again!

As I mentioned earlier, every one used first names in the Oman, but my ex-boss could not bring himself to do so. He always called me 'Chief' (Chief Petty Officer), whilst I used his first name, which made him flinch. I only had a walk-on part in that play playing a surrogate lighting technician called Bernard, but my main job was assisting the stage manager with props. Ex-boss was in the first scene and, with the overture playing, was waiting for the curtain to go up but had forgotten to take with him an important prop. I realised this and was in the wings pretending to ignore him as he tried to attract my attention by hissing 'Chief, Chief' I pretended I could not hear him until in desperation he called 'David, David, I need my prop.' And I answered him 'Yes *****, what do you want? I had won! From then on I was David.

Another hobby I had was photography. Being aircrew, I managed to get commissions to take aerial photographs of hotels and that was very lucrative. Not only being paid cash but also being invited to use the hotels free if I wanted.

I also took some unique photographs of Omani village dwellers. I had a Polaroid camera as well as a 35mm and a large medium format one. When I approached a village the young boys were always the first to greet me and I would take some snaps with the instant Polaroid, which I gave them. They would run back delightedly to show their parents and the father would then appear and greet me. Again, I would take a happy snap with the Polaroid and some with my other cameras. I think that the lined, weathered faces of old Omanis are very photogenic. Father would go back to his house, re-appearing a short time later with his wives and the remainder of his family. Once more, the magic of the Polaroid worked and I was given permission to photo the wives and girls. Soon all the neighbours would turn up asking for photographs. I would always try to return to the villages and present them with good snaps from my other cameras.

As a project, when I returned to Muscat, I purchased a wreck of a GRP (fiberglass) boat of about 20ft. It had no cabin, and one side was completely ripped. It also had no trailer. I had it brought from the beach club to outside my room and spent a year repairing it, using material that I scrounged from various government sources. I paid £27.50, as that was the cost of the repair to the sails. I named the boat Phoenix and painted it fiery red. I sold it, after about 500 hours work for £750. Not a good hourly rate but it was an excellent project to learn about boat repairs and it kept me out of the bar.

I joined the Armed Forces Sailing club and learnt how to sail the Laser dinghy. I had qualified as an RYA dinghy instructor in the UK but the Laser is a completely different boat to sail competitively. The sea around Muscat offers no interesting places to cruise, just miles of golden sands, so racing predominates. Despite my instructor qualification I ended at the back of the fleet continuously. I then discovered how to roll-tack, when you tack by almost capsizing. That took a couple of weeks of every afternoon and dozens of capsizes. After roll-tacking was mastered I spent a month learning roll-gybing. It took about three days before I managed it without capsizing. It would be a lie to say that I never capsized again when tacking or gybing but I became extremely agile at righting the Laser. For the non-sailors, tacking is turning the bow of the boat through the wind direction and gybing is turning the stern.

Eventually I started improving my rating in the regattas. I won my first race by accident, as I did not know what I was doing. After a clash on the start line I had to restart well behind everyone else. It was a race in drifting conditions and I decided not to follow the fleet ahead of me but go in a different direction. I picked up a breeze and rounded the course well ahead of everyone else. I thought that it was just a lucky wind for me but later analysed that I had been using the current to push me into what little wind there was, therefore increasing the apparent wind and thus my boat speed. This is called 'lee-bowing the current' and I knew nothing about it. Luckily no one else did either.

Eventually I became Oman champion and qualified for the World Masters but as that is held in strong winds (Oman usually only has light winds) I knew that I would not stand a chance, weighing only 65 kilos, and opted out.

An annual race for yachts had been inaugurated, from Dubai to Oman. This required sailing eastward through the Hormuz Straits. I had heard about a catamaran (a Woods design 24ft Strider) that had been entered for the race but the owner had sold the boat and departed the country.

I tracked down the new owner and asked if he intended to join in the race but he admitted to being a novice sailor. I managed to persuade him that if he had me as a skipper then we would not disgrace ourselves and he accepted. I told him that he could have any cup we won or anything else that was given out, but that there was a new navigation aid called GPS for the first prize and if we were lucky enough to win it, I would have that. GPS had only just filtered down to the sailing community, replacing Navstar, which earlier had replaced both Decca and Loran, both of which were terrestrial radio beacons. I had never seen a GPS set and could not afford the £1,000 asking price. Although we did not win the race overall, we came second and first in our class and as the winning boat already had GPS it came to us by default. I was a very happy skipper.

I had the navigation equipment, all I needed now was the boat and then I could achieve my aim of sailing the world. I scoured the listings for catamarans, as that was what I decided would be the best choice, and Lis, my girlfriend, and I visited boats in Oman, Wales and Majorca, but nothing suitable was seen. I then read about, a 37ft Flica, in Greece and at a price I could afford. With no hesitation I faxed the broker saying that I would buy it subject to survey. It was a decision I have never regretted. It was my perfect blue water cruising boat and has never been bettered.

My new boat, African Ocean, was laying in Kalamaki marina, Piraeus, and the reason the price was affordable (£25,000 below market price) was because it had been brought with a marine mortgage and the owner had defaulted. It was costing the finance company £1500 p/m for marina fees and they wanted a quick sale. Eight years of Oman pay and not paying income tax had boosted my savings considerable.

I arranged a crew from Oman and we spent a couple of days preparing the boat before leaving. She had been laying in Kalamaki Marina in Greece for a couple of years and had been neglected and abused with much essential equipment 'lost'. The radar and the old satellite navigator did not work but I did have my prize of the Satnav to help with navigation. The log, wind indicator and echo sounder had been installed some 8 years earlier when new, and seemed to work. I noticed that there was no liferaft but the company that had been looking after the boat supplied one and told me it had been serviced. Donning my Survival and Rescue Officer hat I gave an elaborate brief on deploying and using the liferaft to my crew and we set off for the Sultanate of Oman via the Suez Canal.

My girlfriend had to leave at Port Suez and we were joined by a Swedish lady doctor, who had never sailed before. Only the two ladies were allowed ashore, as the rest of us did not have Egyptian visas, and they went shopping for essential supplies, especially beer for our daily aperitif. When the guard at Port Suez saw the beer he had to be subdued with baksheesh.

The first day after leaving Suez was a relief, heading south down the Red Sea for Aden and Muscat. After the hassle of the authorities and paying a thousand cigarettes as 'local taxes' to the soldiers and guards of the canal, we were free and even had some beer for our evening meal, onboard. We stopped over a coral reef and had a quick swim to wash the stickiness of Egypt off our bodies. I decided to head over to the eastern side of the Red Sea and transit down the coast, clear of the shipping lanes. This meant going over a large reef with minimum charted depths of 2 metres. Sunset was about 6pm and I calculated that we would clear it before dusk.

Keeping a good lookout for coral heads we motor-sailed carefully over the reef and satisfyingly saw it disappear into the depths, just about where we expected, as the sun set over Egypt.

I started to cook the evening meal when I heard shouts that the depth was only 1.5 meters, the same as our draft. I rushed up to the cockpit, stopped the engines and dropped the mainsail. The sea was flat, black and impenetrable. The echo sounder showed 1.5 meters. I shone my large lamp into the sea, but the glare showed nothing. It was then that I realised that I had not seen a lead-line onboard. Thankfully, I had bought a roll of nylon line in Greece and spare shackles, so I quickly tied the nylon to the shackles and lowered them over the side. No time to measure and tie knots. The weighted line dropped and ran out - and out - and out. I stopped lowering at over 50 metres with the shackles still not touching the seabed. No reef.

I was weak with relief as I re-coiled the line and cursed the echo sounder as a useless bit of kit. It was not until we had reached shallower water the next day that the depth started to read sensibly again and I then realised what had happened. On my old model of sounder, if the depth was too great, it showed the last recorded depth constantly, which was the return echo of a previous pulse. This was not unusual phenomena but one that I had not encountered before. The latest models have a flashing depth display if this happens.

The lessons learnt are always to have a lead-line that can be used quickly and that electronic instruments are fallible. One other thing, before you bribe the Egyptian guards to allow you to bring enough beer onboard for a 10 day passage make sure it is not non-alcoholic beer!

I had worked out a standing watch system, everyone having the same watch every day as it had been suggested that it was less tiring. I paired the doctor with me, keeping a five hour, 2000 – 0100, night watch. During the first of these I taught her the basic lights of ships that we would see.

The second evening Dr. Greta was looking ahead and reported that she could see a light on the port bow. I asked her what colour. She replied that it was 'White, no, red. No, blue, no, changing colour'. I told her to rest her eyes and look again. After a pause she tried again to identify the colour but once more it seemed to change. Trying not to sound too superior I asked her to give me the binoculars and I would identify it for her. Raising the binoculars to my eyes I had to agree with her, it was constantly changing. For almost 30 minutes we looked at that light trying to determine what it was. We were obviously closing on it as it was getting brighter, on a steady bearing ahead and the elevation was rising. One of us needed to alter course but which one? I got out my cockpit guide and seaman's guide but could find nothing that would show these rainbow-like colours. It was still on a steady bearing and closing but which way to alter course? Then, quickly, it became almost pure white.

Venus is a very beautiful planet, especially as it rises and the light gets reflected and refracted by the heat rising from sun-baked sand of Saudi. There is of course no need to alter course for it. I also do not recommend standing watches; it is very boring having the same watch every 24 hours.

We motor sailed most of the way down to the entrance to the Red Sea, Bab al Mandab, and for us it really was the gate of tears. Unknown to us there was a typhoon in the Indian Ocean and the effect was to produce for us a strong headwind and north flowing current. We spent 12 hours tacking across the strait towards Africa and back and we had made half a mile towards our destination of Aden. I was not sure if we had enough fuel to motor directly into the half gale so decided to call in at Mocha, which we had passed a day earlier and refuel. With baksheesh we had things sorted out and the Chief of Police drove us around in his decrepit car, twisting wires together to start it and having no lights. After two days the wind decreased and we sailed for Aden.

We were quite a few days behind schedule and none of my crew could stay, so I was left alone as they caught the first flight to Muscat. There was nothing for it but to do my first long distance solo sail. It was surprisingly easy. During the day I sailed close to the coast and tacked out to sea at night. When I approached the shipping lanes I tacked back towards the land and made landfall in daylight. The autopilot steered continuously and I just kept a look-out and read books. There was one scary moment when I did a routine engine check at 0100. The port engine was almost underwater but still running. A seawater cooling pipe had swollen and the 'fan' belt had cut into it. It was very nerve racking until I discovered the problem. I did not have a replacement pipe but managed to repair the leak by using rubber tape. It enabled me to carry on motoring to Salalah, where I checked into Oman officially and after a few days home in Muscat a friend's son helped me to sail up to Muscat and then on to the Omani navy base at Wudam, to be lifted ashore for a refit.

Wudam is a purpose built base, with the latest equipment to repair ships as big as destroyers. I motored into a large dock and accurately stopped, assisted by divers. The floor of the dock was raised to dockside level and I discovered that I was on a cradle sitting on railway lines. An engine then chugged onto the raised dock bottom and African Ocean was towed on its cradle along the dock side and taken to her winter quarters. It must have costs thousands to do this and launch me in the spring but I paid nothing as it was a training exercise for them. The Sultan paid.

I removed my liferaft from the boat and took it to the Safety Equipment section at Seeb (Muscat) airport, where I was based. I told the sergeant to inspect and service it and I had just reached my office when the phone rang. It was a call from the SE section, asking me to come and see my liferaft. As soon as I walked in, there was a terrible smell and on asking what was causing it, was told that it was my liferaft. They had unsealed the protective canister and it was half filled with dirty, stagnant, malodourous water. The gas cylinder, unlike the ones being used for the last 10 years, was made of steel and badly rusted. When the slimy fabric of the liferaft canopy was pulled, it came apart at the seams in strips.

The liferaft was completely unusable; a death trap. Beware of Greeks bearing gifts!! The liferaft was easily disposed of but the gas cylinder was a different matter. That could not be thrown away as it had to be assumed that it was fully charged and dangerous. We took it outside, placed some rocks on it to keep it steady, attached a long line to the operating mechanism and, from a safe distance, pulled the line. Nothing seemed to happen so I gave it a harder pull. The bottle broke free of the restraining rocks, leaping off the ground, flying towards us. The SE section staff and I scattered, in case the cylinder exploded, but it just lay on the ground with the operating mechanism still closed, jammed solid by corrosion.

After a pause, we carefully approached the cylinder and decided that desperate times require desperate methods. This time, we dug a hole in the ground and buried it, piling dozens of rocks on top. Two of us got hold of the line, which was led around the corner of the building to protect us, and pulled. Nothing seem to give, so we pulled with all our weight and thought that it had moved a little but maybe the rocks had been dislodged.

Like desperados approaching the scene of a crime, we crept cautiously towards the buried cylinder and carefully removed the rocks and sand. We could hear a faint 'hiss', the bottle was discharging its gas. It took over 24 hours of 'hissing' before we deemed it safe enough to dig up and dispose of the cylinder. It should have inflated a liferaft in about a minute.

So I was now without a liferaft and a new one would cost over a £1,000. That was if I had not been the Survival and Rescue Officer. The RAFO had sold its Defender aircraft and the new owner did not want their 4 man liferafts. I was asked what to do with them and I decided to help the Sultan by taking two of them and keeping the others for evaluation. African Ocean now had liferafts and as they were in soft valises (covers) I could easily carry out an annual survey myself.

That winter was my last in Oman. I had trained up an Omani to take over my job and the previous year two members of my mess had died through heart attack (one in bed with his new Philippine wife). I had achieved what I wanted, an ocean going boat, and Lis and I thought it was the correct time to leave.

There was time for one last performance with the Muscat Amateur Theatre which was outside, at the swimming pool of the Al Bustan Palace hotel and I had an almost non-talking role but it was great fun as I got to fall into the pool and ham it up. There were Hash runs and Hash parties to go to. I also celebrated my 50th birthday by having 50 people at my villa and getting the food cooked by the Sergeants' mess and getting the Omani and Asian staff, in full uniform, to serve and wait.

In the spring I entered African Ocean for the Dubai to Muscat race and again came first in the class. There was a weekend in the Al Bustan Hotel and then it was saying goodbye to Muscat. I had advertised for crew and a young man called James Gibbs agreed to join the boat in Salalah and crew until the Mediterranean. I did not realise that James was a blossoming artist, specialising in fish and later he became very well known. If you Google 'James Gibbs fish artist' you will see his work. Sadly he died earlier this century at, I believe, a monastery, but his beautiful art will be appreciated for many years.

Desert Survival Training

Jkames Gibbs Fish Artist

Chapter 29
Voyages of African Ocean 1994-2004

L is and I sailed to Salalah and this was the first time that Lis had kept a night watch on her own and it was a big learning curve for her. I was awoken three times for the same light, which was a vessel that had overtaken us earlier. Lis became excellent crew and soon was able to manage the boat herself at night.

I wish I could say the same for James. I think that the best way to describe him was aged 27, going on for 12. When he first came onboard Lis was not keen on him but I thought him OK. By the time we had reached the Red Sea I despaired of him but Lis thought that he was funny and sort of cute. Art was everything to James. Every morning watch he would paint watercolour pictures and as it was flat calm and windless he would lay them out to dry on the ample deck space that a catamaran offers. At about 1000 the diurnal sea breeze would kick in and his paintings would blow over the side, disintegrating when they fell into the sea. Tears would follow. This happened day after day. He also used to spend hours in the heads (toilet). On one occasion he was in there so long that Lis was complaining and needed urgent access. I had a gas-canister powered signalling horn, made of red plastic. I leaned over the side, placing the horn in through the heads window and operated it. Being upside down, instead of the expected loud OOOP, it made a spluttering noise and the gas came out in a mist. James dashed out the heads with his shorts around his ankles, almost knocking Lis over screaming that a Martian had put his red nose through the window and breathed fire over him. Lis had to make an even quicker entry into the heads when she heard this, collapsing with laughter. I never told James what really happened.

Unbeknown to us, James was 'water diabetic' and needed to drink at least 6 bottles of water a day. This meant that he had to urinate frequently. I once went into his cabin in the starboard bow and found half a dozen bottles of urine in there. When we asked him why, he explained that he needed to pee at night and didn't want to go to the heads on the other side of the boat. I made some remark about if he could pee in the narrow neck of a bottle he had better not get married and Lis said that as every night had light winds, and the sea was flat, why didn't he just climb through the large hatch onto the fore deck and pee over the side. He thought that this was a splendid idea and the next night, when I was in bed in the port bow cabin, I heard James unclip his hatch and climb up onto the deck. This was followed by a scream from Lis, who was on watch 'No James, the other side!' and James saying 'I can't stop. I can't stop' as he 'got his own back', peeing into the wind. I had a good giggle about this and went back to sleep. Sometime later I heard James again opening his hatch and once again a scream from Lis to use the other side. 'But Lis you told me to use this side last time and I can't stop.' 'James we have tacked!' explained Lis. After this, James always had to ask Lis which side he should use, as he was unable to work out which was the windward and which was the leeward side.

Lis and I have many stories about James, too many to go in this book.

Our plan was to call into Aden to refuel, re-victual (sailors eat victuals, not food!), fill our water tanks and buy James another 60 bottles of water for the 10 day estimated passage up the Red Sea. The night before we were due to arrive, Lis called me on deck and said that there was either a fantastic thunder storm over Yemen or they were having a firework display. It was bombs and rockets exploding; they were at war. Next morning, when closer to Aden, I called Aden port control on the VHF radio and was told to keep away and that the harbour was closed as there was fighting in the town. Plan B would have to be followed – but I had not got a plan B.

I had detailed charts of the Red Sea but the next suitable harbour was either Jeddah in Saudi Arabia or Port Sudan, both hundreds of miles away. I also had a small scale chart covering all of the Red Sea and then saw Djibouti, in the north east corner of Africa, which had a harbour that was easily accessible. That was only a hundred miles away, a day's sail, so we decided to alter course and try to find our way into the harbour and hope that they would allow us entry. I had a book showing all the flags of the world and various coloured cloth and James did a good job in making the correct curtesy pennant (flag) that had to be flown from the starboard yard arm when in their waters. The book had not proven infallible. On the voyage to Oman we made a South Yemen flag before our planned entry into Aden but when our plan changed and we went to Mocha, which was in North Yemen, we made a different flag. When we arrived there, we were told that we had the wrong flag. The book had them the wrong way round!

A visit to Djibouti by yacht is not an experience that I want to repeat. We made our way to the yacht club and were allocated a mooring by a delightful French secretary. She was the only person who spoke to us, from the French expatriate populated yacht club. In Oman, if a visiting yacht was seen in the harbour, they would be welcomed by all sailors and have a very full social programme. In Djibouti we were completely ignored. I thought this was because of our UK Red Ensign but I have since spoken to a Frenchman, who also visited Djibouti, and he said that he had the same treatment, and called the expatriates there French peasants who thought that they were superior beings!

I was offered a lot of money by journalist, who wanted to be taken over to Aden to report on the civil war, but had no difficulty in refusing. If the Yeminis did not kill me, Lis most certainly would have!

The town was very poor but, with help from the secretary, we did manage to re-provision and get 20 cartons of bottled water. I have made it a rule never to bring cartons into the boat and there it paid dividends. Every carton was crawling with cockroaches and the bottles were incrusted with cockroach eggs. We took one box at a time from the inflatable tender onto the stern and scraped off the eggs, before scrubbing each bottle with fresh bleach water. It took hours, delaying our departure. It was worth every minute as we never saw any cockroaches onboard.

Delegating some of the scrubbing to James, I decided to tidy and prepare the boat prior to departure and, spying a black rubbish sack in the saloon, decided to row ashore and 'bin' it. After our anti-cockroach blitz and having used a lot of water from our tanks, cleaning the bottles and washing every crevice where cockroaches could hide, it was prudent to refill them, so we slipped from the buoy and went alongside the jetty and started re-filling the tanks. Whilst alongside, James mentioned that he had just seen a male native wearing a dress just like Lis's. She looked and agreed – and then exclaimed that it was hers and there were also other natives wearing her clothes, clothes which she had carefully laundered and left in a black rubbish sack in the saloon! All three of us rushed ashore and started stripping Lis's clothes of the local men and woman, who vociferously protested about losing their haut couture. We manage to retrieve most of Lis's wardrobe and then spent another hour re-washing everything and a glaring Lis made sure that I carried them back onboard safely before we left the jetty shortly before nightfall, hours later than I had hoped.

As we entered Djibouti harbour, we had passed a departing yacht and spoke to them. They were also proceeding north, to Suez, and we agreed to look out for each other. The second night after leaving Djibouti, we picked up a 'Mayday Relay' message on the VHF. This form of message is a repeat of a Mayday distress call from another vessel. The originator of the Mayday call was the yacht that we had spoken to on VHF when entering Djibouti. I tried calling the yacht directly but it was too far away, although did manage to contact the ship relaying the distress call. The captain told me that the yacht had run aground and was taking on water. He had called the nearest maritime rescue but they would not be able to help for 24 hours. He had then told the yacht that help would be with them soon. I told the captain that he should tell the yacht about the 24 hour wait so they could make appropriate plans, but he said that he did not want to worry the yacht's crew! I never found out what happened to them.

This distress call was also interfered with by the disgusting, dangerous, behaviour of some other ships. During both the southbound and northbound transit of the Red Sea there was serious abuse of VHF channel 16, the distress channel. Ships were singing out, 'Filipino Monkey', followed by crude, vulgar and abusive language. This was being transmitted during, and interrupting, this Mayday relay. The captain of the relaying ship broadcast,' All Philippine ships, please keep quiet during this Mayday'. Another ship then broadcast' It's not Philippine ships it is those Pakistan B********.' Followed by a different voice, saying 'Who are you calling a B******, you Filipino Twat' and so it went on. This abuse often went on for hours and at night I had to turn down the volume of the VHF to get some sleep. I hope that abuse has now stopped. I never heard it outside of the Red Sea.

As often happen at the southern end of the Red Sea, the southerly wind increased, as did the sea state. Waves soon reached 6 meters and African Ocean proved that she was a true blue water cruising boat. We frequently touched 18 knots (21 mph) and the wind vane steering worked well until an out of sync wave caused us to broach (turn to the side). With a loud crack, the wooden servo-power rudder of the steering gear broke and I had to quickly disengage it and revert to hand steering. I had another rudder as spare but if that broke I would have to rely on the electric auto-pilot, which for some reason was temperamental during the heat of the day. James had also already made great inroads in our drinking water, so I decided to call into Jeddah, Saudi Arabia, for a new rudder to be made and for more water.

Jeddah was not chosen lightly, being in a strict Muslim country but it was closer than Port Sudan, an alternative harbour. We called Jeddah port control and they said it was not a problem and would send a launch out to pilot us in to a jetty berth. There was already a Spanish yacht alongside the jetty and we tied up behind her. The Saudi custom officer came onboard and asked the usual questions (any firearms, drugs or alcohol?). When we admitted that we had alcohol, he said that it must be locked up in a cabin. As the cabins had no lock, a strip of security tape was stuck on the door, after the customs officer had suggested that whilst he fetched the tape, maybe we could take out any bottles we wanted.

A soldier was stationed day and night on the jetty and we were not allowed more than 50 yards from the boat. This meant that we could visit the Spanish yacht. Raul, the captain, complained that he had been there three weeks and the Saudis were very unhelpful and also informed us that the Eid, holiday period, after the holy month of Ramadan, had started and would last for days. This was something we had forgotten about. The next day we were ignored and James' drinking water was decreasing at an even greater rate than before. On the third day I decided that we would have to leave and sail over to Port Sudan, but first permission to leave had to be granted by the Saudis. Lis and I went onto the jetty and were stopped by the guard.

We told him he was a smart Jundi (soldier) and a credit to the King and that we would like to speak to his Raqeeb (sergeant). He agreed and took us to meet him. Again, after traditional greetings, he was complimented and we then asked to speak to his Naqeeb (officer). When I say 'we', to be perfectly honest, most of the talking was by Lis, who spoke very good Arabic, whilst after the greetings, my Arabic dried up. The Raqeeb took us to see the Naqeeb, who offered us coffee, dates etc. and was dazzled by Lis and her Arabic. Suddenly, we were interrupted by the arrival of the area commander, who was carrying out his Eid inspection. More, deluxe, refreshments were brought out and again Lis worked her charm and eventually I was asked why we were there. I apologised for taking up their time and said that we would like to leave and go to Port Sudan. 'Why?' I was asked. I replied that we did not realise that it was Eid and, understanding the importance of it to Muslims, did not want to inconvenience them by asking for their assistance. The commander replied that it was no inconvenience and said that we were guests. A new wooden rudder would be made and we could get more water and victuals. When we asked about a visa to go into town, he said that it was not necessary as he would supply transport, driver and guards. Was there anything else we needed? I then mention Raul, on the Spanish yacht, and his problem. 'Yes. He does not know how to talk to us.' was the reply. I refrained from quoting Basil Fawlty and saying that he came from Barcelona, but did say that he was a simple Spanish sailor. Thirty minutes later we were back onboard African Ocean, A carpenter was waiting for us, fuel had been arranged, a staff car and driver was waiting and engineers had come to the Spanish boat. Living for 9 years in Oman and understanding how to behave with Arabs and having female crew who spoke Arabic, opened all doors and, before sunset, we had new rudder (and a spare, spare), were fully bunkered with fuel and water, and had kilos of fresh fruit and lockers that were bulging with food. Next morning we sailed for our next port of Port Sudan. What could go wrong now?

A northerly force 7 that blew up rapidly the next morning! Lis and I were attempting to reef the mainsail and James was steering when he became distracted and allowed the boat to tack. I was hit on the head by the boom and had to lie down for half an hour to recover and the mainsail tore from the luff edge at the front edge to almost the leech edge at the back. It was unusable and we had no spare. When I gathered my wits again, I looked for a sheltered anchorage and found a coral reef marked on the chart, not many miles away. I thought that it may give us some respite from the waves whilst we repaired the sail. In a few hours we were anchored in the lee (sheltered side) of the reef and the waves were much diminished. It was still too windy to lay the sail on the deck to start the repair but the following morning it was calm enough to start work.

I had planned for torn sails but had not expected such a large rip. I cut a long, narrow length of sailcloth and glued it to both parts of the torn sail with impact adhesive, hammering it to make a sturdy join. We than had to spend two days stitching the long, glued patch in-place, adding extra strength to the join. I used a leather-workers awl and a pair of pliers to do the stitching and both Lis's and my hands were sore at the finish of the work. It is very difficult to push a needle through layers of sail cloth.

Just as we completed the work, the wind changed, which meant we had to move the boat as we were now on the windward, dangerous side, of the reef. This southerly wind, which was most unusual at that time of year, was in our favour and blew us north to Port Suez, halving the time we expected to take. The weavers of fate had tested and were now rewarding us.

Amazingly, no cigarettes were required to bribe the military whilst heading north through the canal to the Med. Even the Egyptian pilot refused, saying he hated the baksheesh mentality. He said that he had to give his son money to give to the teacher at his school.

After a short stop in Cyprus we ended up in Rhodes – but you will find that locals call it Rodos. It was here that we said goodbye to James. We did some sailing around the area and as Lis had decided that she enjoyed navigating, I left that aspect of boating to her. I confined my navigating to taking compass bearings and plotting fixes on the chart, whenever the possibility arose.

We were soon joined by Lis's family from Denmark. We were sailing around the Greek island of Symi with the family, which we had circumnavigated before, and Lis explained to her sister how we used the GPS (satellite Global Positioning System), reading the latitude and longitude position, and then transferring that position to the paper chart. Later she came to me and asked if I would check her plotting, as instead of being the expected half a mile to the east of Symi, she had plotted a position on top of a mountain. I promised to do so but after an Ouzo or two that night in a taverna...

Next day, whilst sailing a few dozen yards off the western coast of Symi, Lis asked if I had checked her plotting. I explained about the pressure of Ouzo etc. and went below to plot our position as shown on the GPS. According to my plotting, we were 1.8 miles to the west of Symi, not close to the shore.

The penny then dropped. When I looked at the latest UK Admiralty chart I had bought in Rhodes, it had no Datum printed on it (a datum is the 'anchor' that all land positions are calculated and plotted from) and the GPS had WGS 84 (World Geodic Survey 1984) set, which is the latest datum and used for all new charts that use GPS. All the land on the chart was approximately 1.8 Nm out towards the east. A chronometer problem I assume, whilst being charted over 100 years ago by British seamen. The reason I did not pick this up before was that whenever I had the chance, I used traditional navigating, fixing my position by known objects with a magnetic compass and not using the GPS for harbour entries. By all means use the GPS but always check its (or the charts in this case) accuracy by traditional methods if possible. Even now, the latest issue of charts in the eastern part of the Med. do not all conform to WGS84, some are ED50

(European Datum 1950) and corrections are required before plotting.

A year later an Israeli yachtsman told me that since leaving Israel, his GPS was very inaccurate. When I checked, he still had the Israel chart datum on his GPS, not the WGS84 of his Turkish chart.

Something that I had to learn in the Med. was how to moor stern to the jetty, as the alongside berth is not used. It took a lot of practice before I became competent. I found that the secret was dropping the anchor in the correct position (slightly up-wind). Another trick I learnt was to tie a long rope to the anchor chain (use a Rolling Hitch) and take the other end to a bow. Pulling this rope tight pulls the bow towards the anchor. Because of its width, a catamaran has to be perfectly square to a jetty, or one stern will hit, whilst it is not so critical with a monohull (single hull) boat.

Lis had to go to Denmark and I decided to take African Ocean to the UK for refit. My son, Alexander, came with me to Malta but he had to leave there. Needing crew, especially for sailing in the Med, I printed 'Crew Wanted' notices and stuck them on lamp posts. Within 24 hours an American girl, Jenny, turned up and after we had a test sail, she decided to crew with me to Gibraltar.

It was a light wind sail for most of the trip, the only incident worth mentioning is when, at night, off Algeria, a patrol boat roared up out of the darkness and blinded me with its searchlight. It then started to flash Morse code to me. I was pleasantly surprised when I remembered enough Morse to read it, and managed to flash the answers back, using my torch. Its arrival scared me but we parted as friends, with a 'Bon Voyage'.

At the western end of the Med, the never-had-even-been-hoped-for event, the dream beyond dreams of 15 years earlier, happened. I sailed my catamaran into Shepherds Marina, Gibraltar, and I had the largest sailing boat moored there. It was not as slick as I would have liked, as my inexperienced crew, after being instructed by the marina staff instead of waiting for my command, had dropped the anchor too early and we had to retrieve it and re-moor, but that did not dent my pride. Another great surprise was to meet up with a very good aircrewman friend from my navy days, Bob Venables.

After a few days revisiting once familiar places, it was time to leave Gib. and start the finale leg to Falmouth, where I intended to refit African Ocean ready for further blue water voyaging. Jenny, my crew, decided to stay onboard and accompany me for this leg as well.

A couple of days after leaving, when past Cape Finisterre, we were beset by an Atlantic gale, blowing from the North West. I had a very small storm jib (headsail) hanked on (connected), ready for use but still in its bag, and a reefed (partially rolled up) headsail. With these precautions, and with a small, reefed mainsail, we slowly and comfortably made our way north for the first 24 hours with winds gusting over 40 knots (46 mph). African Ocean showed her true blue water ability and we were able to peel potatoes and cook a proper meal in the pressure cooker on the fixed, non-swinging, gas cooker. As per my daily routine I even managed to go around the boat at first and last light to inspect for damage and wear. Unfortunately there was one place that I missed. In the middle of the second night, the furling line, that kept the headsail rolled up and small, parted where it went through a plastic fairlead (guide), and the big sail rapidly unrolled to its maximum size. This full sized sail was much too powerful and the bow was being forced down into the sea.

The sail was also flogging madly (sails flog, flags flap) and beating against the wire shrouds that held the mast up and it very quickly started shredding itself, with the strips knotting around the wire. This made it impossible to re-reef, even by attaching extra line to the broken one.

Because of the torn strips of sail attaching themselves to the shrouds, it was also impossible to lower the sail and now it was catching the waves, making things even more dangerous. There was only one remedy that I could think of, and that was climb up the mast and cut the sail free with a knife.

Thankfully, African Ocean had steps bolted to the mast, all the way to the top. If not Jenny would have had the almost impossible task of winching me up in a gale from a violently pitching deck in the dark, and she had never done it before, not even in harbour. I got into a 'Bosun's chair', a sit-in safety harness, shackled on a lifting halyard, and instructed Jenny to take the slack down as I climbed, and wrap it around a restraining cleat. Once I was more than head height above her, communications were very difficult because of the screaming of the wind and the hissing crash of the sea, but somehow I managed to reach the top of the sail and slowly cut it free, from top to bottom. Much of the time I was swinging through the air, crashing into the mast, shrouds and sail but after a bruising, exhausting hour, we managed to cut the sail free of the wire shrouds. It was then possible to lower the remains of the headsail, bundle it into a big locker and cut free most of the remnants which were still attached to the shrouds. The remainder was removed after dawn. All I had to do now was hoist the already rigged storm sail and the drama was over. Once again African Ocean made her way slowly and safely towards Falmouth. I think that if we had been on a heeling and rolling monohull instead of a reasonably stable catamaran, it would not have been possible to do this act.

The next day the wind started to decrease in strength, leaving an uncomfortably large sea and by the following morning the wind had almost died away. Jenny and I had just finished breakfast in the saloon and I was considering starting an engine when we heard a strange 'whoosh' from outside. We rushed on deck and saw a large whale, about 100 yards behind us, looking at us with beady eyes. It then dived and a few minutes later surfaced again, this time a bit closer. This was repeated many times, each surfacing closer than the last. When the sounding (diving) time was checked, each one was within a second or so of the last. Eventual it was less than five yards away from the stern and I was worried it might surface directly under us, so I started an engine, which caused it to disappear, never to be seen again.

We had survived the storm but now the problem was the lack of wind blowing into our small storm sail and we were only making a knot or two (about 3mph) and Falmouth was still many miles away. I had another sail, called a drifter, which was used in light winds when going down wind but was not designed for going into wind, so I decided to modify it and sewed a rope to all three edges to strengthen it. I could then use it like a normal headsail, with the luff (front edge) pulled tight and sail towards the wind. With this modified sail we continued towards Falmouth and once there I arranged a re-fit of a different system of mainsail reefing (an attachment to the mast so that the mainsail could be rolled up), three new sails made and an emergency wire stay fitted that could be used if needed. The boat was left at David Calne's chandlery at Penryn and I travelled to Denmark to see Lis, hoping to be able to earn enough money to pay for everything.

Winter in Denmark with Lis was enjoyable and to pay for the refit of African Ocean. I got a job cleaning in the 5 star Hotel D'Angleterre in Copenhagen. Cleaning is a very stress free job, even though it can be quite physical. I was earning £15 an hour when working unsociable hours, which was the same amount as offered to me in Cornwall for an eight hour night shift as a security guard.

Because of a dispute between the cleaning company and the hotel, we were all dismissed after two months and for a week I had the experience of being in a picket line in the snow. Luckily, my reputation as a conscientious worker somehow got to other hotels and I ended up working in three different hotels. I started in one, near home, at 0530. The job was timed at 4 hours but, with the manager's consent, I managed to finish by 0830 and then it was time to go home, have a leisurely breakfast with Lis before she went to work and then on to another hotel until 1300, have lunch and then work for four hours at another hotel. Apart from cleaning I also made up beds. Now whenever I stay at a hotel, I always leave a tip under the pillow for the hardworking staff. Hotel cleaning is not a glamorous job but one that paid very well. After deductions, I was earning over £600 for a 6 day week, a very good sum in 1986. A year later I was sent £300 holiday pay from the Danish Government!

In May I started to look for crew to join Lis and me sailing back to the Med. A crew of four was an insurance requirement to cross the Bay of Biscay in June and we soon found a Danish couple, who proved admirable, and at the end of May Lis and I went to Falmouth and finished off the odd jobs needed after a new reefing system and a small water-maker had been installed and a new electric 'smart' charging system fitted.

I also found time to do a RYA (Royal Yachting Association) course to become a Yacht Master. After four days preparation I had the examination and was asked if I was a Coastal Skipper, the level below Yacht Master. I said no, I had no yachting qualification (I had printed and composed my own qualification in Oman and it had been accepted by the Egyptians to transit the canal).'How about Competent Crew?' asked the examiner, (the lowest, beginner's course). I shook my head and told him that I had recently sailed my yacht to Oman and back to England and showed him my logbook. He agreed that I might pass the exam and he was right. Half of the examinees made it to Yacht Master.

A couple of weeks later our crew joined and then it was goodbye to Cornwall and England and we were heading south to the sun.

It really was a cruise, sailing south, the wind was from the west, giving good sailing conditions and the sun shone. We day sailed down the Portuguese coast and left our crew at Lisbon, then went to Gibraltar (Shephard's Marina again) before leaving for the long leg to Malta. That was our intention but Neptune decided otherwise by blowing an easterly light gale, which kicked up a very uncomfortable sea, so we decided to call in at

Costa de Sol until the wind and swell moderated. I was about to learn a lesson in over-confidence which I doubtless deserved.

After entering the harbour and calling the Marina on VHF, I realised that I had to change course drastically to starboard, but instead of slowing down and using the rudder as any sensible mariner would do, I decided to show off the agility of a catamaran with two engines, by using the port engine 'ahead' and the starboard 'astern'. Instead of turning quickly to starboard, we increased speed, going forward, directly towards the harbour wall. I quickly put the starboard engine hard astern and two things happened. We went faster and started to turn to port, the wrong way. I then realised that for some reason, the starboard engine was still going 'ahead', not 'astern' and turning the boat to port. When I realised that, I turned the wheel rapidly and put both engines in neutral. How we avoid hitting the wall I don't know, I was expecting to feel a crash and hear crushing fibreglass, but nothing happened. I motored slowly into the marine and when I inspected the defective engine found that the gear change cable had broken, leaving the engine in 'ahead'. Lesson learnt was always to expect something to go wrong and plan ahead.

A couple of days later we left the marina at Costa Sol and in calmer seas headed for Malta and then Greece with no drama, just a new experience and finding a new friend.

We were about 10 miles short of Kithara, the westerly Greek island which was our destination, when we received a Pan-Pan call on the VHF radio. This signifies a vessel that has a problem but is not in immediate danger. It came from an Italian yacht that had engine trouble and, in the light winds, was having difficulties reaching harbour. We rigged a tow rope and pulled him into the harbour and arranged to meet that night in a local taverna. The skipper was a well-known, (to the Italians) as a political cartoonist and in the summer he moved onboard his yacht, listened to the news on the radio and drew suitable cartoons. In the evening he would carry his fax machine to the tavern, (before we had smart phones etc.) and fax the cartoons to his editors. I was so envious; what a wonderful use of talent and lifestyle.

Our next port, after Kithara, was Santorini, the magical remains of a volcanic island that exploded thousands of years ago and was probably the origin of the legendry island of Atlantis. The volcano exploded from deep below the earth's surface, which is now a hundred or so metres below sea level. The majority of the original island is far under the turquoise depths that we sailed over when approaching from the west. The town of Santorini is perched hundreds of metres high on the surviving easterly side of the island, with a lift or donkeys carrying visitors up to the town, whilst the sun setting through the haze over Europe is a sight not to be missed.

With Santorini miles behind us and our destination of Rhodes, to the east, miles ahead, Lis took over the watch at 0100 and with only a couple of stern lights of distant ships showing I retired to the after cabin for a few hours' sleep.

I was awoken by a banging on the deck and Lis calling for me to come up quickly. I did so and I was confronted by a large ship, less than a mile away, directly ahead of us. It was a mass of lights of every colour. 'It just came from nowhere' said Lis. 'Which way is it going?' I asked. 'I can't tell' she said. I really didn't need the binoculars as the ship was so close, but used them just the same. I could not distinguish any navigation or steaming lights on the ship. If it had any they were overpowered by the thousands of party lights that were in the rigging, superstructure and around the deck. Although we were sailing and was the 'stand on vessel', I had to alter course but which way was the safe way? I decided to turn to port and tack onto a reciprocal heading as opposed to starboard and gybe.

The vessel overtook us at high speed a few hundred yards away, departing on our port side, eventually showing a stern, overtaking, light. When it was well clear I tacked back onto our original course and asked how this situation happened, as

I knew that Lis was a very conscientious watch keeper and it must have been something abnormal.

She indicated another, more distant, stern light on our starboard side and told me that she had been watching that ship approach from port. It was also garland with coloured lights but its navigation and steaming lights were identifiable and she was happy that it was going to pass well ahead. As it came safely ahead she searched the rest of the arc around us to check that nothing was coming from behind. I had frequently told her that most yachts are hit from abaft the beam (behind) and she had been concentrating for some time on the crossing vessel. When she looked ahead again, the first ship had cleared but the second one had appeared, seemingly from nowhere.

I mused on these details and then I realised what had happened. The first ship, which Lis had seen and which passed safely ahead, had been concealing a second vessel, which also was converging from the east. The hidden vessel's course took it astern of the one seen when just ahead of us, and it would probably not have detected us by radar, as the bulk of the first ship would have hidden us. The party lights of the closest ship had made is impossible for Lis to see the furthest vessel and the more distant, second ship would not have seen ours.

Lesson learnt, beware the hidden ship and from the deck of a yacht it is sometimes impossible to see the navigation or steaming lights of a ship covered in lights, as most Mediterranean ferries and cruise ships are. Also don't expect them to see you.

For the next few months African Ocean was based in Rhodes and we visited most of the islands in the Greek Cyclades. Rhodes is a historically interesting place to visit, even if the purest scoff at the way that Mussolini's Italy rebuilt the citadel – stone cannonballs sticking out of castle walls?! If the Italians had not restored Rhodes, nor would the Greeks, and it would be pile of rubble today. The only drawback to Rhodes is the popularity it has with tourists and that every bar plays 'Zorba's dance' many times every night. We did discover a local, family run, restaurant,

Langanis, close to the western gate, which tourists don't very often find. The seafood platters are excellent – and there is no Zorba dancing! I eat there every time I visit the Island.

In 1996, we had a Danish friend visiting and she asked if we could go to Turkey, which so far we had avoided doing. Lis and I had enough Muslim country experience not to want to go there. For the sake of our friend, we decided to bite the bullet and go. First we needed a Turkish courtesy flag, which I bought from a local chandlery. The owner was quite disgusted that I was deserting Greece and visiting the heathen enemy across the water, and told me stories about how backward and unfriendly the Turks were.

It is only a few hours' sail across the Rhodes channel, past Symi and north to Datcha on the Turkish mainland. We hoisted our Turkish courtesy flag and dressed appropriately for our Islamic hosts. I wore trousers and Lis put on a long skirt, long sleeve top and covered her hair. We were amazed to be greeted by a pretty Turkish policewoman wearing a short skirt with uncovered hair and saw the beach draped in bikini clad women. We were also, very politely told that our flag was not the Turkish flag, and they gave us a real one, free. I did mention that the Greeks hate the Turks and I had bought the flag in Greece...

I did stagger back when told that the charges for entering Turkey was 650,000 lira but then found out that 1,000,000 lira was worth £15.60p. To show you how bad Turkish inflation has been in the last 25 years, £1 in 2021 was worth about 10,000,000 (old) lira. The new (yeni) Turkish lira is worth 1,000,000 old lira so it is now, 2021, 11Tl to £1.

We very quickly fell in love with the country-side and the people. They were the friendliest race we had ever met and we were determined to spend more time with them. It was very enlightening to hear their side of the Greek-Turkish rivalry and obviously the truth of the matter is somewhere near the middle. After a week exploring the Datcha peninsular we changed courtesy as we sailed back to Rhodes.

Autumn was arriving and we had to make the decision where to stay for the winter. It may be a surprise to some people, but the Mediterranean does have a winter, complete with storms, rain (snow has been seen in eastern Med. resorts) and cold. Most 'live-aboards', as full time yacht-folk call themselves, find a snug, safe, mooring or marina. We decided to sail east to Lebanon before cold weather arrived and then probably go to Cyprus for the winter. Why Lebanon? Lis had been told by a friend that it was a to-visit place and I had heard about the Cedar forests. That's enough reason for a live-aboard to move their home a few hundred miles.

Lebanon was not to be a three day dash but a leisurely cruise along the Turkish coast, with no time limit defined. A yachting friend strongly recommended that we visit Göcek, in the North West corner of the large Bay of Fethiye, so that was pencilled into our itinerary, but first we would 'check in' to Turkey at Marmaris, just a few hours sailing time from Rhodes. Arrival was delayed slightly as we discovered a small inflatable boat with an old man and two young children onboard who were trying to paddle unsuccessfully, with one oar, into a bay a mile away, against a very strong wind. We pulled them and the boat onboard and sailed into the bay and, in the calm lee of the land allowed them to paddle the last 10 yards to the beach and their anxious family.

I must confess, Marmaris is not my favourite town. It has a beautiful large harbour, golden sands and the mandatory Byzantine castle. It also has hundreds of bars and thousands of revelling tourists, as well as no curfew on the disco music when all-night clubs crank up the volume to attract customers. If this is your idea of a holiday then you will also like Bodrum, on the western side of Turkey. Personally, I grew out of this form of holiday shortly after being old enough to draw my daily tot in the navy.

Just a day-sail further took us to Fethiye Korfez (Bay) and we entered the little village of Göcek in the top left corner and were instantly enamoured by its charm. The bays and coast around that area are stunning, with ruins of old Christian monasteries, Lycian tombs and cities, Byzantine cities and walls, welcoming restaurants plus many secure, peaceful, anchorages with trees coming down to the shore.

We were hooked; we decided to stay the winter in that area and booked a berth in a little marina, Yes Marine, in Fethiye, 12 miles away in the North East corner of the korfez, for the winter. In no time at all we seem to know, and be known by most of the inhabitants of Göcek. That sleepy little village of 1996 is still a great destination but no longer sleepy. The building of three large marinas has attracted hundreds of yachts and very few of the original buildings remain. A lot of the land surrounding Göcek is covered in (mainly holiday) homes and there are now about a dozen hotels but thankfully not hi-rise. Göcek is still one of the best kept secrets on the Turquoise Coast, as that part of Turkey is called. I have seen Sting, Dustan Hoffman, Naomi Campbell, Tina Turner, Shakira, the late Princess Margret, UK ministers and other famous people there. I was told that Diane, Princess of Wales, went there on her 'Greek' cruise. If you think you have seen someone there that you know, you are probably right. There are also a few UK TV personalities, who have farms and homes locally.

We became particularly friendly with Ali and Aisha Erkman, who ran the Zbar, the only bar and restaurant in the village when it was first 'discovered' by Turkish tourists when it needed a Land Rover to reach it, over the mountainous dirt track. Ali was also a yacht agent and he persuaded us to get a charter licence for the following year. We did not need much persuading, it would be a dream, sailing in that area and getting paid for doing so. There was also the fact that my savings, that were going to support my cruising for about five years, had disappeared, or rather my 'financial advisor', who was based in Dubai, had, with my portfolio! It took two years before I got back the 50% that remained after he had helped himself.

We intended to continue our voyage to Lebanon in the spring of 1997 but in the end decided to join the East Med Yacht Rally, which started in Istanbul and visited Turkish ports before going to North Cyprus, (Kibrus as the Turks call it), and then to Israel and finally to the Bitter Lakes midway along the Suez Canal. We decided to join the rally at Bodrum and leave after Israel. It was a hectic schedule, with parties almost every night. On the leg around Kibrus, we heard a Pan-Pan on the VHF radio from a German yacht on the rally, which had lost its propeller after hitting some of the 'Sargasso Sea' of rubbish which collects to the east of Cyprus. We motored to the yacht and took him in tow, using engine and sails in the light winds. I hoped another yacht had taken a photo of us, but it was not to be. We were very happy to be given a large piece of ham as thanks for our action. Klaus and Hanne, the German owners, became good friends with us.

The last leg from Famagusta (Gazimağusa in Turkish), N Cyprus, to Ashkelon, Israel, was an overnight trip and because of the number of ships around, Lis and I were in the cockpit for much of it. Early in the morning we had a call on the VHF from the Israeli Navy, asking who we were and what we wanted, which we gave the appropriate reply to. A short while later the same female radio operator called another yacht, asking the same questions. That yacht was called Crazy Lady and the radio operator was also a woman. Instead of replying, 'Israeli Navy, this is Crazy Lady' it came out as 'Israeli Nazy this is Crazy Lazy – no, Lazy Crazy – Crazy – Nazy', followed by hysterical giggling. Then a man's voice said 'Give me the microphone woman. 'Israeli Navy this is Lady Crazy – Oh bollocks!' followed by even more giggling from the Israeli navy operator. It certainly made us smile.

For most of us, Ashkelon was not a successful visit. After an all-night sail everyone was tired and very few of us wanted to get onto the arranged coach that was waiting to take us to the Holy sites. We reasoned that as it was a long drive, we could catch up with some sleep on the coach, but it was not to be. The tour guide was a brash American voiced woman who had no empathy with 30 tired yacht-folk. She could not understand our reluctance to sing Hava Nagela or any other jolly song, despite being told that we had been up all night, but an hour's sleep would set us right. She did her best (worst!) to involve us in her version of entertainment but she lost the battle. A bus full of tired and now irate sailors disembarked and started the ritual pilgrimage around the Holy Land sights. Everywhere we went was full of tourists, with guides carrying umbrellas or coloured cards, hurrying their groups along and chivvying anyone who dared to look too long at anything. The word 'Holy' was not in many peoples' minds and we were all very happy to get back on the coach and have a sleep before the evening's party started.

The next port of call in Israel was Haifa and we were lucky enough to meet a Jewish family who hosted us and became friends. They commiserated when we mentioned about the coach trip and tour and told us we must visit the Bahai gardens in Haifa. We asked what was special about them and were told that we would find out.

As soon as we stepped into the Bahai gardens it was like another world: tranquil and serene. It was the most peaceful place I have ever visited, yet I can't explain why. Both of us felt completely relaxed, with an inner calmness. We saw a young lady who was some sort of nun and asked her what Bahaism was, expecting a 'hard sell' but she just led us to a small temple-like structure and told us that there was information and if we wanted more we could write and ask. The information there told us that it was an Islamic sect and anyone could join. If I hadn't discovered that it had temperance – no drinking, I would have joined like a shot. It was a moving experience and the feeling of 'Holiness' there was the only time I felt it in Israel.

We discovered that a Danish friend from Oman was the nurse in-charge of a new hospital being built in Palestine, and we managed to cross the border to see her. What a difference between two countries. On one side of the border, wide roads, green verges and gardens, clean streets, smart houses, the other dirt, old buildings and poverty. Our friend, Anne, told us that the people were so poor that despite having guards, almost every night, equipment and beds disappeared from the hospital. I am sure that things have not improved. There is an old saying; that if what you are doing doesn't work, do something else. It is a pity that the Israeli and Palestinian governments don't listen to that adage. Violence never solves a conflict, only goodwill and talk. There is always a pathway to peace but it may require more intelligence than many leaders have.

On the way back to Göcek we stopped for a couple of days in Akrotiri, South Cyprus, before entering Turkey at Fethiye. It was then time to start our new career as a charter yacht, taking tourists of all nationalities out for weeks at a time.

One of our favourite charters was a South African couple, Leon and Mary. They were a very likable pair but Leon, who enjoyed helping on the boat, was rather accident prone and was the first to admit it. He told us the story of when they and a friend had charted a Greek boat with skipper Yannis.

After a few weeks of cruising around the Greek islands, they had told Yannis that they wanted to go to Turkey. Yannis was appalled; who in their right mind would go to Turkey? They were savages in Turkey whilst the Greeks were the best people in the world and so forth. Leon and company insisted, so, with very bad grace, Yannis agreed to take them to Bodrum, a Turkish harbour in the Aegean Sea.

It seems that Yannis was rather 'laid back' as a skipper, not planning ahead and then doing everything at the rush – the last moment. When the boat arrived at Bodrum they were directed to moor, stern to the jetty and using their anchor, in a narrow gap between two large Turkish boats. True to form, Yannis had nothing prepared for mooring so he shouted out instructions like a machine gun. 'Get the ropes ready, put the fenders out both sides, Leon, untie the dinghy (which was being towed at the stern) and take it to the front, tie it on. Leon, get the anchor ready, untie it, switch the winch on. Hurry, hurry.' The ladies got the ropes and fenders out and tied on, Leon ran backwards and forwards dragging the dingy through the water and securing it at the bow, going below to switch the electric power on and then forward again, untying the anchor and get it hanging, ready for the order to lower it to the seabed from Yannis. This came very quickly as Yannis reversed at high speed between the two Turkish boats. 'Out now Leon, out now, quick quick!' Leon did as he was told and winched out the anchor chain at full speed. When close to the jetty Yannis shouted 'Stop, stop Leon', expecting the anchor, digging into the seabed, to stop the boat but it didn't and only by using full engine power forward did Yannis avoid a crash against the jetty. Yannis let out a torrent of Greek to Leon and then, in English, asked why he had not stopped the anchor going out when told to do so. Leon denied this and then winched in the anchor cable when told to. As the boat, with Greek flag blowing bravely in the wind, motored out of the berth, the noise of Yannis shouting had brought Turkish crews, from the boats both sides on deck and they were busy getting extra fenders out, to protect themselves.

Shouting at Leon that it was his entire fault and this time he must do a better job, Yannis once again started to reverse into the allocated berth. Leon was instructed to drop the anchor and again it required full power to stop hitting the jetty, black smoke belching out of the exhaust. The screaming from Yannis reached a new crescendo as the boat shot out of the berth a second time. 'We are going we are not staying!' bellowed Yannis, as he steered for the exit of the harbour.

It took a lot of persuasion to make Yannis change his mind but eventually he reversed for the third time into the berth and everything went as expected, the anchor dug into the seabed, the boat stopped short of the jetty and the stern lines were attached. This final, successful, attempt was greeted with a round of applause from the not inconsequential crowd of onlookers that had gathered, which enraged Yannis even more. That evening, in the bar, Leon approached Yannis and thanked him for bringing them to Turkey. 'We should not be here,' growled Yannis, 'The Turks are sh*t, the country is sh*t.' 'I think you should know something Yannis,' said a subdued Leon, 'You remember the first two times I dropped the anchor,' Yes, even the seabed here is sh*t' interjected Yannis, 'Well,' said Leon, 'I dropped the anchor into the dinghy,' Leon then, hurried out of the bar as fast as possible and hid for the rest of the night.

I had British (including a Lord), German, French, Spanish, South African, Turkish, Dutch and other nationalities for charters. Mainly it was fun but after a couple of years, Lis decided that it was too hedonistic for her, taking money from people for doing what we enjoyed doing (sailing) and she felt that she needed to go back to Denmark and start nursing again. It was sad to see her go but I understood her reasons. Then world needs more people like her.

African Ocean

Chapter 30
Göcek, Turkey 1998 – 2021

I had already started instructing at the newly opened RYA (Royal Yachting Association) Göcek Sea School, which Duncan Ray and wife Carol managed. Chartering African Ocean was not a weekly event and often I had nothing to do for a month. Chartering alone, with no hostess, was hard work. I was skipper, cook, cleaner, engineer, plumber, deckhand and tour guide. The chartering became less, the instructing more, until I realised that the cost of the charter license was not worth the money. I decide that my chartering days were over.

Teaching sailing allowed me to meet many interesting people, from all over the world. Starting on Boxing Day, on a six day course, I had a father and son from Alaska. When I asked why they wanted to go sailing mid-winter, the reply was 'It's better than being in Alaska at this time of year.' I suppose they had a point.

Another time I had a couple of newly emigrated, Russian Israelis. We were anchored by an island covered in Byzantine ruins, lit by a full moon and were dressed in shorts, finishing off a bottle of good red wine after a meal of wild boar. It was a typical fourth evening of the sailing course. I then noticed that one of the men was crying and asked his friend why. The reply humbled, and reminded me, of how lucky I was in life. 'He is crying because one year ago today, in Russia, he got his permission to emigrate. Never did he dream that a year later he would be sat on a yacht, and in such beautiful surroundings.' Tears rose in my eyes also.

One of my biggest successes was with Professor Peter, from Canada, who came for a two week, Day Skipper course. He said that he had managed to fail two sailing courses in Canada. After the first week I could understand why, His navigating, especially his plotting of fixes was abysmal. When we sat down at the chart table he was good, but at sea he was a long way out. I thought that I had sorted the problem out when, checking the bearings he had taken with the hand held compass, found that they were out by a significant amount of degrees. He could not read a compass, but how was that possible? The night sail provided the answer. When Peter took and plotted the bearings they were spot on, unlike the ones he took during the day. I asked if he had anything different in his pockets that might cause a magnetic deviation during the day, and the answer was negative. I also inquired if he was wearing the same glasses and the answer was yes. Peter then remembered that he had clip on sun filters for them and they were magnetic! His glasses with sun filters were causing the deviation to the hand held compass. I was extremely happy at solving the conundrum and Peter got his certificate.

Sometimes very intelligent people make mistakes that are hilarious to all onboard. Towards the end of one course, a student, who was a senior lawyer, asked why an oil tanker showed a black ball. I said that it didn't and described the symbols and lights that a tanker might display. The lawyer shook her head and said 'No David, you said on the very first day that a black ball meant that I'm a tanker.' The other students and I almost collapsed with laughter. What I had said, was that a black ball means that I'm at anchor. Thereafter it has been called a tanker ball!

My students gave me good feedback about my instructional ability so I decided to put it to the test and try to become a Yacht

Master Instructor. Again I was part of the 50% that passed and I could now instruct on all sailing courses. Duncan and Carol decided to move back to Australia for the education of their two children, and I became the Chief Instructor at Göcek Sea School from 2003 until I gave it up in in 2021.

In case you are rushing off to train as a skipper, I had better remind you that it is not always an idyllic life. I also did charter skippering on other boats and one of these was a boat with the sewage tank (also known as the phew tank) positioned high up in the engine compartment. The tank had become blocked and it was going to require drastic actions to fix it.

We were secured in a secluded bay, with the guests swimming. I had a hostess onboard and I asked her to call the guests onto the land, and I filled two buckets with seawater. When the guests were safe on land I put on my swimming costume, a face mask and snorkel, and told the hostess that I was going into the engine room to clear the holding tank, and she must open the engine compartment door and throw in both bucket of water when I shouted. She then had to stand well clear.

Once closed in the compartment, I used my spanner and unscrewed the outlet pipe at the bottom of the raised tank and as the pipe became detached the inevitable happened, the entire contents of the tank poured over my head. I screamed, two buckets of water hit me and I ran to the upper deck and dived into the once pristine blue water, oozing filth. I did get a large tip from the guests but I do not recommend this action to obtain one.

Have you noticed that we can do good actions and nobody notices, yet make one small slip and everyone knows about it?

African Ocean was in Marmaris, 40 miles west of Göcek, for the winter period. In the spring I decide to bring her back to Göcek. Duncan, who I worked for, had his father from New Zealand visiting and he said he would like to accompany me on the sail east. When I tried to start the starboard engine it refused to work, but that was no problem as the port engine worked fine. We motored out of Marmaris Bay and as the wind picked up, started to hoist the mainsail, only to discover a small tear that would quickly get very long in the freshening wind. That was only a minor problem as the wind would be behind me and the big genoa foresail was all I needed to get to Göcek. I also decided to hoist my large drifter, another sail that was used going downwind, and set it on the other side, so I now had two headsails, wing on wing. It was a wonderful sail, averaging 15 knots as the wind increased. I realised that I was on the very limit of wind speed for the drifter but knew that I could drop that sail as I got in the sheltered lee of the headland west of Fethiye Bay. As I rounded the headland and started heading north towards Göcek, I was surprised that there was no sheltered lee, the wind continued. I was not at all fazed as I was sure that the wind would drop before my last alteration of course, west, into Göcek. Sure enough, there was a lull and I dropped and bagged the drifter. All I had to do now was to start the port engine, roll the genoa away and motor the last mile in and pick up my mooring.

The engine burst into life instantly but sounded different. I checked over the side and there was no cooling water coming out of the exhaust. I now had no serviceable engine and no mainsail and had to sail down a narrow entrance to my berth directly into a force 7 wind. This meant tacking side to side of the channel which was not so bad but the last half mile was cluttered with boats at anchor swinging wildly in the erratic wind. With much hard work we managed it and I briefed John, Duncan's dad, that I had the only mooring buoy in the harbour, and to tell me when he could see it. It was getting dark when I was told that it could be seen and, under sail, I came up to the buoy, furled the genoa and John picked up the buoy and secured us to it. It was an inch perfect manoeuvre in difficult conditions and as I walked from the cockpit to bows I felt extremely pleased with myself. That was until I realised that someone else had laid a mooring that winter and it was not my buoy we had tied up to! Mine was 30 yards away. There was no way that I could set sail in that crowded anchorage and reach it; I had to risk starting my non-cooled engine and motor across to it.

That night, ashore, I meet up with an Australian couple I knew, from a multihull called 'Linga Longa'. The first words they said were 'I saw that you picked up the wrong mooring buoy!' When I asked if they had seen the skilful way I tacked in, avoiding the anchored boats, they replied 'No, just you picking up the wrong buoy.'

A good friend of mine, and popular with all the live-aboards, was a Dutch sailor named John. John, usually sailed his yacht alone, and eventually he 'came out 'as Gay, much to the surprise and dismay of the many young ladies who had fallen in love with him.

One winter, when secured alongside a jetty, in a small marina attached to a hotel in Fethiye, I managed to have two accidents in two weeks, cracking four ribs. I was living alone on African Ocean at the time. Every morning, other yacht-folk (usually the females) would call in on me and ask what I needed at the shops and if I needed anything doing on the boat.

On a cold February night, awoken by a banging on the boat, I painfully crawled out of my bed, and looked onto the jetty to see who wanted me. The jetty was empty, and the banging had stopped. I then looked over the other side to see if there was a boat along-side. There was nothing there also.

I hobbled back to bed and again heard banging. I was now feeling rather peeved. The air was cold and my broken ribs made movement difficult, but once again, I made my way to the cockpit and looked over both sides and onto the jetty, which was still deserted. I continued to hear the banging, so, painfully, I stepped onto the jetty and hobbled up to the bows. There I discovered John, in the water, kicking my boat and hanging onto his semi-submerged dinghy, which was still tied to the jetty.

John was calling 'Save me, help me, I'm drowning' and splashing the water in an attempt to stay afloat, as he kicked African Ocean to awake me for help. It appeared that after enjoying the party spirit too much, he had decided to return to his yacht, which was at anchor 100 yards away. Unfortunately, he had fallen into the sea whilst trying to get into his dinghy, and in an attempt to climb up into his wooden dinghy; it had capsized and partially sank. Only the securing rope on the bow, tied to the jetty, had stopped the dinghy sinking completely.

After re-assuring John that I would not let him drown, I clambered back onboard, passed the end of a rope to John and pulled him to African Ocean's stern, where I had a swimming ladder. After he managed to climb the ladder, I narrowly avoided a dripping wet 'thank you' embrace, took him into the saloon (main cabin) and gave him a towel and dry clothes.

I could see that John was in the first stage of hypothermia; he was pale and had uncontrollable shivering. Luckily, being a survival instructor I knew what to do; get a large sleeping bag, and both of us get into it, naked, and use 'body warming' to raise his core temperature,. This would be much safer for him than a hot shower. I then remembered that in the morning the yacht girls would be around to do my shopping and would find me naked in a sleeping bag with John, who was Gay...

You could say that I could 'talk the talk' but not 'walk the walk', but John had his own sleeping bag and extra blankets for the remainder of the night and I ignited my Taylor Yacht Heater to heat up the saloon. When I said that John was a good friend, I didn't mean that good! The ironic thing about Johns unplanned midnights swim was that the water was only 4ft deep, and he could have walked ashore or to my stern if he had been sober enough to think.

Now, in 2021, I have stopped being a RYA chief instructor and am concentrating on my new career as the inventor and owner of SeaStrop, a revolutionary rescue device. I have not cut all ties with the yacht world, as I skipper for people cruising, do yacht deliveries, and skipper for races. I have also just finished refitting a 30 year old 37 ft Jeanneu Voyager monohull. I have brought it into the 21st century with solar panels, USB chargers in all cabins and thick, thermal headlining. It took 18 months of hard work but she is now a classy cruising yacht.

The idea of SeaStrop came about many years ago but only recently have I found the right materials. A lot has been written about how to find a Man overboard (MOB) but then there is a gap. If the MOB is conscious, they can get a rescue strop (loop of canvas material) over themselves but if unconscious or incapacitated it usually requires another person to get into the sea to help them. Not popular in bad weather or icy seas and I have mentioned the difficulties I had in helicopters when recuing survivors. I managed to think of a way of getting a strop around a person, even in a choppy sea, and then bring them to safety. It is now possible for a couple to go sailing and rescue each other without third party help. Also, as it is low tech, the strop can be used for training and, apart from an inspection for damage and a wash, can be used many times. I have a patent pending.

As for the plan to go to Lebanon, so far it has not happened. I have been told that the cedar forest has almost disappeared, whilst the largest, which I have visited and camped in, is in Turkey. Maybe I will sail there one day in my monohull (African Ocean was sold in 2004). Perhaps there will be another sea change, but I don't think that it will be a cold UK one. I wonder what the snorkelling is like in Cuba...

Culdrose Revisited 2016

The end

(For the moment)